Manifest Destinies

Manifest Destinies

The Making of the Mexican American Race

Laura E. Gómez

NEW YORK UNIVERSITY PRESS
New York and London

NEW YORK UNIVERSITY PRESS
New York and London
www.nyupress.org

Library of Congress Cataloging-in-Publication Data
Gómez, Laura E., 1964–
Manifest destinies : the making of the Mexican American race /
Laura E. Gómez.
p. cm. Includes bibliographical references and index.
ISBN–13: 978–0–8147–3174–1 (cloth : alk. paper)
ISBN–10: 0–8147–3174–0 (cloth : alk. paper)
1. Mexican Americans—Race identity. 2. Mexican Americans—Legal
status, laws, etc. 3. Mexican Americans—Colonization—History—19th
century. 4. Racism—United States—History—19th century. 5. United
States—Race relations—History—19th century. 6. Mexican Americans—
New Mexico—History—19th century. 7. Racism—New Mexico—
History—19th century. 8. New Mexico—Race relations—History—19th
century. I. Title.
E184.M5G625   2007
305.8968'72073—dc22   2007026486

New York University Press books are printed on acid-free paper,
and their binding materials are chosen for strength and durability.

Manufactured in the United States of America
10 9 8 7 6 5 4 3 2 1

For my son—Alejandro

Contents

Acknowledgments

Although I completed this book in Albuquerque, where I have lived and taught at the University of New Mexico for the past few years, its genesis was at two earlier points in my life, when living away from New Mexico provided me with different perspectives about my home state. The first was more than twenty years ago at Harvard College, when I tried to understand New Mexico's racial dynamics by taking African American and Latin American studies courses (there were no courses on Chicanos or Latinos, nor were there any Chicano faculty) and writing a senior thesis called "What's in a Name? The Politics of *Hispanic* Identity." The second point was about a decade ago when, in the wake of California voters' ban on affirmative action, a group of law school faculty formed the Critical Race Studies Concentration as a way to consolidate our intellectual interests and attempt to recruit students of color to UCLA. I began teaching a course on comparative racialization and the law in the United States, which, in retrospect, started me thinking along the lines developed in this book. At both of these points, it proved intellectually fruitful to have been in a milieu outside New Mexico; I had to work harder to define and explicate those features of the New Mexico social landscape that might have otherwise seemed deceptively obvious.

To give birth to this book, however, I ultimately returned to New Mexico, where my perspective again shifted. During the 2004–5 academic year, I was fortunate to hold a residential fellowship at the School for American Research (now the School for Advanced Research on the Human Experience) in Santa Fe. On weekly drives to Albuquerque to visit family, I marveled at the tangible difference perspective makes in simple, everyday ways—like how the Sandia Mountains look when viewed from Albuquerque's North Valley, where I grew up, as opposed to how they look driving south on Interstate 25 from Santa Fe. Like differences resulting from viewing the Sandias at different times of day or different seasons of the year, various geographic perspectives highlight different peaks, crags, or tree lines in the mountain range. On those drives I would ponder the meaning the Sandias must have had for the various pre-nineteenth-century communities along the route from Santa Fe to Albuquerque—Las Golondrinas, Santo Domingo Pueblo, San Felipe Pueblo, Bernalillo, Sandia Pueblo. In this book, I have tried to be true to my perspective on events—as a sociologist and a legal scholar, as a Chicana whose roots in New Mexico range from three to eight generations—even though I do not claim my perspective is "representative" in any sense.

I owe a large debt to UCLA, my intellectual home for so many years, and, in particular, to the School of Law (and Deans Prager, Varat, Abrams, and Schill), the Sociology Department, the Institute for American Cultures, the Center for the Study of Women, the Chicano Studies Research Center, and to the colleagues in those departments who supported me and my research. In addition, I received great research assistance from the staff of the Hugh and Hazel Darling Law Library.

I am grateful to the Stanford Humanities Center (1996–97) and the School for American Research (2004–5) for providing me with generous in-residence fellowships—the former as I was beginning research related to this book and the latter as I was starting to write. Just as important, each of these institutions provided working environments where I found invaluable intellectual stimulation and collegiality.

I received valuable feedback from presentations related to this work from the following audiences: School of Law (King Hall), University of California, Davis; UCLA School of Law; School of Law, University of Colorado, Boulder; University of Houston Law Center's Conference on *Hernandez v. Texas*; Institute for Legal Studies at the University of Wisconsin, Madison; New York Law and Society Colloquium (co-sponsored by New York Law School and New York University); and annual meetings of the Law and Society Association, the American Sociological Association, and LatCrit, Inc.

As with raising a child, it takes a village to produce a book. For the past few years, my village has been the University of New Mexico. I have received generous support from UNM's Center for Regional Studies (Tobias Durán, director), the College of Arts and Sciences, and the School of Law (including Dean Suellyn Scarnecchia and the Keleher and McLeod Professorship). I have also benefited from presentations of this work to the American Studies Department, the Anthropology Department, the Southwest Hispanic Research Institute, and the School of Law. I am grateful to my colleagues at the Law School who have not tired of hearing the various iterations of this project as it has evolved (or, if they have grown weary of it, have kept me blissfully ignorant). A special thanks to the entire staff of the UNM School of Law Library, especially Eileen Cohen, Barbara Lah, Lorraine Lester, Michelle Rigual, Alexandra Siek, Sherri Thomas, and Ron Wheeler. I am grateful to Barbara Jacques and Melissa Lobato for assisting me with preparing the manuscript and for their good cheer. Thanks also to other UNM support staff who were generous with their time. Amy Lammers, Adolfo Méndez, and Michael Wilson provided excellent research assistance.

Over many years, I have relied on the expertise of librarians and archivists to find and access various government documents and special collections. I thank the staffs of the New Mexico State Records Center and Archives, the Office of the State Historian of New Mexico, and the Center for Southwest Studies at UNM's Zimmerman Library.

For providing suggestions at various stages of this project, I thank the following people: Rick Abel, Kip Bobroff, Carole Browner, Devon Carbado, Ernie Chávez, Sam Deloria, Toby Durán, Lawrence Friedman, Eileen Gauna, Carole Goldberg, Alyosha Goldstein, Em Hall, Joel Handler, Cheryl Harris, Sandra Jaramillo, Susan Johnson, Jerry Kang, Ken Karst, Jake Kosek, Gillian Lester, Ian Haney López, Alex Lubin, Roberto Martínez, Joe Masco, Margaret Montoya, Maria Montoya, Alfonso Morales, Rachel Moran, Michael Olivas, David Reichard, Sylvia Rodríguez, Manuela Romero, Mark Sawyer, Rebecca Schreiber, Clyde Spillenger, Quiche Suzuki, Eddie Telles, Gloria Valencia-Weber, Leti Volpp, and Jessica Winegar. I am especially indebted to the following people for extensive feedback: Antonio Gómez, Felipe Gonzáles, Jerry López, Estévan Rael-Gálvez, Sherene Razack, and Mary Romero. My thanks goes out to the entire staff at New York University Press but especially to Deborah Gershenowitz, whose insight has improved this project at every step of the way.

I have been lucky in many ways, one of which has been to be surrounded by caring friends and relatives; for the good food and wine, babysitting, and good company, thanks to Miguel, Mitchie, Kip and Michele, Camille, Manuela and Alfonso, Quiche, Juan and Estévan, Cristina and Gabriel, Juli, Kat, Kris, Aunt Elida, Aunt Naomi, Aunt Virgie, Aunt Norma, Tina and Michael, Vilma, Lorie, Lillie, Jessica and Hamdi, Marina, Margaret and Charles, and the families of the Alameda Avengers. For providing constant support of every imaginable variety, I am forever grateful to my parents, Eloyda and Antonio Gómez. Special thanks to my Dad, for encouraging my sociological imagination and taking my ideas seriously. My deepest thanks go to my son Alejandro, who keeps me focused on the important things in life and whose hugs matter more than he can know.

Introduction

More than a century-and-a-half ago, a series of events occurred that resulted in the formation of Mexican Americans as a *racial* group in the United States. For complex reasons that I explore in this book, Mexican Americans often have been portrayed (and sometimes have portrayed themselves) as an ethnic group that eventually will assimilate into American society, just as European immigrant groups once did. I will argue that given the early history of Mexicans in the United States, it is more accurate to treat Mexican Americans as a racial group.

Two common misconceptions lie at the root of what most people take for granted about Mexicans in the United States. The first is that Mexican Americans are not a *racial* group at all, but instead merely an ethnic group. Race in the United States has historically been viewed as a matter of black/white relations and, more specifically, as about white subordination of African Americans. Despite the fact that the United States has always been a racially diverse society, non-white groups other than blacks often have been overlooked.[1] Although Indian tribes were recognized as constituting independent nations (who could, for instance, freely enter nation-to-nation treaties with the United States until 1871), Indians were just as surely recognized as a racial group and as racially inferior to Euro-Americans.[2] The arrival of more than 400,000 Chinese immigrants in the first century of the nation's existence added to America's racial diversity.[3] The United States has always been a multiracial nation, even though it has become popular only in the past twenty-five years to talk in those terms.

The second misconception is that Mexican Americans are a "new" group that consists primarily of recent immigrants and their children. Mexican Americans have been a significant part of American society since 1848, when more than 115,000 Mexicans became U.S. citizens. It was well into the twentieth century before the U.S. government seriously regulated Mexican immigration to the United States.[4] For 160 years, the Mexican

American population has been continuously replenished with new immigration from Mexico, with the pace especially strong since 1965.[5] Consider that in 1970 less than 20 percent of Mexicans in the United States were born in Mexico—in other words, more than 80 percent of Mexican Americans were American-born. Today, just over half of Mexicans in the United States were born in Mexico and just under half of them were born in the United States.[6] While the Mexican American group continues to grow due to ongoing immigration from Mexico, it includes a large proportion of people whose American roots go back many generations.

The status of Mexican Americans as a racial group is rooted in their long history in this nation. In making this argument, I draw heavily on the experiences of the first Mexican Americans, those who joined American society involuntarily, not as immigrants, but as a people conquered in war. As Mexican Americans sometimes say, "We didn't cross the border, the border crossed us." Moreover, Mexicans joined American society at that time as citizens, albeit, as second-class citizens in many respects. *Manifest Destinies* excavates the history of Mexican Americans as an American racial group that was uniquely situated as "off-white."[7] It analyzes the larger American racial order as it evolved in the late nineteenth century and the social process of racialization—or how groups come to be identified and to identify themselves in racial terms and learn their place as deserving or undeserving in the racial hierarchy.

Race and ethnicity overlap in important ways—and, in fact, race as it operates in the United States generally subsumes ethnicity. For example, black Americans are a racial group composed of a variety of ethnic groups, including African Americans, Afro-Caribbeans, and African immigrants from various countries. Of course, race and ethnicity are used in varied ways across many disciplines. I employ them here in a conventional way to emphasize the quality of *assignment* associated with race—racial group membership is assigned by others, and particularly by members of the dominant group—and the quality of *assertion* associated with ethnicity—ethnic group membership is chosen by members of the ethnic group.[8] Used in this way, race involves a harder, less voluntary group membership (though, as we shall see, not as inflexible as is typically assumed). By using race rather than ethnicity to describe the Mexican American experience, I intend to invoke what sociologists Stephen Cornell and Douglas Hartmann have called the legacy of race as "the most powerful and persistent group boundary in American history, distinguishing, to varying degrees, the experiences of those classified as non-white from those classified as white, with often devastating consequences."[9] While ethnicity has been and continues to be an important marker of difference and inequality, especially outside the United States, it pales in comparison to the role race has played and continues to play in American society in shaping both group relations and individual life chances.[10]   — race

Racial categories and racial difference are socially constructed; rather than having inherent significance, race is historically contingent and given meaning by persons, institutions, and social processes.[11] In recent years, a growing body of scholarship has explored how specific groups have become white, as well as the larger significance of white racial identity.[12] As historian Matthew Jacobson has put it: "[R]aces are invented categories. . . . Caucasians are made not born. White privilege in various forms has been a constant in American political culture since colonial times, but whiteness itself has been subject to all kinds of contests and has gone through a series of historical vicissitudes."[13] Yet the literature has implied that the process of becoming white is relatively straightforward—once a group is on the path to becoming white, whiteness becomes inevitable and occurs within a matter of decades. For Mexican Americans, as historian Neil Foley has explained in a study of Mexicans, blacks, and poor whites at "the fringe of whiteness," the process has been more complex and less straightforward.[14] *Manifest Destinies* illustrates that complexity as a byproduct of Mexican Americans' relationships with whites, Indians, and blacks, examining these relationships from 1846 to the turn of the century to reveal the dynamic, non-linear nature of Mexican Americans' off-white status.

Many Americans view the concept of Manifest Destiny positively, as a shorthand reference to a period in history (the 1840s) during which Americans' unbounded hunger for national growth was satiated by the acquisition of the Oregon Territory, Texas, and the Mexican Cession, including California as its jewel. For many, Manifest Destiny conjures a moment of national triumph before the dark years of conflict over slavery that culminated in the Civil War.[15] This book views Manifest Destiny quite differently—as a cluster of ideas that relied on racism to justify a war of aggression against Mexico. As historian Reginald Horsman has observed,

> In the middle of the nineteenth century a sense of racial destiny permeated discussions of American progress and of future American world destiny. . . . By 1850 the emphasis was on the American Anglo-Saxons as a separate, innately superior people who were destined to bring good government, com-

mercial prosperity, and Christianity to the American continents and to the world. This was a superior race, and inferior races were doomed to subordinate status or extinction.[16]

Manifest Destinies, as used in this book's title, embraces the idea of Manifest Destiny as inexorably entwined with race and racism. At the same time, it refers to how the competing *destinies* of many groups ultimately produced the Mexican American race and fundamentally changed the American racial order in the half-century following the U.S.–Mexico War.

Three themes drive this book. The first is that colonialism was central to the origin of Mexican Americans. Manifest Destiny fueled American imperialism and the expansion west and south into Mexico. Acquisition of northern Mexico, and especially of Alta California, now the state of California, was essential to several goals: securing massive amounts of mineral and other natural resources; acquiring land to expand the public domain and to construct a transcontinental railroad for transporting goods and people; and accessing Asian economic markets by way of the Pacific Ocean.[17] If Manifest Destiny was the ideology that justified the American colonization of Mexico, its material consequences were the American occupation of New Mexico, California, and Mexico City by ground and naval forces and the ratification of a peace treaty in 1848 under which Mexico ceded more than half its territory to the United States—approximately 1.3 million square miles, an area 50 percent larger than the Louisiana Purchase of 1804.[18] This additional territory more than tripled the size of the young nation, adding what is today all or parts of the states of Arizona, California, Colorado, New Mexico, Nevada, Texas, Utah, and Wyoming.

This book's second theme is the central role that law played in the creation of Mexican Americans as a racial group. *Manifest Destinies* illustrates the larger process of the social construction of race, focusing specifically on how law fundamentally created and expressed race, racial categories, and racial dynamics as they affected Mexican Americans. The central paradox was the *legal* construction of Mexicans as racially "white" alongside the *social* construction of Mexicans as non-white and as racially inferior. The book explores how these contradictory legal and social definitions coexisted and how the legal definition of Mexicans as white affected other non-white racial groups, eventually helping to entrench white supremacy in the United States. Following the U.S–Mexico War, Euro-American elites actively contested and negotiated racial categories among themselves and with Mexican elites, who in turn accommodated, contested, and negotiated their position in the new American racial order, often navigating legal institutions to do so. Ultimately Mexican Americans in New Mexico became a wedge racial group, between Euro-Americans above them and Pueblo Indians below them in the racial hierarchy.

The third theme of *Manifest Destinies* is that the construction of Mexicans as an American racial group proved central to the larger process of restructuring the American racial order in a key period stretching from the war to the turn of the twentieth century. Ironically, the emphasis on white-over-black relations during this period (due to the Civil War and Reconstruction) has obscured the significant role played by Manifest Destiny and the colonization of northern Mexico in the racial subordination of black Americans. The absorption of the Mexican Cession brought to a head the question of whether slavery would be allowed to expand beyond the South. In the infamous *Dred Scott* case, the Supreme Court answered this question in a way that made the Civil War all but inevitable. After the Civil War, black slaves were emancipated and, through the Reconstruction amendments to the Constitution, African American men were endowed with political rights. During this period, the majority of Mexican American men, who had received *federal* citizenship under the peace treaty of 1848, held a kind of second-class citizenship in which their rights were limited because Congress refused to admit New Mexico as a state due to its majority Mexican and Indian population.

Moreover it was dual, if nearly opposite, ideologies of race that helped enshrine the twentieth-century racial hierarchy that placed African Americans at the bottom with Mexican Americans above them so that, in the national racial hierarchy, Mexican Americans became a wedge racial group between whites and blacks. While Mexican Americans were relegated to second-class citizenship in virtually all areas, they had access to legal whiteness under a kind of reverse one-drop rule: one drop of Spanish blood allowed them to claim whiteness under certain circumstances. The separate racial ideologies that developed with respect to Mexican Americans and African Americans highlight the complexity and contradictions within white supremacy. Whereas the racial ideology that we most commonly associate with this period of American history resulted in the hardening of categories that governed African Americans (under the one-drop rule), with respect to Mexican Americans a racial ideology emerged that depended on those boundaries being flexible and inclusive. Both ideologies reproduced the racial subordination of blacks and Mexicans, but they did so in very different ways. Without understanding how they worked—

and how they worked in tandem—we cannot fully understand American racial dynamics in the twentieth century and beyond.

I intend this book to be an antidote to historical amnesia about the key nineteenth-century events that produced the first Mexican Americans—the U.S.–Mexico War, the Mexican Cession, and the peace treaty that extended American citizenship to Mexican citizens living in what is today the American Southwest. Placing Mexican Americans at the center of the analysis reveals how their entrance into the United States shaped the larger racial order. Mexican Americans interacted with and impacted the destinies of American Indians, African Americans, and Euro-Americans, and these interactions, in turn, shaped the destiny of Mexican Americans. Excavating the nineteenth-century history of Mexican Americans as a racial group erases their racial invisibility and thereby reveals the complex, sometimes contradictory evolution of nineteenth-century racial dynamics as involving both multiple racial groups and competing racial ideologies.

The Mexican Cession consisted of Tejas, Alta California, and Nuevo México. A year before the start of the war, in 1845, Texas had joined the Union as a slave state. California joined the Union as a free state in 1850, soon after gold had been discovered there. This book principally focuses on the remainder of the newly annexed territory, New Mexico, which at the time was much larger than Texas and California combined, including all of present-day New Mexico as well as all or part of eight other U.S. states.[19] New Mexico's Mexican population was also far larger than those of California and Texas combined, with nearly two-thirds of Mexicans in the Mexican Cession living there.[20] Although Congress would eventually divide New Mexico into smaller components, the vast majority of the non-Indian population living in this vast region in 1848 resided in what is today north central New Mexico.[21]

To speak of the nation's first Mexican Americans, then, is to speak substantially about Mexicans living in New Mexico.[22] It was not, however, raw numbers alone that made New Mexico's Mexican population significant— it was numbers coupled with the proportion of Mexicans to Euro-Americans and to Indians, especially Pueblo Indians. At the outset of the war with Mexico, fewer than a thousand Euro-Americans lived in New Mexico. In contrast, Euro-Americans outnumbered Mexicans in Texas as early as 1830, due to Mexico's liberal immigration policies (that is, liberal relative to the restrictive policies of Spain prior to 1820).[23] And, due largely to the discovery of gold in California in 1848, Euro-Americans outnumbered

Mexicans there by 1850.[24] The small number of Euro-Americans in New Mexico allowed Mexican Americans to remain demographically dominant well into the period of American rule, and led the American colonizers to devise ways to incorporate and co-opt them.

Another key aspect of New Mexico's demographics was the size and diversity of its Indian population at the time it was annexed to the United States. Comparatively, the rest of the Mexican Cession had fewer and less diverse Indian tribes. New Mexico's population included 15,000 Pueblo Indians and perhaps 60,000 other Indians.[25] Mexicans and Pueblo Indians had much in common culturally and geographically, even though they shared a long history of conflict in New Mexico. When Euro-American colonizers arrived in New Mexico, one of their goals was to cement the divide between Mexicans and Pueblo Indians. One way to do this was to allow Mexican Americans to designate themselves as legally white while preventing Pueblo Indians from doing so.

Two-thirds of Mexicans in the Mexican Cession lived in New Mexico, making it a target for U.S. military occupation during the war and, later, establishment as an American colony. Although New Mexico became a federal territory in 1850, its status was in many ways different from that of non-contiguous U.S. colonies such as Puerto Rico and the Philippines. One of the chief differences is that Puerto Rico and the Philippines were not seen as colonies in which Euro-American "settler citizens" would eventually predominate, and therefore were not seen as candidates for statehood.[26] In contrast, both New Mexico and Hawaii were seen as places where white settler citizens eventually would outnumber the non-white native population, thereby facilitating statehood. At the same time, the racial complexion of New Mexico and Hawaii caused Congress to delay statehood, keeping these regions in a colonial status for many decades.[27] These political realities contribute to the centrality of New Mexico in this study.

Manifest Destinies reflects my efforts to engage three distinct disciplines. In terms of methodology, this book is grounded in history: it draws heavily on data from primary historical documents and from secondary studies of archival materials. Yet I have approached these documents (or studies of them) as types of social facts, within a broader empirical emphasis that stems from my training in sociology. I have attempted to tell a story, using historical documents, that is analytically driven by sociological concepts and understandings of race and racial ideology, politics, and colonialism.[28]

The third disciplinary home of this book is law, defined broadly to include positive law ("laws" themselves, enacted by legislatures or made by courts); legal institutions such as the police, the courts, and trial by jury; and actors in the legal system such as lawyers, prosecutors, judges, and jurors. *Manifest Destinies,* then, is a sociological study of race that focuses on law, legal institutions, and legal actors in a particular historical context.

This book started to take shape in the late 1980s, when I began an archival project on the legal system in nineteenth-century New Mexico. By this time, I had lived away from my home state of New Mexico for almost as many years as I had lived in it. My time away increased my awareness of the region's peculiar racial dynamics, or what can be described as New Mexico's exceptionalism within the Chicano experience. As someone who possessed a dual vantage point as both insider and outsider, I thought there was something to the exceptionalism thesis, but I also believed it was flawed. The notion that New Mexico's Mexican Americans are a breed apart from other Mexican Americans remains robust not only in scholarship from diverse disciplines, but also in popular culture. In a nutshell, the exceptionalism thesis emphasizes New Mexico's unique status among southwestern states—as having, for example, a long history of Mexican American elected officials at all levels of government, relatively low levels of racial oppression of Mexican Americans (compared to Texas and California), and an intense, long-standing claim to Spanish, rather than Mexican, heritage.[29] The exceptionalism thesis often attributes these facts to New Mexico's relatively limited Mexican immigration in the twentieth century (compared to California, Texas, and Arizona) and to the related persistence of cultural and other characteristics of the Spanish settlers of the region.

An additional dimension of the exceptionalism thesis has been the marked tendency to view Mexican Americans as regionally distinctive, rather than as a group with one national history.[30] Local social histories in Chicano studies have contributed to the notion that there is not a coherent *national* story to be told about Mexican Americans. To be sure, there is much to be learned from highly localized studies, but it is also important to see the connections between local, regional, national, and even transnational levels of analysis.[31] This study situates New Mexico in a national and hemispheric context.

In short, the claim of New Mexico's exceptionalism has obscured these larger dynamics. For example, the historical record suggests that New

Mexico was deeply Mexican in the late Spanish period, the twenty-five-year Mexican period (1821–46), and well into the American period. Why have proponents of the exceptionalism thesis—and the historical actors whom they studied—downplayed New Mexico's Mexican legacy in favor of its Spanish heritage? In addition, in both historic and contemporary contexts, the degree of racial oppression of Mexican Americans by whites and the level of racial conflict between Hispanics and Anglos (as Mexican Americans and Euro-American whites are more commonly referred to today in New Mexico) was and is actually much greater than typically acknowledged. What historic factors and dynamics led and continue to lead us to systematically understate the level of racial conflict in New Mexico?

In answering these questions, I have continually been drawn back to the early decades of the American colonization of northern Mexico. American colonization was most visceral in New Mexico as measured by the intensity of the Mexican resistance to the Americans and the sheer brutality of the American military and legal responses. Moreover, anti-Mexican racism was most evident in the refusal of Euro-American elites to annex New Mexico as a state precisely because of its majority-minority population. These factors, coupled with the fact that most Mexicans who joined the United States in 1848 lived in New Mexico, suggest that, if New Mexico is in fact exceptional, its exceptionalism works in the other direction. It counsels us to pay more attention to the ways in which Mexicans in New Mexico were typical and to how that shaped, first, the strategies of the American colonizers, and, second, those of the first Mexican Americans. Viewed in this way, we might well see New Mexicans' continuing claims to "Spanish" heritage as a tactic that evolved from the intense anti-Mexican racism of the 1800s.

Manifest Destinies tells the story of how Mexican Americans became an American racial group. The first chapter begins with the American colonization of northern Mexico, focusing on the American invasion of the vast region known as New Mexico. It reveals that ideas about Mexicans' racial inferiority animated the American war against Mexico and the later efforts to colonize New Mexico under civilian authority. At the same time, the chapter brings to light the unique features of New Mexico that led to the enfranchisement of Mexican men and, thus, the legal construction of the first Mexican Americans as "white" rights-holders. In short, the Americans had no viable alternative to allowing Mexican elites to share in governing this vast region because the American military presence in New Mexico was too small to sustain martial law and because there were too few Euro-American immigrants to implement a civil government without Mexicans' participation.

Chapter 2 focuses on how, in the decades following the initial American occupation, the question of where Mexicans fit in the American racial order was negotiated among Euro-American elites. The dominant view, articulated by most congressmen and the national press, was that Mexicans were a racially inferior people, no better than blacks and Indians and, thus, unfit for self-government. Adherents of this position vigorously opposed admission of New Mexico as a state until Euro-Americans outnumbered Mexicans. What I term the progressive view was developed by some Euro-American elites living in New Mexico as a counter-narrative to the dominant racial story and, specifically, as a strategy to achieve statehood. Proponents of the progressive view posited a notion of race that emphasized culture over biology and harmony over conflict and sought to rehabilitate Mexican elites as the descendants of the initial European colonizers of the region. The progressive view fostered an unprecedented level of incorporation of a non-white racial group, but it also served to promote white supremacy.

A central part of the second chapter is its analysis of nineteenth-century New Mexico as the product of a unique process of "double colonization," first by the Spanish and later by the Americans. Significantly, both the Spanish and the American colonial enterprises were grounded in racism, though their precise ideologies of white supremacy differed. American colonizers in New Mexico thus did not start with a clean slate, but rather developed a racial order in the looming shadow of the Spanish-Mexican racial order. American sociologists who study race often have cited Latin American contexts as illuminating counter-examples to American racial dynamics, but these studies have overlooked the substantial ways in which American racial dynamics are themselves substantially evolved from Spanish colonial models of race. The myopic tendency to view American race relations as about white-over-black relations and as centered on a North/South axis has obscured the ways in which Latin American–style race relations have existed historically in the United States and continue to exert a powerful legacy.

The third chapter highlights the actions and motives of Mexican American elites, from whose ranks the majority of the elected officials in New Mexico came, making them the co-citizens who governed the region with

Euro-American officials appointed by the American president. With the quiet blessing of Congress, Mexican elites defined themselves as *white* rights-holders, even as they often were politically subordinate to the Euro-American appointed officials sent by Washington to govern the region. This chapter explores the fragility of Mexican Americans' legal whiteness, in a context in which both Mexican Americans and Euro-Americans understood that Mexicans occupied a racially inferior niche in American society. I argue that Mexican elites struggled mightily with this tentative off-white status, constantly seeking to shore up their whiteness by distancing themselves from other non-white groups. One result was Mexican elites' disenfranchisement of Pueblo Indians, despite the many commonalities Mexicans and Pueblo Indians shared and despite their history of alliance against the American colonizers. A second dynamic was Mexican elites' anti-black and pro-slavery actions, despite their earlier anti-slavery positions. I close the third chapter by looking at Mexican elites' moves to protect their ideological and material interests in enslaving Indians captured or traded from the various non-Pueblo tribes in the region.

The final chapter considers how New Mexico's racial dynamics fit within the larger picture of American race relations as they evolved in the middle to late nineteenth century. It explores each of the book's three themes in a national context. First, the centrality of colonization in the Mexican American experience is explored through the lens of land and the transition from a Spanish-Mexican to an Anglo-American property regime. Second, the racialization of Mexican Americans is linked in important ways to the racial subordination of blacks by examining the connections among Manifest Destiny, the infamous *Dred Scott* case, and the Civil War. The book's third theme, law's key role in the social construction of race and racial ideology, is explored by contrasting the legal definition of Mexicans as white under naturalization laws with the consolidation of black subordination in the Supreme Court's *Plessy v. Ferguson* opinion of 1897. We explore the co-evolution of opposite "one-drop" rules that governed African Americans and Mexican Americans: for blacks, one drop of African ancestry justified legal disabilities, while for Mexicans, one drop of Spanish ancestry at times conferred legal whiteness.

The book closes with an epilogue in which we travel forward one hundred years from the study's end at the beginning of the twentieth century to the present. I move from a focus on the macrohistorical context to the question of racial identity, both collective and individual. I consider the legacy of Mexican Americans' off-white status for understanding Mexican American identity today. This includes a discussion of how Mexican Americans compare to other Hispanic subgroups and how the increasing proportion of Mexican immigrants affects Mexican American identity.

In this study, I use the terms "Mexican" and "Mexican American" to describe the people of mixed Spanish, Indian, and African ancestry who lived in the Spanish colony of New Spain known today as the American Southwest. I intend to distinguish Mexicans from Euro-Americans (white Americans of European origin, both citizens and non-citizen immigrants, who were not black, Indian, Asian, or Mexican), African Americans, Indians, and Asians. Although the meaning of these various labels or their application in particular situations was hardly simple and uncontroversial, the adoption of terminology facilitates our discussion.

I eschew the terms Spanish, Spanish American, Hispanic and Hispano to describe the majority of Mexican Americans, who lived in what is today New Mexico, although these terms appear frequently in the literature.[32] I do so for two reasons. First, "Mexican" was the term most consistently used in the historical records of the nineteenth-century, regardless of whether the speaker was Mexican or Euro-American and no matter the forum or the language. Second, it more accurately describes the population's mestizo—or mixed Indian/Spanish/African—racial heritage. As the chapters to come will show, by the early nineteenth century, very few of these people were born in Spain or had parents or even grandparents who were Spanish, although they spoke the Spanish language, were practicing Roman Catholics, and otherwise conformed to cultural practices consistent with having been colonized by Spain. In terms of ancestry, the vast majority of these people were more indigenous than Spanish, and some of their religious, cultural, and political practices had indigenous origins.

The skeptical reader already may be wondering whether she is about to read a tale of grand conspiracies carried out by myopically racist actors. The story I will tell, however, is not one in which coordinated social action on the part of Euro-Americans led inexorably to the racial subordination of non-white people. Racial dynamics were considerably more complex— just as they are today. Two core beliefs about historical actors have shaped this book. First, race and racism were powerful realities in the social world in which these people lived. When Euro-Americans moved to Mexican Texas in the 1830s, when American volunteers headed off to war against Mexico in the 1840s, and when Euro-American governors followed the president's orders to go to New Mexico in the 1850s, ideas about race were deeply embedded in their consciousness and experience. Second, social actors generally behave in self-interested ways. I understand self-interest broadly to include material interests and also people's interest in how they perceive themselves individually and collectively. Combining these two ideas, it would be natural for social actors to deploy race and racism in a variety of ways, even as that was only a part of the story of their motives and strategies. As in other parts of the United States at other times, material interests and collective and individual self-perceptions came together to shape group interactions in the lands recently taken from Mexico.

1

The U.S. Colonization of Northern Mexico and the Creation of Mexican Americans

The morning of April 9, 1847, was in many respects a typical spring day in Taos. The early morning air was crisp and the big sky was blue except for some fleeting clouds. Snow-covered Wheeler Peak, the highest point in New Mexico, would have been clearly visible from the village center.[1] That Friday was anything but ordinary, however, in this far northern Mexican territory that the United States had recently invaded. On that day in 1847, the Americans executed six Mexican men for their roles in the attack on the highest-ranking American civilian in the region. During Holy Week, these Catholic men were tried and convicted under American law; four days after Easter, they were given their last rites by the local priest and hanged.[2]

The Americans erected the scaffold in the central plaza so that the hangings would be visible not only to those present, but also to those who watched from more distant rooftops.[3] The hangings of García, Lucero, the two Romeros, Salázar, and Trujillo must have been an amazing spectacle in Taos, probably drawing people from other communities to witness this violent exercise of American power. The sole surviving eyewitness account of the executions offers a vivid description of the men's last moments: "The bodies swayed back and forth, and coming in contact with each other, convulsive shudders shook their frames; the muscles contracting would relax, and again contract, and the bodies writhed most horribly. While thus swinging, the hands of two came together, which they held with a firm grasp till the muscles loosened in death."[4] Their martyred bodies remained hanging for forty minutes before the American sheriff cut them down, surely sending a powerful message to the Mexican and Indian people of the Taos Valley.

A few months earlier, dozens of Mexican and Pueblo Indian men had joined together to attack the American civil governor, Charles Bent, killing him and five other Americans and American sympathizers (those killed included three Euro-Americans, one Mexican, and the half-Mexican teenage son of a prominent Euro-American).[5] Bent, a Taos merchant, had been appointed civil governor by the army commander who had invaded New Mexico nine months earlier. In the weeks following Bent's assassination, thousands of Mexican and Indian people, including many civilians, died from attacks by American soldiers. Dozens more eventually were arrested on charges of murder, despite the fact that there was little evidence as to Bent's actual killers. The same men were charged with being traitors to the United States, despite the facts that they were Mexican citizens and that Mexico was at war with the United States. In 1847 when the Taos executions occurred, the United States claimed military authority over New Mexico, but it did not establish political sovereignty over the region until May 1848, when a peace treaty officially ended the war. Congress did not authorize a territorial government or a legal system until late 1850.

The first American executions in the Southwest raise questions about how Americans imagined themselves at mid-nineteenth century and about how they collectively recall this era. In the main, Americans tend not to think of themselves as colonizers—and when they do, they tend to associate America's colonial exploits with places like the Philippines (or, less frequently, Hawaii or Puerto Rico). Americans tend, perhaps conveniently, to forget that their nation attacked Mexico in a war of aggression and that Americans were unwelcome invaders of Mexico's northern frontier. Popular culture and mainstream American history teach that the "frontier" (a concept connoting an empty, unpopulated region) was "settled" by brave and hearty pioneers (with the notion of settlement itself implying a benign presence, rather than a military occupation).[6]

Writing two decades ago, historian Patricia Nelson Limerick presented a different account, self-consciously using the word "conquest" to describe Euro-Americans' entry into the American West at mid-century. Limerick foregrounded the conflict inherent in the American colonization of northern Mexico, as well as the competition over land and labor that was heavily shaped by race.

Happily or not, minorities and majorities [in the American West] occupied a common ground. Conquest basically involved the drawing of lines on a map, the definition and allocation of ownership (personal, tribal, corpo-

rate, state, federal, and international), and the evolution of land from matter to property. The process had two stages: the initial drawing of the lines
(which we have usually called the frontier stage) and the subsequent giving
of meaning and power to those lines, which is still under way. Race relations
parallel the distribution of property, the application of labor and capital to
make the property productive, and the allocation of profit.[7]

Whereas Limerick provided a general account of this process, here I consider the American conquest of Mexico from a different vantage point,
with the aim of situating the subsequent formation of Mexican Americans
as a racial group. The common misperception of Mexicans as an ethnic
group new to the United States obscures the legacy of American colonization in shaping the Mexican American experience. The evidence reveals
that the U.S. colonization of northern Mexico should be understood as the
moment in which Mexican Americans first became constituted as a racial
group.

The Mexican Problem and the Outbreak of War

The acquisition of northern Mexico, and especially of New Mexico, as an
American colony raised thorny questions of inclusion and exclusion in the
American nation and polity. These questions led elite Euro-Americans to
engage in conversations about the racial character of American citizenship
and of national belonging more generally. As sociologist Rogers Brubaker
has explained, citizenship "is inevitably bound up with nationhood and
national identity, membership of the state with membership of the nation."[8] Questions about race, citizenship, and belonging were at the heart
of the national debates about the U.S. declaration of war against Mexico
and about the ratification of the peace treaty that ended the war. The core
issue, both for pro-war Democrats and for anti-war Whigs, was the "Mexican problem": what was to become of the more than 115,000 Mexicans
who lived in the conquered lands?

What animated both the pro- and anti-war factions was a racist fear
about incorporating Mexicans as rights-holders. This had not been viewed
as a problem with the annexation of Texas because Euro-Americans (largely
immigrants from southern states) had established both demographic and
political dominance more than a decade prior to Texas's admission as a
state in 1845.[9] For the pro-war faction, the goal was to maximize the ac-

quisition of Mexican territory while minimizing the acquisition of Mexicans.[10] Many of those who opposed the war did so in part because the annexation of territory also meant the acquisition of Mexican people. In the end, Congress compromised by ratifying the Treaty of Guadalupe Hidalgo to achieve two ends: the cession by Mexico of half its territory, but with the barest guarantees regarding the citizenship and property rights of the Mexican people living in those lands, two-thirds of whom lived in New Mexico.

The origins of the U.S.–Mexico War lay in the breakaway of Texas from the Mexican Republic. Although Texas declared independence in 1836 and became a U.S. state eleven years later, Mexico did not abdicate its claim over the territory until its legislature ratified the Treaty of Guadalupe Hidalgo in 1848. In the 1820s, Mexico had adopted liberal immigration policies designed to encourage Euro-Americans to settle its northern frontier.[11] These efforts were most successful in Texas, where by 1831 Euro-Americans outnumbered Mexicans.[12] These Euro-American settlers, who came disproportionately from the southern states and brought with them large numbers of slaves, resented the regional and national legislatures' efforts to curtail slavery, culminating in 1829 with the abolition of African slavery in Mexico.[13]

Their response was to flaunt Mexico's anti-slavery laws and, at the same time, to foment rebellion against the central Mexican government among Euro-American settlers and elite Mexicans. These activities reached a climax in 1836, when a group of Americans, backed by some Mexican supporters, declared the establishment of the Republic of Texas and independence from Mexico. Mexico refused to recognize the new state and pursued a number of military and diplomatic avenues to pull Texas back into its fold. After independence, Mexicans increasingly feared that the United States would annex Texas, and that this, in turn, would lead to American claims on its other northern territories, Nuevo México and Alta California.[14] In 1845, Mexico's fears were realized when Texas was admitted to the Union as a slave state. Between 1850 and 1860 the U.S. Census showed a three-fold increase in the number of black slaves residing there.[15]

Historian Reginald Horsman concludes that "the Texas Revolution was from its beginnings interpreted in the United States and among Americans in Texas *as a racial clash*, not simply a revolt against unjust government."[16] The American senators who eventually would come to play a major role in backing the declaration of war against Mexico received their training during congressional debates about Texas, in which Senators Thomas

Hart Benton, Sam Houston, and Robert J. Walker played prominent roles. Walker, a Mississippi senator and a Democrat, frequently compared Mexicans to American blacks and Indians. Arguing in favor of American recognition of Texas's independence from Mexico, Walker urged that Americans rejoice that "our kindred race, predominated over that fair country, instead of the colored mongrel race, and barbarous tyranny, and superstitions of Mexico."[17] A few years later when he argued for the annexation of Texas as a slave state, Walker characterized "five-sixths" of Mexico's people as "the mixed races, speaking more than twenty different languages, composed of every poisonous compound of blood and color," and, ultimately, "semi-barbarous hordes."[18]

From the Mexican point of view, the U.S. annexation of Texas was tantamount to an act of war. For the Americans' part, there was an ongoing debate about the southern boundary between Texas and Mexico, made more urgent with Texas statehood.[19] Historians on both sides of the border acknowledge that President James Polk sought to provoke Mexico by moving U.S. troops into the disputed boundary zone.[20] Mexico responded by firing, and on May 9, 1846, Polk informed his cabinet that he would seek a declaration of war from Congress. Although some historians suggest that opposition to the war with Mexico was substantial, the declaration easily passed both houses of Congress.[21] Ultimately, even the anti-war Whigs found it hard to oppose the war with Mexico, as this passage from the *American Whig Review* written during the war, reveals: "Mexico was poor, distracted, in anarchy, and almost in ruins—what could she do to stay the hand of our power, to impede the march of our greatness? We are Anglo-Saxon Americans; it was our 'destiny' to possess and to rule this continent—we were bound to it!"[22]

The U.S.–Mexico War of 1846–48 was a landmark war for the United States in several respects. It was the first American war fought on foreign soil.[23] It was the first in which the United States occupied a foreign capital, first holding Mexico City on September 14, 1847.[24] As the first American military conflict since the War of 1812, it gave the nation an opportunity to test its new weaponry and other technology. Moreover, the war provided crucial experience to both military branches that existed at the time, the army and the navy. While the army moved west and south into Mexico, American naval forces proceeded to California and to Mexico's eastern coast to erect a blockade.[25] For American naval forces, the Mexican exercises represented their first large-scale operations and proved a training ground for the Civil War.[26]

The timing of the U.S.–Mexico War was important to national development more generally. Historian Robert Johannsen argues that the war, which began just over half a century after the ratification of the Bill of Rights, became "an exercise in self-identity" for the young nation.[27] By this time, the revolutionary generation had passed the torch to a new generation of political and military leaders who would prosecute the Mexican War and then go on to hold prominent positions in national affairs. Two key officers in the Mexican War went on to become U.S. presidents, and countless numbers of officers and soldiers went on to become congressmen. General Franklin Pierce, who led supply convoys into Mexico City as part of the American occupation, served as president from 1853 to 1857. One of the war's greatest heroes, according to some American historians, was Zachary Taylor, who ran successfully for president just as the peace treaty was being ratified, serving from 1849 to 1850. Johannsen notes that Taylor's upbringing in Kentucky may have prepared him well to be a soldier, since "his nursery tales were stories of Indian butchery."[28] Like many officers from the southern states, Taylor was accompanied by his slave Ben on his Mexican campaigns.[29]

Many of the officers who led the Union and the Confederate armies during the Civil War honed their skills in the U.S.–Mexico War. The best known are Ulysses S. Grant and Robert E. Lee. Grant fought under General Taylor in the earliest battles along the Rio Grande; Lee was an aide to General Winfield Scott, who led the assault on Mexico City, and was twice promoted during the war (first to major and then to lieutenant colonel). During the Civil War, Grant rose to be the General-in-Chief of the Union Army and Lee commanded the Confederate forces. Once comrades-in-arms, the two men ultimately met in battle during the Civil War, with Grant gaining Lee's surrender at Appomattox on April 9, 1865. More generally, the war with Mexico served as a training ground for military officers who were among the first generations trained at the West Point Academy.[30] Grant and Lee both studied at West Point; the Mexican War in some respects legitimized elite military academies, which many had previously criticized as anti-republican.[31]

One of the most important aspects of the U.S.–Mexico War was the fact that it was fought primarily by volunteer, rather than professional, soldiers. Of the nearly 78,000 American men who served in the Mexican War, 70,000 were volunteers.[32] Within the national imagination, the fact that the war was fought by volunteers made it appear more democratic and, in turn, generated a grass-roots patriotism that swept the young nation.

> The rush of volunteers simply confirmed the superior nature of the republican government and proved that even republics could respond quickly and decisively to national crisis. ... The reliance on volunteers gave the Mexican War an immediacy that could be felt by all the people. It was a civilian war from the outset, clothed with all the romance of a conflict that touched the popular imagination.[33]

In short, the volunteer army was seen as the hallmark of a republican government. Historians have noted that, in the context of the times, a volunteer military was seen as positively reflecting a true democracy, whereas the regular, career soldier was seen as elitist and an affront to democracy.[34] The war was democratic in another sense, as well, serving as a leveler of social difference and status.[35] In particular, it served to bring white ethnics and new European immigrants into the American fold. In her study of American popular literature and the Mexican War, Shelley Streeby identifies the central role that pro-war patriotism played in uniting Euro-Americans of diverse ethnic backgrounds. During a period of increased Irish and German immigration, the war became a vehicle for incorporating these then-marginal whites into a *racialized* national polity: "This vision of a united, more inclusive, white American race defined through a hierarchical relationship to Mexico is entirely consonant with the politics of manifest destiny."[36]

Moreover, the war's grass-roots popularity made it harder to criticize. Historian Paul Foos notes, "Leading political figures felt compelled to praise volunteers even if they opposed the Mexican War, and supporters of the president found it expedient to criticize his policies when he gave preference to regular over volunteer soldiers."[37] Ironically, the anti-war argument (made mostly by Whig congressmen in the northeast)—that the war was unjustified and hypocritical in that it involved a republic seeking its own colonies—was undercut by the promotion of the war as one fought by volunteer soldiers who performed democracy by their act of enlisting. The preponderance of volunteers among the war's soldiers gave it a populist cast that legitimated the war, despite the fact that it essentially was fought to further quite anti-democratic, colonialist aims.

The Military Conquest of New Mexico

Just a few months after the Texas skirmishes, volunteers led the invasions of New Mexico and California. Colonel Stephen Watts Kearny proceeded with 1,700 troops from Fort Leavenworth, Kansas, in June 1846 with orders to subdue New Mexico and proceed to California before winter.[38] While Kearny was moving ground forces into northern California (after the capture of New Mexico, to which we will return in a moment), General Taylor was moving American naval forces to Monterey. American ships arrived in northern California just two days after Independence Day 1846, raising the flag without Mexican resistance. The American invasion of southern California was more challenging because far more Mexicans lived there. The Mexicans in Los Angeles successfully resisted the Americans over the course of several months in the fall of 1846. It was not until January 1847, six months after the occupation began, that American military commanders could safely declare that they had subdued California.[39]

Colonel Kearny and his troops left Kansas under presidential orders to secure New Mexico "with the least expenditure of blood and money."[40] Secretary of War William L. Marcy's letters to Kearny were blunt about the president's priorities: "It has been decided by the President to be of the greatest importance in the pending war with Mexico to take the earliest possession of Upper California [Mexico's Alta California, the present-day state of California]."[41] Kearny did just this, declaring New Mexico under American military rule as of August 18, 1846, when he reached Santa Fe. For his speed in occupying New Mexico, Kearny was rewarded with a promotion to Brigadier General.[42] In a letter to his superiors, Kearny bragged about taking New Mexico "without firing a gun or spilling a single drop of blood," leading historian Hubert Howe Bancroft to describe Kearny's reception by the Mexicans in New Mexico as "friendly."[43]

Writing a half century after the war, Bancroft concluded, "Thus was the capital of New Mexico occupied without the shedding of blood," ushering in the still-dominant mythology of the bloodless conquest of New Mexico.[44] Yet Bancroft's assessment was true only inasmuch as the Mexicans did not immediately greet the Americans with armed resistance. As historian Tobias Durán has explained, however, Mexicans demonstrated their displeasure at the American invasion in other ways. For example, in a speech following Kearny's pronouncement of American authority at Santa Fe, the acting Mexican governor of New Mexico said, "[D]o not find it strange if there has been no manifestation of joy and enthusiasm in seeing this city occupied by your military forces. To us the power of the Mexican Republic is dead. No matter what her condition, she was our mother."[45] Moreover, as the opening discussion of the Taos executions showed, Mexicans and Indians in New Mexico did not remain acquiescent for long.

As Kearny entered each successive New Mexican village—Las Vegas, Tecolote, San Miguel del Vado—on his way to Santa Fe, he addressed the native people, often from the rooftop of an adobe building.[46] In these speeches, he asserted U.S. authority over the region, warned his audience not to resist or to risk death, and then made promises about how the Americans would improve the lives of the native people. Seeking to mollify resistance, especially from Mexican elites, Kearny emphasized the principle of religious freedom and said his troops would respect Catholic religious institutions.[47] In what would later be used against him, he said that the Americans' intent was to provide a government "similar to those in the United States." The American strategy in New Mexico was dictated by President Polk, who, through Marcy, directed Kearny "to conciliate the inhabitants and to let them see that peace is within their reach the moment their rulers will consent to do us justice [by surrendering]."[48] Even as Kearny bragged to his superiors about his bloodless conquest, his speeches revealed his appreciation of a more complicated and potentially dangerous reality.

Over the next five weeks, before departing for California with most of his troops, Kearny fortified the American military presence in New Mexico by constructing a permanent fort (which he named Fort Marcy, in honor of his superior).[49] But he spent most of his time during those weeks implementing the president's orders to establish a civil government under American authority.[50] Kearny already had reappointed a number of local officials, having, in his initial speeches to native New Mexicans, asked local officeholders to "take an oath of allegiance to the United States" in order to continue in their posts.[51] A month later, on September 22, Kearny went further, invoking the president's orders to appoint a civil government for what he termed "New Mexico, a Territory of the United States."[52] In so doing, Kearny overstepped his role as military commander: only Congress could establish new territories. Indeed, when word of Kearny's actions reached Washington four weeks later, several members of Congress reacted with swift criticism of the administration, and Congress voted to launch an investigation.[53] Although the president distanced himself from Kearny, the correspondence between Marcy and Kearny suggests Kearny was executing the President's orders. None of this, however, was known in

New Mexico. By the time Kearny received word of the controversy in late December, he was in California.[54]

Meanwhile, Kearny's new civilian appointees, most of whom had no prior governing experience, set out to oversee what they incorrectly assumed was a newly organized American territory. Of course, the real power remained in the hands of the military commander, now Colonel Sterling Price. Of the nine appointments Kearny made in September 1846, seven were of Euro-American merchants. Kearny appointed a "superior court" consisting of three judges.[55] He ordered drafted and then promulgated a code of law drawn from those of the Missouri Territory, Texas, and Mexico. Revealing again his over-reach, the opening sentence read, "The government of the United States of America ordains and establishes the following organic law for the Territory of New Mexico, which has become a Territory of said government."[56] Although Kearny submitted the so-called "Kearny Code," Congress refused to authorize it, signaling its disapproval of the Polk administration and its failure to reign in military officers—disapproval that, once again, was largely unheard in New Mexico.[57]

Kearny's relationship with the man he appointed as civil governor, Charles Bent, was sealed at Bent's Fort, the trading post on the Arkansas River that he co-owned with his brother George. Kearny's forces camped there in August 1846 on their way to Santa Fe so that Kearny could enlist Bent's help in the invasion of New Mexico.[58] Bent had been actively trading in New Mexico since 1829, making him one of the best-known Euro-Americans in northern New Mexico. Bent also lived with a Mexican woman, Ignacia Jaramillo, whom many mistakenly assumed was his wife; in fact, Kearny referred to Bent's "marriage" to a native woman in his announcement of Bent's appointment.[59] From the base at Bent's Fort, Kearny sent out two advance parties, each led by merchants, to ascertain Mexicans' likely resistance and to enlist Mexican merchants in the American invasion. Bent's spy party went to Taos and returned to inform Kearny to expect heavy resistance from the Mexicans.[60] The second spy party, led by trader James Magoffin, who was fluent in Spanish and married to a Mexican native, apparently bribed the New Mexico governor in exchange for an agreement not to resist the Americans.[61]

The American military strategy was to conserve military resources in New Mexico in order to hold them in reserve for later battles in California and, especially, central Mexico.[62] The Americans hoped not to have to waste manpower in taking control of New Mexico. Instead, they planned to exploit what they perceived as divisions in Mexican society. That understanding—one shared even by President Polk and his cabinet—was in every way racial, paralleling in important respects racial dynamics in the United States. Letters from Marcy to Kearny spoke of racial and class divisions among the Mexicans that might provide a wedge for the American invaders. In a letter of July 9, 1846, for example, Marcy described Mexico as a country "so divided into races, classes, and parties" that it provided "great room" for "inducing them to wish success to an [American] invasion."[63] In the letter, Marcy highlighted the racial division "between the Spaniards, who monopolize the wealth and power of the country, and the mixed Indian race, who bear[s] its burdens."[64] Here, Marcy sought to educate Kearny about the different between elite Mexicans, who perhaps claimed Spanish ancestry, and the vast majority of Mexicans, who had far more Indian than Spanish ancestry. Later in the same letter, Marcy also spoke about the division between Mexicans and "the Indians," by whom he meant not "Indian Mexicans," but the diverse nomadic and semi-nomadic tribes whose territory included New Mexico. As to these Indians, Marcy advised pacifying them by "increas[ing] your supply for goods to be distributed as presents" to them.[65]

No Longer a Bloodless Conquest

As Kearny prepared to head west to California, military intelligence reported that New Mexico and its natives were "contented" and "perfectly tranquil."[66] Within months, however, the Americans realized how wrong they were, as a widespread anti-American rebellion took shape. According to some, most of the high-status Mexican families had members among the leaders of the resistance, which was based in Santa Fe but spread across many northern New Mexico communities.[67] No written documents survive that describe the rebellion from the point of view of its Mexican proponents, but we can piece together a partial account from the official reports by the American military and civil authorities, as well as from American newspaper accounts. José María Sánchez, one of the alleged opposition leaders, was captured and in his confession to American soldiers described an elaborate series of secret meetings held at various private homes over many weeks, the election of resistance officers, and the drafting of proclamations to be carried to villages around New Mexico.[68]

Similarly, Bent reported a well-organized resistance that had been sending representatives to "the different towns to incite the lower classes of Mexicans and [P]ueblo Indians."[69]

The uprising was to have begun with a Christmas Eve attack, the idea being that the American officers would be occupied with festivities, inebriated, and otherwise less mindful of their weapons. According to Bent's report, less than a week before Christmas, an unnamed woman notified military officials of the rebellion plan.[70] All but two of the resisters were caught and arrested, but none was punished because they confessed and promised to cooperate with the Americans in the future. The official reports provide little information about the female turncoat (not even her name), but contemporary accounts arose about her identity and motives for cooperating with the Americans. These stories took on a life of their own, appearing in various newspapers, likely more fiction than truth, but the fiction too suggests the dynamics of gender and sexuality that permeated the U.S.–Mexico War. In a New Orleans newspaper account, she was portrayed as a virtuous Mexican woman of mixed indigenous and African descent, while American soldiers were praised for "winning the hearts" of native women like her.[71]

If masculinity was defined in part by "winning the hearts" of females, in New Mexico this meant Mexican and Indian women. One way for Euro-American men to challenge Mexican men was to portray "their" women as voluntarily choosing loyalty to the Americans over the Mexicans, as the New Orleans newspaper account suggested. A poem published in a Boston newspaper shortly before the outbreak of the U.S.–Mexican War, entitled "They Wait for Us," conveys the presumption that Mexican women would gladly choose American over Mexican men, portrayed by the author as lazy and undeserving of feminine attention.

> The Spanish maid, with eye of fire,
> At balmy evening turns her lyre
> And, looking to the Eastern sky,
> Awaits our Yankee chivalry
> Whose purer blood and valiant arms
> Are fit to clasp her budding charms.
> The man, her mate, is sunk in sloth —
> To love, his senseless heart is loth:
> The pipe and glass and tinkling lute,

A sofa, a dish of fruit;
A nap, some dozen times by day;
Somber and sad, and never gay.[72]

At a broader level, the larger war implicated gender roles in American popular culture, with the United States gendered as male and potent and Mexico feminized as weak and vulnerable.

American attitudes toward Mexican women oscillated between the view that they were prizes to be won from the feckless Mexican men to the view that they were, literally, "contaminating" American soldiers.[73] Often Mexican women were described by Euro-American travelers as being sexually promiscuous, a racial stereotype that persists today.[74] There were undoubtedly native women who were prostitutes, including some who made successful careers of serving American soldiers. To what extent did they freely choose prostitution or feel they had no alternative to survive? Keep in mind that there were only a handful of Euro-American women living in all of New Mexico during the war. Native women had a variety of relationships with Euro-American men. Consider the relatively affluent Jaramillo sisters of Taos, for example, who married or lived with Kit Carson and Charles Bent, two of the earliest American immigrants to New Mexico. In 1843 Josefa Jaramillo married Carson, who had converted to Catholicism and become a Mexican citizen prior to the marriage. Her sister, Ignacia, became a widow at a young age, and, perhaps sometime in the late 1830s or early 1840s, established a household with Bent. (We can only speculate, but one reason they did not marry may have been his unwillingness to convert to Catholicism.) Historian Deena González has shown that marriages between Euro-American men and Mexican women never involved more than a tiny percentage of Mexican women, although we know little about less formal relationships.[75]

The official story of the December uprising was that it had been stopped in its tracks. It became at once a cautionary tale for the Mexicans and, at least briefly, an opportunity for the military and civil governments to brag to Washington. Bent, as civil governor, and Price, as military commander, both took credit for stopping the coup, and both were confident that there would be no future rebellions. Two weeks before he was assassinated, Bent penned a conciliatory, if also hortatory, letter "to the inhabitants" of New Mexico, signing it "your best friend." The letter referred to the Mexican rebels as "anarchists" and ambitious men who sought to control the masses, whom Bent urged to embrace democracy: "you [New Mexicans] compose a part of the Union, the cradle of liberty."[76] But Bent seriously misjudged the mood of New Mexico's natives.

His false confidence prompted him to leave his well-guarded Santa Fe lodgings to return home to Taos, where, within a month of the arrests in the Santa Fe rebellion, he was murdered by rebels. Teresina Bent Scheurich, who was around five years old in 1847, later recalled the attack on her father:

> We were in bed when the Mexicans and Indians came to the house breaking the doors and some of them were on the top of the house tearing the roof. So we got up and father stepped to the porch asking them what they wanted, and they answered him: "We want your head *gringo*; we do not want for any of you gringos to govern us, as we have come to kill you."[77]

According to Price's report, Bent's attackers scalped and beheaded him.[78] They also killed five others that January morning, including two other Euro-American officials (the sheriff and the district attorney), a young man who was the son of one of the judges Kearny had appointed, Ignacia Jaramillo's brother, and a Mexican justice of the peace who had pledged loyalty to the Americans.[79]

In his official report, the military commander concluded, "It appeared to be the object of the insurrectionists to put to death every American and every Mexican who had accepted office under the American government."[80] Whether or not they were coordinated, events at Taos appear to have triggered other anti-American attacks. Later that same day, eight Euro-Americans (including at least one Englishman) were killed at Turley's Mill, a distillery owned by an American in the village of Arroyo Hondo, north of Taos. Two other Americans were also killed that day in Rio Colorado. Within a few days of Bent's assassination, Lawrence Waldo's eight-man trading party was killed near the village of Mora.[81] Price reported contemporaneously that the rebellion was gaining supporters from each village along the way.[82]

Little in the existing historical record allows us to conclude definitively that the December plot and the Taos uprising were connected. Indeed, several contemporary accounts by Euro-Americans go out of their way to claim that the two rebellions were unrelated and quite different in their origins and style—suggesting the Santa Fe plot was carried out by Mexican elites, while the Taos uprising was the work of peasants—but they do so based on little evidence. When news of the Taos uprising finally reached the American public two months later, the press portrayed the Taos rebels as "greasers," "loafers," and "rabble."[83] Yet at least one elderly man from a prominent Mexican family eventually was convicted of treason and sentenced to die (though he was never executed). Over time, the Santa Fe plot came to be associated with Mexicans alone, although the scant evidence suggests Pueblo Indians also were part of the conspiracy, if not in leadership roles. The Taos "massacre" came to be portrayed as the work of "savage" Indians, despite the fact that all contemporary accounts of the attack on Bent described the rebels as both Indians and Mexicans.[84] For example, an 1847 Euro-American account presented the Taos rebellion as one exclusively committed by "the Pueblos of Taos [who] were accounted the most warlike and the bravest race in Mexico" and emphasized the "extreme brutality" and "savage barbarity" of the attack on Bent.[85] These characterizations also fed into the racist current of the time that portrayed Indians as more brutal than Mexicans, even as they buttressed the stereotype of Mexicans as lazy and inefficient (the explanation given for the failed December plot).

The military response to the murders of Euro-American civilians and government officials was immediate and unequivocal.[86] While the native resisters fought mostly with bows and arrows along with a few guns, the Americans responded with cannons. Over the course of a few weeks, the U.S. Army engaged in battles against the native population at Santa Cruz de la Cañada, Embudo, Mora, Taos Pueblo, and Las Vegas. Four days after Bent's murder, Colonel Price left Santa Fe with 353 men and four twelve-pound cannons (supplemented soon thereafter with two more howitzers), to be employed against an enemy that Price estimated to number roughly 1,500 men.[87] The winter of 1846–47 was especially harsh, with deep snow on the ground in the Taos area in January and February, a special hardship for soldiers on foot (only the company of volunteers rode horses).[88] The natives had the advantage of knowing the local terrain, but they were outgunned by the Americans, resulting in lopsided casualty numbers. For instance, eight Americans were killed or wounded at Santa Cruz, but more than four times that many Mexicans and Indians lost their lives.[89] The Americans headed north toward Taos, and in the village of Embudo, which lies at the bottom of the canyon that is the principal route into Taos, encountered more than six hundred resisters on January 29, according to Price. By this time, Price had 479 troops and six cannons. He reported that one American and twenty natives were killed.

While Price was moving toward Taos, another American contingent was moving from the northeast through the village of Mora, near where Waldo's trading party had been murdered January 19. Five days after these murders, the Mora rebels successfully repelled the American forces, which then retreated. But the Americans returned a few days later, this time under the command of Captain Jesse I. Morin and anxious for revenge. The Americans reported no enemy casualties from this attack, but it is likely that many villagers were killed, save those who could escape to the mountains. In addition to razing the village, the Americans destroyed communal food supplies, which probably resulted in the later starvation of those who initially fled to the surrounding mountains.[90] The *New Orleans Daily Delta* portrayed Captain Morin, a native of Platte, Missouri, as a hero for his attack on Mora, saying he "burned to ashes every house, town and rancho in his path [and that was] just retribution for assassination of innocent people [in Waldo's party]."[91]

Price continued moving toward Taos, reporting that he arrived at the summit above Taos in two feet of snow on February 1, the same day that Morin's forces razed Mora. It took Price and his troops another two days, marching down the mountain through the snow, to reach Taos, where Bent had been murdered.[92] At this point, Price learned the rebels had barricaded themselves in the San Geronimo Catholic church at Taos Pueblo, north of the village where Bent lived. Price described the Pueblo's church as well-fortified: "calculated for defense, every point of the exterior walls and pickets being flanked by some projecting building." According to Price's report, the troops arrived at the Pueblo mid-day on February 3 and, starting at 2 P.M., pounded the western side of the adobe church with five cannons for more than two hours. Meanwhile, a company of volunteers on horseback, led by one of Bent's long-time trading partners, Charles St. Vrain, blocked access to those who might have escaped to the mountains. The next morning, Price stationed cannons on the west and north sides of the church and continuing pounding it for two more hours. After an unsuccessful effort to storm the church at mid-day, Price moved the largest cannon, a six-pound howitzer, from a position 250 feet west of the church to one 60 feet away and then continued firing until there was a large opening in the adobe wall of the church.

At least two hundred Mexicans and Pueblo Indians died that day at Taos Pueblo, including fifty-one killed as they tried to flee to the mountains.[93] But the number of officially reported deaths only begins to tell the story. Because the Pueblo itself was destroyed, along with all food supplies, many more Taos Pueblo residents (including women, children, and elderly men) must have starved to death over the months to come. Never once in the official reports did Price express concern that he had stormed a church to achieve his end. But a young American adventure-seeker named Lewis Garrard described what it was like to visit the ruins of Taos Pueblo shortly after the battle:

> [We entered] the church at the stormers' breach, through which the missiles of death were hurled. Above, between the charred and blackened rafters which leaned from their places as if ready to fall on us, could be seen the spotless blue sky of this pure clime—on either side, the lofty walls, perforated by cannon ball and loophole, let in the long lines of uncertain gray light; and strewed and piled about the floor, as on the day of battle, were broken, burnt beams and heaps of adobes. Climbing and jumping over them, we made our way to the altar, now a broken platform, with scarce a sign or vestige of its former use. . . . A few half-scared Pueblos walked listlessly about, vacantly staring in a state of dejected, gloomy abstraction. And they might well be so. Their *alcalde* dead, their grain and cattle gone, their church in ruins, the flower of the nation slain or under sentence of death, and the rest—with the exception of those in prison—refugees starving in the mountains.[94]

The First American Trials in the Southwest

The first American trial in New Mexico was the court-martial of one of the leaders of the Taos revolt. Price reported capturing alive the two reputed leaders of the uprising, Tomás Romero of Taos Pueblo (whom Price refers to by first name only, a sign of his inferior treatment of Indians) and a Mexican named Pablo Montoya. Romero was "one of [the enemy's] principal men, who had instigated and been actively engaged in the murder of Governor Bent and others," according to Price; his capture was a principal goal of bombing the church at Taos Pueblo. Price reported that Romero was killed in military custody by a "Private Fitzgerald." Price did not provide any additional details or indicate that Fitzgerald was punished or otherwise reprimanded for Romero's murder, perhaps a further indication of Price's low value of Indians.[95] Montoya was captured at Taos Pueblo, court-martialed, and executed a day later.[96] Newspaper accounts describe the court-martial charges against Montoya as murder (the January attack on Bent) and "exciting the people to rebellion," based on a letter he authored a week after the assassination.[97]

In the aftermath of these military executions, New Mexicans witnessed their first trials under U.S. civil law. It was these trials that culminated in the Easter hangings of 1847 described at the outset of this chapter, as well as eleven to sixteen additional executions.[98] Stemming from the uprising by Mexicans and Pueblo Indians against the Americans, more than one hundred native men were arrested and jailed under military guard in Santa Fe and Taos. The Euro-American prosecutor sought an incredible seventy-nine indictments against Mexican and Pueblo Indian men for Bent's murder.[99] The two resulting sets of trials—one series in Santa Fe in March 1847 and one series in Taos in April of that year—were conducted as civilian trials, but they occurred very much in the shadow of military rule. It does not appear that the "superior court" constituted by Kearny so early in the American invasion had functioned prior to these trials. The war did not end until May 1848, and Congress did not authorize a civil government and legal system in the region until late 1850. Thus, these trials fell somewhere between martial and civil law.

The trials would have seemed foreign not only to Mexicans and Pueblo Indians in New Mexico, but also to those in the rest of the United States. We can therefore understand the trials by comparison to two relevant benchmarks: the Spanish-Mexican legal system that pre-dated the American occupation, and the criminal justice system that Americans aspired to in the mid-nineteenth century.

Under Spanish and Mexican authority, the local *alcalde* system was the primary means for adjudication of disputes, and, by Kearny's design, this system remained in place during the U.S. military occupation. As with the early American justice of the peace, formal legal training was not a requirement for being an *alcalde*; instead, men were chosen for this role because they were prominent in their community, literate, and probably frequently relatively wealthy due to ranching or mercantile enterprises.[100] Rather than relying on procedural formalities or legal precedent, the *alcalde* system put a premium on reaching a settlement that maintained the relationship between the parties in a land where life was challenging and highly interdependent on kin, neighbors, and community.[101] There were no lawyers (although parties occasionally brought along an adviser to assist them in making their case), nor were there juries or other mechanisms for public participation, outside the parties and witnesses. The community, however, which was generally small and interdependent, functioned as a check on the *alcalde*, since the efficacy of resolutions depended on their widespread acceptance in the community.[102]

A second benchmark against which to understand these first American trials in the Southwest is to consider how trials looked elsewhere in the United States at the time.[103] As they do today, prosecutions of persons for major felonies (burglary, robbery, arson, major fraud, manslaughter, assault, rape, and murder, among them) involved juries composed of laypersons at two major stages: (1) at the indictment stage, a grand jury composed of laypersons decided whether or not to accept a prosecutor's recommendation to indict and what crime(s) to charge;[104] and (2) at the trial stage, a petit jury of laypersons decided whether the defendant was guilty or not and sometimes had the discretion to determine punishment in cases of guilt.[105] Looking at the United States as a whole, we know that all grand and petit jurors were men and that the vast majority of them were white.[106]

One distinguishing feature of nineteenth-century criminal trials was that the defendant frequently was not represented by a lawyer, especially when less serious crimes were involved.[107] Perhaps the irregular presence of lawyers influenced the pace of criminal justice in the nineteenth century. In one California county, researchers found that the average criminal trial in the 1880s lasted 1.5 days,[108] and in some jurisdictions, entire trials concluded in less than an hour.[109] Finally, convicted defendants had the right to appeal—to ask an appellate court to review and reconsider their conviction.[110]

Another aspiration of the U.S. trial system was that the trained legal experts, in the form of prosecutors and presiding judges, and the laymen who served as jurors would hold each other in check. Citizen grand juries checked the power of the prosecutor and petit juries checked the power of the trial judge. Writing about nineteenth-century trends, legal scolar Lawrence Friedman argues that, over the course of the century, judges became less powerful and petit juries gained power, even as what he terms a "fundamental ambiguity" about Americans' beliefs of juries persisted: "Juries were, on the one hand, supposed to reflect popular norms; but, on the other hand, they were not supposed to indulge in popular stereotypes. On the one hand, they were lionized; on the other, mistrusted."[111]

These two benchmarks—the Mexican legal system that existed prior to the American invasion and the practices that governed criminal trials elsewhere in the United States—reveal what the expectations of the native people of New Mexico and of the Americans in the region would have been on the eve of these first American trials in the Southwest. The trials themselves unfolded in ways that would have seemed foreign to both audiences. This is true because the trials ultimately must be seen as "war trials," in that they aimed to accomplish the ends of war, rather than in any sense meet the standard of being a coherent adjudication system. They were war trials despite the fact that Mexicans participated in them as grand and petit jurors, defendants, and witnesses. Indeed, it may have been precisely the fact of Mexicans' participation that resulted in the successful imposition of American colonial rule in New Mexico during the coming decades.

During his brief stay in New Mexico, Kearny appointed three judges to the "superior court": Antonio José Otero, Charles Beaubien, and Joab Houghton. Otero was a well-to-do Mexican merchant and rancher, who had served in the Mexican legislature and helped draft Mexico's constitution.[112] Beaubien was a French Canadian trapper and trader who had become a naturalized Mexican citizen and married a Mexican woman, and who had served as an alcalde under the Mexican government.[113] Of the three, only the Euro-American merchant Houghton had no prior legal or governing experience.[114] It is hard to believe that Kearny imagined the newly conceived American court actually conducting business during the wartime occupation, but that opportunity came with the Taos uprising. The previously inactive court system provided a way both to mete out punishment to the surviving rebels and to consolidate American rule. The Americans probably expected the trials to result in an undeniable display of American authority and a dramatic warning—in the form of public hangings—to any natives still contemplating rebellion.

There were numerous ways in which the trials were illegitimate as judged by contemporary American standards. Despite the fact that his son Narciso had been killed along with Bent, Beaubien convened the Taos court as judge. He appointed George Bent, brother of the slain governor, as foreman of the grand jury, though typically the grand jury would have elected its own foreman. Not surprisingly, given the judge's and foreman's relationships to the murder victims, the grand jury returned indictments against thirty-eight of the forty men brought before it. Yet the nineteen-man grand jury also included fourteen or fifteen men with Spanish surnames, likely members of high-status Mexican families in the Taos area.[115] Given the relative isolation and small size of these villages, we can assume that these and other jurors were related to or otherwise connected to those charged with crimes (several shared surnames with defendants).

Although the majority of the grand jurors were Mexican men, Euro-Americans seem to have been over-represented, given their small numbers in New Mexico at that time. It appears that virtually all Euro-American men present in Taos who were not part of the occupying military force served as jurors. Thus, the presiding judge very likely overlooked any requirement of residency for jurors (under typical rules, only men who had resided in the region for six or more months would have been eligible). Amazingly given their numbers, the juries in at least three murder trials involving a total of ten defendants—those of José Manuel García, of the five Pueblo Indian defendants tried jointly, and of the four Mexicans tried jointly—were composed entirely of Euro-Americans. An American eyewitness reported that several juries included a Frenchman who spoke very little English and whom he characterized as "with not two ideas above eating and drinking."[116] He reported overhearing the French juror ask the jury foreman what he should do, to which the Euro-American foreman's response was, "Why, hang them, of course; what did you come here for?"[117]

In Taos, more than thirty men were indicted for serious crimes. Five were indicted for "high treason" for their activities on January 19: Polio Salazar, Francisco Ulibarri, Varua Tafoya, Felipe Tafoya, and Pablo Guerrera. Of these five, only Salazar was convicted of treason; he was tried, convicted, and hanged within a few days without the opportunity to appeal his conviction. Ulibarri was tried for treason April 12, but his case ended in a hung jury and the court ordered him released. Perhaps the jury was influenced by the hangings of five native sons they had witnessed three days earlier. More than a week into the court session, prosecutor Frank Blair dropped the treason charges against the remaining three men, and they were released. Although the high number of returned indictments suggests that the grand jury chose not to exercise its authority to "check" the prosecutor's power in this case, the petit jury in the Ulibarri case did. Because at least one juror refused to acquiesce in the conviction for treason (which, from the hanging of Salazar three days earlier, they knew would result in death to the defendant), the Euro-American prosecutor received the message that it was not worth pursuing treason charges against the remaining men accused of that crime.

Seventeen men were charged with Bent's murder. This charge suggests that Blair put forward a theory that the men were accomplices in the murder of Bent. This theory would seem implausible under these circumstances, since it was not known who Bent's actual killers were, substantial time had passed since the murders, and many of those in a position to provide evidence to the jury about Bent's murder had been executed by the Americans, killed at Taos Pueblo, or had escaped capture by the Americans.[118] On April 7, José Manuel García was convicted of murder and sentenced to die; he was hanged at Taos plaza two days later. Pedro Lucero, Juan Ramón Trujillo, Manuel Romero, and Isidro Romero were tried jointly, convicted, and sentenced to death all in the same day. On April 8, Francisco Naranjo, José Gabriel Samora, Juan Domingo Martínez, Juan Antonio Lucero, and "El Cuerro" were convicted of murder and sentenced to die.[119] On April 10, Manuel Miera, Manuel Sandoval, Rafael Tafoya, and Juan Pacheco were jointly tried, convicted, and sentenced to die. A defendant listed in the court records only as "Ascencio" was tried and acquitted of murder on Monday, April 12. Juan Antonio Avila was convicted of murder and sentenced to die on April 13. In addition to the treason and murder cases, the grand jury indicted sixteen other native men for property crimes (larceny, theft of animals, receipt of stolen property) in connection with the Taos uprising.[120]

Once Congress officially established courts in New Mexico in 1850, they operated with two official Spanish translators, one to translate the court proceedings and another to translate for the grand and petit juries. This was not, however, the case in April 1847. There the official translator was Charles St. Vrain, who in addition to leading the volunteer forces against the rebels in the Santa Cruz, Embudo, Mora, and Taos Pueblo battles, was also the slain governor's business partner.[121] It appears that his only role was to translate the testimony of Spanish-speaking witnesses into English (including that of sisters Ignacia and Josefina Jaramillo, respectively, Bent's common law wife and Kit Carson's wife). His role did not include translating the proceedings from English into Spanish for the benefit of the defendants.

The only trained lawyer in the courtroom (including the judge) was prosecutor Frank P. Blair, another Kearny appointee, a young man who had only recently become a lawyer in the Midwest. He had come west for health reasons when the war with Mexico broke out, so he traveled from Bent's Fort to New Mexico with the army.[122] Given Blair's youth and novice status, it is likely that he made numerous errors, at least some of which would have harmed the Mexican and Pueblo Indian defendants. Whatever his limitations, at least the prosecutor was trained as a lawyer. Garrard describes one defense lawyer (perhaps the only one for all thirty-eight defendants) as "a volunteer private."[123] José Manuel García, whose trial for

Bent's murder was the first in the court session, was indicted early on the morning of April 6 (the day after the court convened and appointed the grand jury). At that time his lawyer asked for a brief adjournment to prepare for the trial; the judge granted the request and the court reconvened a few hours later to convict García in one afternoon. By the second trial, the defense lawyer had improved: in representing four defendants tried together for murder (Pedro Lucero, Manuel Romero, Juan Ramón Trujillo, Isidro Romero), the judge considered but rejected a defense motion to quash the indictment. According to a letter from Blair to the U.S. Attorney General (which was received in Washington weeks after the trails had ended and the executions had occurred), the defense lawyer objected repeatedly to the court's authority to hear *any* case against Mexican citizens. But both Houghton and Beaubien summarily overruled the defense objections.[124] Over the course of two weeks, thirty-nine native men were indicted at Taos, nineteen of whom faced the death penalty. Yet none had the right to appeal.

More than thirty native men captured in the army's attack at Taos Pueblo were held prisoner in Santa Fe. The prosecutor eventually sought indictments for treason against twenty-nine of them. On March 8, 1847, Judge Joab Houghton convened a grand jury to consider whether to approve or reject the indictments. Although we do not know who served on the grand jury, the demographics of Santa Fe suggest that it likely contained a substantial number of Mexicans. The grand jury rejected twenty-five indictments on the grounds of "insufficient evidence."[125] It returned four indictments for "high treason" against the United States. The first and only treason defendant to stand trial was seventy-five-year-old Antonio Maria Trujillo, the father-in-law of Diego Archuleta, one of the leaders of the thwarted December 1846 plot, who eluded capture by the Americans. Three other native sons who were indicted for "high treason" were Pantaleon Archuleta, Trinidad Barcelo, and Pedro Vigil.[126] The three were tried separately after Trujillo, with each trial ending in a hung jury. These outcomes suggest juries' unwillingness, after the Trujillo case, to pass the defendants on to Judge Houghton for sentencing. In other words, majority-Mexican juries really were checking the power of Euro-American prosecutors and judges.

Trujillo was convicted by a jury on March 12 and sentenced to be hanged four days later. In sentencing Trujillo, Judge Houghton said, "You have been found seconding the acts of a band of the most traitorous murderers that ever blackened with the recital of their deeds the annals of history. . . .

For such foul crimes, an enlightened and liberal jury [has] been compelled . . . to find you *guilty of treason against the government under which you are a citizen.*"[127] Previously at trial Trujillo's lawyer challenged the court's jurisdiction, apparently arguing that the court system created and appointed by Kearny was illegitimate because it was beyond the bounds of a military commander's authority to take such actions.[128] Houghton rejected the defense argument and refused to allow the jury to consider these issues. After Trujillo was convicted, Trujillo's lawyer again raised the issue, this time moving for a mistrial and requesting a new trial.[129] Perhaps it was these concerns that prompted Houghton, Blair, and scores of other Euro-American and Mexican elites to seek Trujillo's pardon.[130] In a June 11, 1847, letter to Colonel Price, then military commander of New Mexico, Secretary of War Marcy reported that he had "conversed" with President Polk about "the pardon of Antonio Maria Trujillo" and that, while the president would leave the matter to Price to decide, it was his view that Trujillo's life should be spared.[131]

At the national level, two additional questions about the American court's legality persisted well beyond the trials themselves. In part the life of these questions beyond New Mexico was due to the fact that it took news from New Mexico from four to eight weeks to reach Washington, D.C. The first, broader question was whether these courts were legitimate at a fundamental level, given their creation by Kearny, as the leader of the invading forces, rather than by Congress. This question is, of course, related to the larger criticism that the Polk administration overstepped its prerogative in prosecuting the war; in short, congressional leaders (especially Whigs) accused Polk of illegally authorizing the invading army to do things only Congress could do (such as establish federal territories and civilian governments in those territories, including courts).[132] Without addressing the New Mexico situation specifically, an 1850 Supreme Court opinion suggests that Kearny had overstepped his boundaries in establishing a civil government. In that case, the Court considered whether the Mexican port city of Tampico was a foreign or domestic port when it was under control of American naval forces during the Mexican war.[133] With only one dissenting vote, Chief Justice Roger Taney wrote that the port remained a foreign port, even though it was under U.S. military control. At the crux of the opinion was the belief that the power of the executive branch was inherently limited in a military context.

The second question was whether it was legal—under U.S. law—to accuse and convict Mexican citizens of treason against the United States. The

Supreme Court's decision in the Tampico case is relevant once again. The corollary to the President's (and military's) inherently limited power was the fact that foreign citizens in the military zone were in no sense American citizens:

> While it was occupied by our troops, they were in an enemy's country, and not in their own; *the inhabitants were still foreigners and enemies, and owed to the United States nothing more than the submission and obedience*, sometimes called temporary allegiance, which is due from a conquered enemy, when he surrenders to a force which he is unable to resist.[134]

Although the legality of the court conducting the 1847 treason trials was never litigated before an appellate court, this Supreme Court opinion calls it into question. Indeed, an essential element of the crime of treason is the act of belonging to a community: "It was necessary to prove that the person accused [of treason] had intentionally performed acts conflicting with his obligations as a member of the community."[135] Because they had not willingly joined the community, the Mexican and Indian rebels did not owe allegiance to the United States, for Kearny's proclamations alone had not created such a duty. Thus, the prosecutions, convictions, and, in one case, execution, of the rebels for treason were illegal.

Despite the numerous and significant flaws apparent in the 1847 treason trials, they may have worked in two fundamental respects. In the wake of the deaths of perhaps thousands of men, women, and children in the winter of 1847, American civil authorities arrested another hundred Mexican and Pueblo Indian men for participating in the resistance. The American prosecutor attempted to obtain indictments against nearly four-fifths of these men, yet he was rebuffed in most cases by majority-Mexican grand juries. In the end, grand juries approved treason indictments against nine men, a far cry from the scores indicted for murder and other violent crimes associated with the January attack on Bent. Only two of the nine Mexican men charged with treason were convicted by juries and, although both were sentenced to death upon conviction, only one was executed for that crime. After the first treason conviction and execution in Taos, and after the first treason conviction in Santa Fe, it appears that majority-Mexican juries refused further convictions for treason, although they were willing to convict (and mete out death sentences) to those accused of murder. In this respect, the system worked as it was designed to, with lay jurors operating as a check on prosecutors and judges.

What differed is that, in this instance, the judges and prosecutors were part of a colonizing force only marginally removed from the military occupiers. The trials occurred during the war, and military leaders might well have killed all of those captured or executed them after courts-martial. Instead, it seems that military and civilian authorities decided jointly that martial law without the cooperation of the native population (at least without the native Mexican population, if not the Pueblo Indian population) was necessary to assure the Americans' long-term control of the region. Thus, the hastily pulled together legal system had to seem legitimate *enough*, a key aspect being the incorporation of lay grand and petit jurors. This aspect of the trials worked to co-opt some Mexicans in the conviction and punishment of the anti-American rebels. Yet the Americans did not anticipate that, at least some of the time, Mexicans would exercise their authority as jurors, such as by refusing to acquiesce in indictments or convictions.

It is the treason charges that most fundamentally present the paradox at the heart of this book: at this wartime moment, some Euro-Americans moved to treat Mexicans as American citizens even before the Senate had ratified the peace treaty and even before Congress had declared New Mexico a territory. A charge of treason only made sense if someone was seen as part of the political community, even if peripherally so. Moreover, it was Mexican jurors—presumptive "citizens" in their role as jurors—who decided the fate of their countrymen. With the military campaign against the native Mexican and Indian resisters complete, the civil authorities entered to consolidate American power over the natives. In 1846, the Americans understood the need to co-opt Mexican elites, even as they looked ahead to a time when Euro-American immigration would allow them to control the region without native complicity. While some members of elite families had been charged with crimes in the Taos and Santa Fe trials, most of those charged were not elites. Mexican elites' allegiance to the Americans was strengthened by their incorporation into the system as jurors. Additionally, their incorporation by the Americans served to divide Mexican elites from other Mexicans and to divide Mexicans from Pueblo Indians, who, despite having many reasons to distrust Mexicans, had worked together with them against the Americans in Taos and other communities in the January 1847 rebellion.

Official executions were uncommon in New Mexico, both before and after American rule. Reporting on the Spanish colonial and Mexican periods, historian Robert Tórrez found that only a handful of executions occurred. During the official U.S. territorial period (1850–1911), fewer than fifty men were executed. Tórrez speculates that majority-Mexican juries retained a collective memory of these first American executions that made them wary of convicting for first-degree murder, knowing that hanging was the mandatory sentence.[136]

I am left wondering about the significance of these legal executions for the Catholics who were martyrs in that 1847 Easter season and their relatives, then and now. For instance, should we now remember those executed as traitors to the United States, the nation of their future relatives? In a conversation with a descendant of a Taoseño who participated in the rebellion against the Americans, I learned that the story of the treason trials lives on in stories passed down through the generations.[137] For this descendant, the story was mixed in that, on the one hand, elders told of the family's ancestors who were "traitors" to the Americans, thus bringing shame upon the family. Yet the elders told their younger listeners that their ancestors "had good reasons to do what they did" as patriotic Mexicans at war with the United States. Instead of largely ignoring these events (or talking about them in whispered, "private" conversation), we should embrace them as part of the complicated, messy history of the Southwest.

Race and Citizenship after the War

If the first prong of the legal colonization of New Mexico was these early trials for treason and murder in connection with the 1847 resistance to the American invasion, the second prong was the broader effort by the Americans to establish political authority over the region, first through military rule and then by civilian government. Two years after the war ended, Congress admitted California as a state and designated the remainder of the Mexican Cession as the Territory of New Mexico. New Mexico remained in this ambiguous political status for the next sixty-four years, until it was admitted as the forty-seventh American state in 1912.[138]

In large part, New Mexico's status as a contiguous colony was due to the racial composition of its population. American ideas about the racial inferiority of its Mexican enemies had been in wide circulation during the debates leading up to the war and during the war itself, as we have seen.[139] But they came to a head in 1848, as the question of how much territory Mexico would cede to the United States became paramount. Debates in Washington, D.C., and in the nation's major newspapers reflected racist concerns about incorporating "too many Mexicans," and the goal of ending the war became entangled with the goal of getting the most land from Mexico with the smallest number of Mexicans.[140] The thorniest problem was the question of citizenship and what precisely the relationship of the people in the new lands would be to the nation. Secretary of State Buchanan spoke for many when he pondered the question: "How should we govern the mongrel race which inhabits [the new territory]? Could we admit them to seats in our Senate and House of Representatives? Are they capable of Self-Government as States of this Confederacy?"[141]

On two days in February 1848, President Polk's cabinet debated whether the President should recommend ratification to the Senate of the proposed treaty ending the war with Mexico.[142] About a week later, the treaty went to the Senate for approval, where it weathered eleven days of secret deliberations before being approved by a vote of thirty-eight to fourteen.[143] The purpose of the treaty was to end the war in a way that was mutually acceptable to both nations. The Americans insisted on a sizable cession of Mexican territory (ultimately about half of Mexico's total territory at the time), and the boundaries of the cession were laid out in the treaty.[144] The Mexicans negotiated a sum of $15 million to be paid to indemnify Mexico for claims against its citizens and for the war more generally. The Mexican negotiators also sought to include provisions for the protection of the political, religious, and property rights of its citizens living in the ceded territory.

The Senate's modifications were significant and nearly caused the Mexican legislature to reject the treaty, which would have prolonged the war.[145] The Senate voted to strike entirely proposed Article X of the treaty, which pertained to the fate of Mexican and Spanish land grants in the ceded territory (which will be discussed in detail in Chapter 4). The Senate also voted to modify Article IX, which, as it was originally drafted, sought to protect the rights of the Mexican citizens by assuring that the ceded territory would be admitted as one or mote states of the Union "as soon as possible."[146] Instead, the Senate altered Article IX to more vaguely refer to when the ceded lands might become states: Mexicans living in the ceded territory who chose not to retain their Mexican citizenship "shall be incorporated into the Union of the United States and be admitted, *at the proper time (to be judged of by the Congress of the United States)* to the enjoyment of all the rights of citizens of the United States according to the principles of the Constitution."[147] Some of the Mexican legislators debating ratification after the U.S. Senate's amendments strongly feared that the Mexican citizens were doomed to ill treatment by the Americans: "The North Americans hate us, their orators deprecate us even in speeches in which they recognize the justice of our cause, and they consider us unable to form a single nation or society with them."[148]

In its approval process, the Senate left intact Article VIII of the treaty, dealing with the citizenship rights of the Mexican citizens living in the ceded territory. Under that provision, Mexicans living in the ceded region had three options.[149] First, they could choose to leave their homes in order to relocate south of the newly established U.S.–Mexico border. An estimated four thousand people chose this option, an astounding number given the trauma and cost such moves must have entailed at that time.[150] A second option for the former Mexican citizens was to remain in their homes, now in the United States, but elect to maintain their Mexican citizenship.[151] Given conflicts during the early 1850s about who was eligible to vote and hold office, it appears that numerous Mexicans elected to maintain their Mexican citizenship in the period immediately following the ratification of the peace treaty. In one instance in 1853, forty Mexicans were indicted by the Euro-American prosecutor for falsely claiming they were U.S. citizens in order to vote. When the prosecutor produced records showing these men had elected to retain their Mexican citizenship, the judge ruled the records unreliable, invalidated the 1849 process for retaining Mexican citizenship (which had been established by the military commander), and dismissed all the cases, with the result that the Mexican men could vote.[152] The third option operated by default: if the former Mexican citizens remained in their homes and did not formally elect to retain Mexican citizenship, they would be presumed to be U.S. citizens after one year.

Ultimately, however, the nature of "citizenship" rights conveyed to the Mexicans under Article VIII was, at best, legally vague and, at worst, a deliberate attempt to mislead the Mexican negotiators. With the citizenship provision, the Mexican legislature believed it had protected the rights of its citizens to retain Mexican citizenship or elect American citizenship. What the legislators probably did not understand, however, was that *federal* citizenship was inferior to *state* citizenship in the United States.[153] Writing in 1828, Supreme Court Chief Justice John Marshall distinguished between the rights of federal citizens and state citizens: those citizens who held *only* federal citizenship (this case dealt with citizens of the Florida Territory) had the protection of the Constitution ("the enjoyment of the privileges, rights, and immunities of the citizens of the United States"), but they did not have political rights. Political rights, Marshall wrote, would not accrue to Florida's citizens until they became *state* citizens as well.[154] By 1870, when the American citizenship of Pablo de la Guerra, a Mexican American living in California, was challenged, Marshall's distinction had become settled law and was applied to the former Mexican citizens incorporated under the Treaty of Guadalupe Hidalgo. The California Supreme Court candidly acknowledged that the treaty provided only *federal* citizenship. Federal citizenship extended the protections of the Constitution and provided "a shield of nationality" abroad, but it did not convey political rights. Instead, political rights stemmed only from being a citizen of a *state*.[155]

Under Article IX, the treaty left it to Congress to determine the political status of the former Mexican lands, which left the question of Mexicans' access to full political rights, as state citizens, subject to politics. Congress's first move was to divide the ceded territory into two parts, California and New Mexico. As noted previously, it was the acquisition of California that largely fueled U.S. military aggression against Mexico in the first place. When gold was discovered there in early 1848, near the end of the war, it became obvious that California would be admitted as a state. California's statehood was made part of the so-called Compromise of 1850, which bundled together a variety of congressional measures related to the former Mexican territories and to slavery. With California's fate sealed, the remainder of the ceded territory was organized into a federally controlled "New Mexico Territory."[156] The newly created federal territory was a vast area including almost all of present-day New Mexico and Arizona, as well as substantial portions of present-day Colorado, Nevada, and Wyoming.[157] Territorial status, rather than statehood, proved an effective way for the federal government to establish political authority over New Mexico, while extending the bare minimum of the right of self-governance to the majority-Mexican and Indian population and small (but growing) minority of Euro-American residents of the region.[158]

There were three profound ways in which New Mexico's status as a territory shaped its history as part of the United States. First, New Mexico's status as a federal territory meant that its residents held a hollow federal citizenship. They were governed by the federal government, but they had no elected representatives in that government. Under the act creating the territory, New Mexicans elected a nonvoting delegate to Congress. Second, territorial status precluded New Mexico's population from controlling the *territorial* government. Instead, New Mexico's governor, three Supreme Court justices, and about a dozen additional territorial officials were appointed by the President (subject to approval by the Senate). Over the course of New Mexico's 64-year territorial period, these appointees were overwhelming Euro-Americans.[159] The congressional legislation creating the New Mexico Territory provided for the establishment of a territorial legislature, which was dominated by Mexican men well into the American period of rule. However, territorial legislation was subject to nullification by Congress. Congress rarely overrode the territorial legislature, but it is reasonable to conclude that majority-Mexican territorial legislatures sometimes decided to forego or to enact legislation to appease congressional leaders.

By 1860, it became clear that New Mexico's status as a federal territory placed it in a kind of political limbo. In the Compromise of 1850, when New Mexico was declared a federal territory, Congress admitted California as a free state. Five years earlier, Congress had admitted Texas as a state in which slavery was allowed. In the coming decades, New Mexico would be carved into a variety of additional regions, including Arizona and Colorado, and several parts of the Mexican Cession would become states. Although some Mexicans and Euro-Americans repeatedly argued for New Mexico's admission as a state throughout the territorial period, New Mexico's status differed strikingly from that of its neighbors in the West. New Mexico existed for sixty-four years in an ambiguous political relationship with the United States, part colony and part territory-to-be-annexed.[160]

More than anything, it was New Mexico's racial make-up that accounted for its lengthy status as a federal territory. Though substantial numbers of Indians lived in the region, they were disenfranchised. It was the majority-Mexican federal citizens whom Congress objected to including as state citizens. Although Congress allowed Mexican men to enfranchise themselves as "white" rights-holders, it would not yield to the notion that Mexicans were true Americans, entitled to state citizenship alongside federal citizenship. Instead, Mexican Americans entered the nation as second-class citizens very much identified as racially inferior to white Euro-Americans.

2

Where Mexicans Fit in the New American Racial Order

The stock story of westward expansion portrays Americans as courageous settlers welcomed by the Mexican people living in what would become the U.S. West and Southwest. The previous chapter provided a very different history of the American encounter with the native Mexican and Indian peoples of the region. Instead of peaceful annexation and conflict-free settlement, the Southwest came to be part of the United States via a conquest that was frequently violent, with law playing a central role in perpetrating that violence. Moreover, the American conquest, as well as the specific violence inflicted by troops and by law, reflected and expressed Americans' convictions about white superiority and about the racial inferiority of everyone else, including Mexicans.

In describing the military and political conquest of New Mexico by the United States, I have emphasized the region's status as an *American* colony. However, the American colonization of the region in the nineteenth century was grafted onto the Spanish colonization of the sixteenth, seventeenth, and eighteenth centuries. The Southwest developed in what I term a "double colonization" context. Both the Spanish and American colonial regimes imposed a system of status inequality grounded in racial difference. While a central aspect of both the Spanish and American conquests was a racial ideology of white supremacy, the particular variants of the ideology differed under the two regimes.

Double colonization meant that the various racial groups who inhabited the region in the mid-nineteenth century were forced to navigate two different racial regimes simultaneously. For example, those native to New Mexico—the Mexican, Pueblo Indian, and other Indian communities—negotiated the American racial order in the shadow of the Spanish-Mexican racial order. Similarly, white Euro-Americans who immigrated to New

Mexico, as well as those who lived elsewhere, experienced the addition of Mexicans and Indians to the nation against the backdrop of the prior Spanish-Mexican racial order. Double colonization resulted in a situation in which everyone, including elites of all races, jockeyed for position and defined themselves and others in an undeniably multi-racial terrain. To fully grasp the nature of the changes in the racial order after the American occupation, we must first come to terms with the prior Spanish-Mexican racial order. Only then can we explore how the two systems of racial sub-ordination interacted with each other to produce the new American racial order.

The First White Man Was a Black Man

Pueblo oral history tells of their first encounter with non-Indians. In 1539, the Spanish Crown sponsored an expedition led by Fray Marcos de Niza. De Niza was dependent on the linguistic and geographical knowledge of a man named Estevan, who had amassed experience from earlier Spanish expeditions to Florida, Texas, and central Mexico.[1] Spanish accounts describe Estevan as dark-skinned and, often, as an African slave.[2] Jemez Pueblo historian Joe Sando relates that Pueblo Indians today often say, "The first *white* man our people saw was a *black* man."[3] Indeed, Jemez Pueblo still commemorates the encounter with a dance that includes roles for Estevan and De Niza. According to Sando's description, De Niza is portrayed by a dancer with his face painted white who wears "a long black coat with a knotted white rope tied around his waist in the fashion of a Franciscan priest," while Estevan is portrayed by a dancer with his face painted black—a "black sheep pelt covers [his head] to indicate curly hair."[4]

There are multiple and conflicting accounts of Estevan's death at the hands of the Zuni people. According to the most frequently cited account (that of De Niza), Estevan led an advance party traveling about two days ahead of De Niza. Arriving at Zuni Pueblo, Estevan was warned to turn back; when he did not do so, and when he informed the Zunis that the rest of his large, well-armed party would soon be joining him, he was killed in the hope that word of his death would discourage the rest of his party from approaching further.[5] In one Zuni telling of the story, the Zunis were awed by Estevan's size and various powers and so decided to cut off his feet so that he would be unable to flee and would live among the Zuni people, eventually dying there as "an old deity."[6] Some anthropologists have attributed the Hopi and Zuni story about a man known as Nepokwa'I to that of Estevan, noting that the former is portrayed as a black-colored *katsina* who was stoned by the Zunis for seeking sexual relations with Zuni women.[7]

The story of Estevan as the first non-Indian to explore New Mexico and meet the Pueblo Indians evokes the complexity of the Spanish conquest of New Mexico. From the Pueblo point of view, the story illustrates the irony and confusing nature of Spanish racial categories. To the Indians, the Spanish were "white men," and yet their ranks included "black men" whom the Spanish had enslaved. In the Pueblo world of today, they are neither white nor black and thus wear "whiteface" or "blackface" to underscore their exclusion from these racial categories in their contemporary dance marking the infamous encounter.

From another point of view, Estevan's story raises more questions than it answers about his slave status. Anthropologist Martha Menchaca has concluded that Estevan was an African slave (probably, she says, brought to New Spain by his owner, Andres Dorantes, who was part of the Florida expedition of 1528).[8] Based on circumstantial evidence, she believes he came from Africa's west coast, from which Spain was heavily importing slaves in the early sixteenth century.[9] Another account suggests different African origins for Estevan. According to an exhibition on the first Arabs in North America at the Arab American National Museum in Dearborn, Michigan, Estevan's Arabic name was Zammouri, which means a person from Al-Zammour, a city in Morocco.[10] The exhibit reports that Estevan was captured in 1511, when Portugal invaded Morocco, and then likely sold into slavery, along with more than 12 million North African Arabs.[11]

Yet another account argues that Estevan was not a slave at all, but would more accurately be characterized as "a political or economic refugee" who probably fled Morocco during the early sixteenth century, when 60,000 Moroccans went to Spain or Portugal.[12] Anthropologist Hsain Ilahiane cites Spanish accounts describing Estevan as a Moor born in Morocco, and he also concludes that the Spanish would not have given him such latitude (and the concomitant opportunity to escape) if he had been a slave.[13] Ilahiane goes so far as to dispute that Estevan was black, concluding that he was most likely "an Arab Muslim."[14] Of course, it is possible he could have been both black and an Arab Muslim. At least some of the confusion results because Estevan did not tell his own story—we do not have his written account, as we do that of Marcos. That significant limitation has been compounded because the nomenclature used to describe Estevan has varied. First, racial terms have been inconsistently translated from Spanish to English. For instance, various English translations of Spanish descriptions of Estevan use the terms "Negro," "black," "brown," "Moor," and "North African Arab" to describe him. In addition to the considerable problem of reliable, contextualized translation, there is the dilemma of the nomenclature of racial categories themselves, which have been contested in both Spanish and English.

Seen through a wider lens still, Estevan's story opens the door to a conversation about African slavery in the Americas more generally. The Spanish importation of African slaves into Mexico began in the mid-sixteenth century, almost as soon as the Spanish colonization did. During the first century of Spanish conquest of Mexico, there were about as many African slaves brought to Mexico as Spaniards who emigrated there, about 200,000 in each category.[15] Over time, African slaves mixed with Spaniards, Indians, and mestizos (people of Indian and Spanish ancestry) in Mexico to produce a racially mixed population. From the beginning, then, the racial encounter between Spaniards and Indians was ambiguous and nuanced, even as it was eerily clear in terms of who occupied positions of domination and subordination. What is crucial to understand is that both the Spanish and the American regimes of colonization imposed a hierarchy grounded in race, and, thus, each heralded a new system of racial inequality.

The two hallmarks of the Spanish racial order as it was expressed in the "New World" were, first, the identification of the indigenous population as "savage" others and, second, the use of the first claim to legitimize Spanish conquest. As historian Ramón Gutiérrez has concluded, the moment of Spanish conquest in New Mexico in 1540 was marked with racist claims by the Spanish that the Pueblo Indians of the region were uncivilized, unintelligent, and "a people without capacity."[16] These racist conclusions, based on virtually no significant encounters with the Pueblos, allowed the Spanish to justify their wholesale appropriation of Pueblo property, their execution of Pueblo men, and their sexual exploitation of Pueblo women at the moment of initial Spanish–Pueblo contact.[17] The key distinction in the Spanish racial cosmology was one between Spaniards (in general) and Indians (in general), which corresponded to other key binaries: civilized/savage, Christian/heathen, pure/impure, honorable/shameful, European/indigenous. At the same time, the Spanish early came to distinguish among Indians–between those whom they felt they could colonize ("civilized Indians" or neophytes, referring to their conversion to Christianity) and those over whom they did not hope to assert authority ("barbarous Indians"). In New Mexico, Pueblo Indians were "civilized Indians," while the Apaches, Navajos, Comanches, and other tribes that refused to submit to Spanish authority were considered "barbarous."

But the dilemma for the Spanish colonizers in New Mexico, as it had been throughout Mexico and Latin America, was the almost immediate social-sexual interaction and blending between colonizers and natives. The result was an elaborate hierarchy of race-based inequality built around combinations and degrees of racial mixture among Spaniards, Indians, and African slaves who had been brought to the Americas. The foundation for this *"régimen de castas"* (caste regime) was phenotype, expressed as difference, most importantly in skin color, but also in hair type, eye shape, facial structure, and the like. These external differences among a population rapidly mixing "became the visible indexes of what were construed as *natural* inequalities of social being," according to anthropologist Ana Maria Alonso.[18] She describes the end result as a system of race-based inequality in the Spanish colonies:

> A hermeneutics of descent based on a calculus of types and mixtures of pure and impure blood, specified the quality (*calidad*) of social subjects and endowed them with a differential value that defined their place in society. Religion, color, blood, and descent became fused in the calculation of status and in the determination of class membership.... Through this logic of racial difference, power was personified and embodied; relations of domination and exploitation were produced, naturalized, and legitimized.[19]

While specific categorizations were complex and localized, the general hierarchy placed Spaniards at the top, Indian/Spanish mestizos in the middle, and Indians, blacks, and Indian/black mestizos at the bottom.

In Mexico (including "New Spain," as New Mexico was then known), the demographics of racial mixture overwhelmed the system, causing the formal regime to collapse of its own weight. Consider that, in 1646, Mexico's population contained roughly equal numbers of those claiming Spanish descent (a minority of whom had been born in Spain) and of those persons identified as black, but ten times as many mestizos and Indians as either of those groups, so that an inevitable mestizo population eventually resulted.[20] Historian Alan Knight has noted that, in Mexico, "miscegenation proceeded apace" so that "no rigid apartheid could be sustained, and the sheer proliferation of 'racial' subtypes attested to the impossibility of thorough categorization."[21] Partly because of the dearth of pure Spaniards and partly because of mestizos' demands for greater civil and economic rights, the turn of the nineteenth century was a period in which the Spanish racial legacy was softening, so that some mestizos were able to claim entitlement to the privileges of whiteness formerly limited to Spaniards. Spanish racial categories became increasingly fluid throughout the former Spanish colonies, so that in colonial Latin America, white skin, wealth (including land ownership), and other attributes of social mobility (such as occupation) were perceived as being able to "whiten" otherwise disadvantaged mestizos.[22]

While it is difficult to document, it appears that the Spanish racial order was especially susceptible to challenge in frontier areas such as New Mexico.[23] In these settings, even those with "impure blood" (i.e., indigenous ancestry) could transform themselves into "civilized" people in the context of a generally uncivilized, Indian-dominated frontier.[24] Moreover, the Mexican government began to use the promise of upward mobility to induce settlers to its remote northern frontier. Anthropologist Martha Menchaca concludes that, over the centuries, "Blatant racial disparities became painfully intolerable to the non-white population and generated the conditions for their movement toward the northern frontier, where the racial order was relaxed and people of color had the opportunity to own land and enter most occupations."[25] These fluid and dynamic processes suggest that the Mexican frontier, and probably Latin America generally, were places where racial identity had a strong performance aspect—where people knowingly and variably performed race in different social contexts.[26]

The racially mixed people who settled Mexico's frontier regions of Nuevo México, Alta California, and Tejas were only nominally "Spanish," bearing out the phenomenon described by Menchaca. Consider, for example, the first Mexican census of Los Angeles, which in 1781 listed twelve settler families. Four of the twelve male settlers were described as Indian, two as Spanish, two as black, and four as some combination of those three groups; their twelve female partners were identified as Indian, or as mixed Indian/black, or their race was not listed.[27] In other words, among the two-dozen first "Spanish" settlers of Los Angeles, only two settlers claimed to be Spanish, while twenty-two claimed other racial statuses. Spanish colonial officials and priests frequently characterized settlers in New Mexico as "*mestizos, mulatos,* and *zambohijos*," that is, deeply mixed among Indians, Africans, and Spaniards.[28]

The very first Spanish settlers, who arrived with Francisco Vásquez de Coronado's expedition of 1540 included twice as many mestizos and Indians as Spaniards.[29] Fifty-eight years later, the 130 settlers in Oñate's group included only thirteen married couples, so that the remaining men in the party turned to "Indian women, black slaves, and to Apache captives" for sexual and marital partners.[30] In his pathbreaking study of New Mexico's Spanish colonial period, Gutiérrez concludes that extensive racial mixture characterized the earliest waves of Spanish settlers.

> Those who called themselves Spaniards in seventeenth-century New Mexico were biologically a motley group. At the time of the colony's conquest, the soldier-settlers were almost equally of peninsular and creole origin ... [although they] proclaimed themselves *españoles*. They did so primarily to differentiate themselves ethnically as conquerors from the *indios*, and not as statements of pedigree.[31]

With little additional migration from Spain to the region, by 1680 New Mexico's "Spanish" population consisted overwhelmingly of persons born in the region and of mixed racial ancestry.[32]

What is more, the most active period of Spanish settlement in New Mexico did not occur until after the Pueblo Revolt of 1680.[33] In what one scholar has labeled "the most successful native revolt against European occupation in America," the Pueblo Indians succeeded in completely removing Spanish settlers from New Mexico for twelve years.[34] During that time, key leaders of the revolt died and the Pueblos struggled to maintain their unity in the face of linguistic, cultural, and other differences. Remarkably, a truce occurred in 1692, when the Pueblos allowed the surviving Spanish settlers who had retreated to El Paso to return to New Mexico (though smaller anti-Spanish rebellions continued to occur through 1700).[35]

In one of the most comprehensive analyses to date, historian José Antonio Esquibel has documented the efforts to recruit settlers to New Mexico after 1692. Such recruitment was necessary because relatively few of the pre-Revolt settlers chose to return. According to Esquibel, the lure of settling the frontier was especially strong for those people of mixed Indian/Spanish and black/Spanish parentage, who, by virtue of signing up as frontier settlers, "were given access to these opportunities for upward social mobility and other privileges denied them in their places of origin."[36] For instance, it was settlers recruited mostly from Mexico City who traveled nine months to reach New Mexico in 1694 to settle Santa Cruz de la

Cañada (one of the sites of the rebellion against the Americans described in the previous chapter). Although more than 90 percent of the adults in this group were born in Mexico, they were listed as Spaniards (*españoles*).[37] Overall, Esquibel concludes that the settlers who traveled to New Mexico in the late seventeenth and early eighteenth centuries were "ethnically and culturally diverse," coming from fifteen regions and sixty-three towns in Mexico, as well as from other countries, including those in Africa, Asia, and Europe.[38]

On the eve of the nineteenth century, New Mexican society was characterized by a five-tier racial hierarchy.[39] The highest status racial group— and numerically the smallest—consisted of those individuals who had emigrated from Spain or who had two parents of Spanish descent. Below them was a much larger group of Indian/Spanish mestizos, many of whom had become settlers in order to gain the advantages of upward racial mobility. Most Mexican elites were mestizos, but all Spaniards (in the top group) were elite as well. The third group—known as *genízaros*—consisted of Indians who had forcibly or voluntarily left their communities to join Spanish settlements and who had acculturated to Spanish norms to varying degrees.[40] Below *genízaros* were Pueblo Indians, who had independent communities but who regularly interacted with mestizo settlements. At the bottom of the racial hierarchy were other Indians—the Apaches, Comanches, Navajos, Utes, and others—who resisted Spanish domination to the extent that they operated outside the colonial society.

To describe this hierarchy is not to deny the extensive mixture that existed in this society, as we have described. Thus, the five-tier hierarchy obscured extensive racial mixture, even as it sought to naturalize the five categories as formally comprehensive. Indeed, it is ironic that neither blacks nor Afro-mestizos appear as discrete groups in this hierarchy. Their official omission reflects the extent of racial mixture and also the fact that, precisely because of anti-black racism, blacks and black mestizos had even greater incentives to "improve" their racial status via strategies such as marriage, moving to the frontier, or wealth accumulation. Anthropologist Paul Kraemer points to the "disappearance" of blacks from Albuquerque to illustrate the plasticity of race. For example, Albuquerque's 1750 census showed a mixed black population of 14 percent, but forty years later it had fallen to .5 percent, despite the presence of the same families in the two censuses.[41] Kraemer would accordingly urge us to view skeptically New Mexico's official 1750 census showing nearly six thousand "Spanish" settlers; the evidence suggests that the vast majority were racially mixed persons.[42] Additionally, cutting-edge DNA research suggests that New Mexico's Mexican American population is significantly more Indian than European in ancestry.[43]

Looking from a distance at the Spanish colonial racial order in New Mexico at the turn of the nineteenth century, two contradictory trends are notable. On the one hand, there was increasing and inevitable racial and cultural mixture. The five categories in the hierarchy already represent extensive racial mixture, but additional racial mixture occurred across these racial categories, though the record does not tell us how large such subgroups may have been. For example, with *genízaro* slaves living in mestizo households came the promise of additional sexual unions (within the household, as between a male head of household and female *genízaro* servant, and across households) and the question of whether the children of those unions would blend into the mestizo settler population or inherit their parents' status as *genízaros*. Kraemer speculates that "by marriage or some degree of economic success, the transition from genízaro to *vecino* [status as a Spanish settler] occurred almost routinely in the late colonial period."[44] Additionally, there were mestizo-Pueblo social-sexual unions. Based on his exhaustive analysis of census records, sacramental records, and muster rolls, Esquibel concludes that there were mestizos who lived in Pueblo communities and Pueblo Indians who lived in Spanish settlements, and they "straddled the cultural boundaries between the Pueblo Indian communities and the Spanish communities."[45]

On the other hand, it was precisely such ubiquitous and multidimensional racial mixture that spawned a hardening of formal racial categories. It is at times of great racial mixture, in other words, that we would expect to see the rhetoric of racial difference and accentuated discourses of racial purity/impurity. The ultimate effect of the solidified racial order, in turn, was to facilitate and justify the Spanish colonizers' exploitation of indigenous peoples. Literary scholar Rosaura Sánchez has observed a similar dynamic in eighteenth-century California:

> The othering of the Indians, both neophyte [Christian] and gentile ["heathen"], perceived by the *Californios* as culturally, linguistically, and ethnically different, serves therefore not only to mask the fact that a large percentage of the original colonists as well as later arrivals from Mexico shared the same Indian blood but more significantly to legitimate the conquest and exploitation of the Indians on the basis of a racial and cultural superiority.[46]

In this way, the fiction of racial difference as signified by the "pure," oppositional categories of "Spanish" and "Indian" became naturalized and taken for granted in Spanish colonial New Mexico.

Race in New Mexico on the Eve of the U.S. Invasion

By the early nineteenth century, the pressures on the caste system from an increasingly mestizo population had become too great for Mexico and the other Spanish colonies; too many mestizos who had been arbitrarily denied rights and privileges were growing wary of Spanish rule. Consider that by 1810 more than 80 percent of Mexico's population of 6 million was either mestizo (Spanish/Indian mestizo and/or Spanish/African mestizo; more than 1.3 million) or Indian (almost 3.7 million).[47] Motivated largely by the need to incorporate the majority of Mexico's people (as well as those of other tenuously held colonies) culturally and economically, and in an attempt to block Mexican independence, the Spanish legislature in 1810 initiated a variety of changes to improve the position of Indians and mestizos.[48] These changes included lifting occupational restrictions on mestizos and Indians, releasing Indians from paying tribute to the crown, and, instead, making them liable for taxation like other subjects. Two years later, the Spanish legislature abolished the racial castes and promised formal equality regardless of racial status. In large part, these changes reflected Spain's instability as a colonial power and proved a harbinger for Mexico's independence from Spain in 1821. The Mexican republic declared mestizos and Indians equal citizens. The fledgling Mexican legislature banned the future importation of slaves from Africa and mandated that current black slaves would be free after an additional ten years of servitude.

What were the effects of these liberal trends on New Mexico, the most populous of Mexico's northern provinces? The immediate impact of the new racial equality legislation was to endanger Pueblo Indians' property rights. Mestizo settlers quickly seized on the equality initiative to challenge the size of land grants to the Pueblos and to encroach on Pueblo lands that adjoined mestizo settlements.[49] Sando thus notes that the equal rights legislation, in New Mexico, "soon became the right for all equally to take Pueblo land."[50] At the same time, the liberalization of racial restrictions went hand in hand with an anti-clerical, republican effort to secularize the missions, which substantially increased Pueblos' autonomy. Anthropologist Alfonso Ortiz notes that, by the 1830s, only five priests were assigned to the Pueblos, leaving them "free to openly pursue the rich ceremonial life and ways of being that had secretly sustained them through the long years of persecution and oppression."[51]

A final noteworthy shift that occurred during the twenty-five-year Mexican rule of New Mexico was the liberalization of immigration restrictions in 1824, which allowed Euro-Americans to settle Mexico's northern frontier.[52] Given the dual problems of a large, hostile Indian population in these regions and the paucity of federal resources to suppress them militarily, Mexico believed encouraging immigrants to settle in these regions was the only feasible alternative to maintain control of its frontier. Mexico actively encouraged Mexican migration to its northern regions, but also American immigration. In order to be legal settlers, those emigrating from the United States were required to become naturalized Mexican citizens and to convert to Catholicism if they were not already Catholic. Historian Richard White estimates that as many as 40 percent of the American immigrants to Texas in the 1820s ignored those requirements—thus becoming "illegal aliens" to Mexico.[53] Euro-American immigration to New Mexico, both legal and illegal, proceeded at a much slower pace. Only small numbers of Euro-American men arrived in northern New Mexico before 1850, primarily to engage in fur trapping or trading along the Santa Fe and Chihuahua trails. Some of these immigrants married or lived with native Mexican and Indian women, producing yet another class of racially mixed persons in New Mexico, however small it might have been.[54]

In considering how the Anglo-American racial order intersected with the Spanish-Mexican racial order in the Southwest in the middle of the nineteenth century, we must begin with the preceding two centuries of Anglo-American presence in the Americas.[55] Anglo-Americans' relations with various Indian peoples were heavily shaped by two related demographic facts.[56] First, Anglo-Americans were heavily outnumbered by indigenous people, whom they considered culturally and racially inferior. In this context, there was no possibility of either short-term military conquest or large-scale enslavement of Indian peoples. Second, the indigenous population of North America consisted of thousands of linguistically and culturally diverse tribes. Thus, while Indians outnumbered Anglo-Americans, "Indians" were not one group but many, and Anglo-Americans adopted the strategy of dealing with them on a tribe-by-tribe basis.

Early Anglo-American settlers (sometimes in conjunction with one or more tribes) variously engaged in warfare, trading, treaty formation, and land purchase from Indian tribes. The result during the first two centuries of Anglo-American occupation of North America (in competition with French, Dutch, and other European colonizers) was reliance on alternating strategies of military struggle and treaty formation with Indian nations. Writing in 1783, George Washington opined that the latter was more cost-effective:

> The Indians . . . will ever retreat as our Settlements advance upon them and they will be as ready to sell, as we are to buy; That is the cheapest as well as the least distressing way of dealing with them, none who are acquainted with the Nature of Indian warfare, and has ever been at the trouble of estimating the expense of one, and comparing it with the cost of purchasing their Lands, will hesitate to acknowledge. . . . I am clear in my opinion, that policy and economy point very strongly to the expediency of being upon good terms with the Indians, and the propriety of purchasing their Lands in preference to attempting to drive them by force of arms out of their Country; which as we have already experienced is like driving the Wild Beasts of the Forest which will return to us as soon as the pursuit is at an end and fall perhaps on those that are left there.[57]

Twenty years later, on the eve of the Louisiana Purchase, Thomas Jefferson wrote that the twin keys to dealing with what he characterized as the few remaining "obstinate" tribes was, first, to "encourage" their assimilation to farming and stock-raising and, second, to incorporate them into the capitalist economy in order to provide an incentive for them to sell their land—in order to have money to make purchases.[58] Both strategies would become mainstays of federal Indian policy in the nineteenth and twentieth centuries. By 1823, leaders of the still young American nation were comfortable asserting "the discovery doctrine" as the rationale for taking title to Indian land based on racist assumptions.[59]

The Anglo-American racial order at mid-century rested on the legacy of European colonialism in North America that was openly and forcefully justified by defining Indians as racially inferior. Another crucial dimension of the U.S. racial order was the legalized enslavement of African peoples on the basis of race, justified with claims of blacks' racial inferiority. Beginning with the first arrival at the port of Jamestown in 1619 of a ship carrying Africans, "slavery developed quickly into a regular institution, into the normal labor relations of blacks to whites in the New World."[60] Even in those states in which slavery was not legal (and even among most abolitionists), the idea of black inferiority went largely unchallenged, whether speaking of slaves or free blacks.[61] Thus, from before the nation's founding, racism legitimated different Anglo-American strategies toward blacks and Indians: for Indians, it justified the wholesale dispossession of their land, while for blacks it justified exploiting their labor by treating them as property rather than human beings.

When American settlers and traders first encountered Mexicans in the nineteenth century, it was by no means clear where Mexicans would fit within the American racial hierarchy. Historian Reginald Horsman has written about Manifest Destiny and the problem of the Mexicans: "The Americans had two immediate racial models—the Indians and the blacks. Wherever the whites had moved in large numbers the Indians had disappeared. . . . The blacks were not disappearing but were increasing in numbers."[62] Politicians and newspaper editors publicly wondered which fate would await Mexicans: should they be treated like blacks or like Indians? Contemporary commentaries were split between the views that Mexicans were "really Indians" (a view emphasizing Mexicans' predominant Indian ancestry) or more comparable to blacks in color, custom, and overall depravity (a view emphasizing culture over ancestry).[63] In particular, American southerners were ambivalent about the nation's expansion to Mexico because they considered "the Mexican race" a suspect, colored race "but little removed above the Negro."[64] It was southerners, in turn, who were the majority of the early American migrants to Texas and who had the earliest sustained contact with Mexicans. As historian Neil Foley has emphasized, Euro-Americans in Texas were adamant that "whiteness meant not only *not black* but also *not Mexican.*"[65] Given that, the outcome of whether Mexicans were treated "like Indians" or "like blacks" in the American context may have been inconsequential, since both groups were excluded from the rights and privileges accorded whites. Yet it was precisely the ambiguity of Mexicans' racial status that positioned them to play a role as an intermediate group, between whites and non-white groups like blacks and Indians. Mexicans' status as a racially mixed group both made it possible for some Mexicans to occupy an "off-white" position and for the group overall to be classified as an inferior "mongrel" race. It may well have been the variations among Mexicans—due partly to perceptible differences in the extent of indigenous versus Spanish ancestry and partly to how individual Mexicans performed their racial identity—that placed Mexicans as a *group* in an ambiguous racial position within the U.S. racial terrain.

We can glean a great deal about the racial attitudes of Euro-Americans by reading the narratives of early foreign visitors to the region, who produced a substantial travel literature.[66] These early accounts were often serialized in eastern newspapers and then published in book form. They appeared during a period of increased literacy and high demand for reading material about "exotic" lands.[67] Particularly relevant for this study is a narrative written by William Watts Hart Davis, who was one of the first Euro-American lawyers in the region and the first U.S. Attorney assigned to the New Mexico Territory. Prior to his appointment, Davis had not had any contact with Mexicans or Pueblo Indians. He arrived in northern New Mexico in late November 1864, after four weeks of difficult stagecoach travel from Independence, Missouri. His book is a diary of his travels around New Mexico from late February to early June 1865, while serving as prosecutor.

Davis's often-lively accounts give new meaning to the judicial concept of "riding circuit" (a term describing a court that is held in different locations, such as the twelve federal courts of appeal that hold court in various states within their jurisdiction). Davis literally rode circuit via horseback, covering thousands of miles, including one thousand miles in New Mexico's first judicial district alone. He slept outdoors at times or in modest indoor accommodations at lodging houses or private homes (there being no hotels in the territory at this time). Prior to his appointment as U.S. Attorney, Davis had not had any contact with Mexicans or with Pueblo Indians. Moreover, it is clear that most of his interactions with Mexicans were superficial and quite limited in nature and time. Judging from his journal, he did not have Mexican intimates, and he interacted even less with Pueblo Indians. From his standpoint, however, drawing group-based conclusions about racial inferiority was not empirically or morally problematic. Indeed, it was eminently natural given the racial order from which he came. In that world, Davis took for granted the inherent inferiority of blacks and Indians, and it was within this framework that he approached his experience in New Mexico. It would have been no leap for him to lump Mexicans and Pueblo Indians with the blacks and Indians at the bottom of the American racial hierarchy. In this way, Davis's diary simply recorded "the truth" as he and other white Americans understood it.

Early in the book, Davis reveals his understanding of the racial hierarchy he took for granted when he describes the stagecoach crew that took him west: He identifies Euro-Americans by last name, without a racial designation, and often with some personality trait that humanizes and individualizes them (e.g., "Jones, a clever Kentuckian"); he identifies Mexicans by first name only, always indicating their race (e.g., "Jose, a Mexican"); and he does not even name black crewmembers (e.g., "the colored out-driver").[68] Davis frequently remarks on the "semi-civilized" character of Pueblo Indians, calling them a "primitive race" replete with "drunkards" and "beggars."[69] At one point in the journal, he purports to provide a complete dictionary of the many Pueblo languages that he says consists of fifty-nine words in total.[70]

At times Davis seems genuinely perplexed about Mexicans, not knowing quite where they fit in the American racial hierarchy. Because they were "a mixed race," Mexicans presented peculiar problems of categorization, but, in the end, it was mixture itself that signaled inferiority, relative to Euro-Americans and, especially, Anglo-Saxons: "Here was a second blending of blood and a new union of races; the Spaniard, Moor, and the aboriginal were united in one and made a new race, the Mexicans."[71] Davis was adamant about the physiological consequences of such race mixture on skin color (very dark with "no present hope of the people improving in color"), and he ridiculed "greasy" and "Indian-fied" Mexicans who tried to act or appear white (via attempts to lighten their skin or keep out of the sun to avoid getting darker).[72] Just as important as these physical descriptions, however, were what Davis considered Mexicans' inherent, inferior cultural traits. According to him, Mexicans had an "impulsive nature," were too obedient, tended toward "cruelty, bigotry, and superstition."[73] In this way, Mexicans, like blacks, were stereotyped as essentially child-like, a characterization that implied they were unfit for self-government and for citizenship. At the same time, Davis characterized Mexicans as "possessing the cunning and deceit of the Indian." Contradictions notwithstanding, what was important for Davis—and very likely for his audience in the East—was that Mexicans were far inferior to Anglo-Saxons: "They have a great deal of what the world calls smartness and quickness of perception, but lack the stability of character and soundness of intellect that give such vast superiority to the Anglo-Saxon race over every other people." Mexican women were singled out for special criticism, with Davis concluding that "the standard of female chastity is deplorably low" in New Mexico.[74]

Competing Narratives of Race

As Euro-Americans increased their presence in New Mexico over the course of the 1850s, 1860s, and 1870s, they differed among themselves about how to understand and characterize New Mexico's racial landscape. Under what I label the "dominant view," Mexican Americans were characterized as unfit for self-government because they were of inferior racial stock (compared to Euro-Americans). Under what I label the "progressive view," Mexican Americans were considered a more benign presence, largely because its proponents emphasized Mexican Americans' "glorious Spanish past" as conquerors of Indians.[75] Significantly, both the dominant and progressive views of race were *racist*: both assumed white racial superiority and Mexican racial inferiority.[76] Where they differed was in the extent to which they sought to exclude Mexican Americans from full citizenship and civic life. As New Mexicans (Euro-Americans and Mexican Americans alike) increasingly lobbied for admission to the Union, the differences between these competing racial narratives became crucial.

Over a period of years, the perception of Mexicans popularized by travelers like Davis who published their diaries in the popular press crystallized into the dominant view about race in New Mexico. In this view, popular among many Euro-Americans who lived in New Mexico but especially among Euro-American elites at the national level, Mexicans' racial inferiority justified their continued exclusion from the national polity (and, hence, the rejection of New Mexico's ongoing bids for statehood). Indians (both Pueblo Indians and other Indians) were ranked below Mexicans in the racial hierarchy and, within the dominant view, they fell entirely outside the polity.[77]

The dominant view surfaced in the New Mexico press, which until the 1880s remained dominated by Euro-American editors. But the national press most consistently articulated this idea of race in New Mexico. For example, in the 1870s, in the midst of one of several congressional debates about statehood, the *New York Times* ran articles that presented the tenets of the dominant view. First, Indians essentially were perceived as being outside the political system, which involved "Mexicans" and "Americans" or "whites."[78] Second, Mexicans were a race deeply inferior to white Americans. Indeed, the stereotypes of Mexicans as lazy and backward, which persist today, were generated by the leading American newspapers of the era.[79] Third, racial conflict, especially between "Mexicans" and "Americans," was prevalent in New Mexico, leading journalists to comment frequently on Mexican Americans' resistance to assimilation (used to counter the claim by some Euro-Americans that Euro-Americans would quickly overwhelm "the Mexican element" of New Mexico).[80] Finally, because Mexicans were unfit for self-government, New Mexico should not be admitted to statehood.[81]

In an 1879 front-page article with the subhead "Progress Retarded by a Want of Energy, Lazy Mexicans the Chief Inhabitants," the *New York Times* began by noting that "whites" were far outnumbered by "Mexicans," making it clear, as well, that Indians were irrelevant to the discussion.[82] The centerpiece of the article was the claim of Mexicans' inherent racial inferiority, and in particular what the newspaperman termed their "natural indolence," which made statehood out of the question:

> The women, with the inevitable shawl about their heads and muzzling their mouths, so that all one sees of them are the coal-black eyes and tips of tawny noses, go in bunches [to the Catholic churches], and the men lag along lazily behind, with about as much care for their appearance as the average tramp. Indeed, the Mexican, on the average, is the very personification of tramphood, seldom or never turning his hand to the extent of sweating his brow if his daily bread can be secured by any other means.[83]

Another article similarly claimed that conflict between "greasers" and "Americans" ran high in New Mexico. The *New York Times* pointed to territorial politics, noting that both the Republican and Democratic parties had nominated for nonvoting delegate to Congress men "from the old Spanish families."[84] The correspondent viewed these nominations as evidence that "the Mexicans have stood it as long as possible and now break out into open revolt" and joked that, no matter which party wins, a Mexican will be New Mexico's congressional delegate and thus require "Congress [to appoint] a Spanish interpreter to guess what the nominee says if he ever says anything."[85]

The national press frequently and uncritically referred to Mexicans as "greasers."[86] In an 1855 California law, "greaser" was defined as "the issue of Spanish and Indian blood," and the epithet quickly gained popularity across the nation.[87] An article published in 1882 in the *New York Times* revealed as much in its lengthy headline as it did in its text: "GREASERS AS CITIZENS. What Sort of State New-Mexico Would Make. The origin and character of the so-called 'Mexicans' of that Territory—their hatred of Americans, their dense ignorance, and total unfitness for citizenship—the women of New-Mexico."[88] Mexicans' inferiority, according to the article, stemmed from their status as a mixed race: "the mongrel breed known as Mexicans—a mixture of the blood of Apache, negro, Navajo, white horse-thief, Pueblo Indian, and old-time frontiersman with the original Mexican stock."[89] Not atypically, the prime indicator of Mexican inferiority was racial mixture, yet this article was unusual in asserting two tiers of racial mixture. The reference to "the original Mexican stock" invokes the racial mixture of Spanish and Indian ancestry. Yet greater virulence seems to be reserved for what the author believes is racial mixture of a more recent vintage, perhaps since the Americans took control of the region, drawing on a range of negatively stereotyped Indian groups (Apache, Navajo, and Pueblo Indians), American blacks, and even whites (apparently only low-status whites had mixed with Mexicans, white criminals and mountain men). The author's intent was not to get caught up in the details of how Mexicans got to this point, but rather to deliver the bottom line: Mexicans were unfit for citizenship because they were too deferential (having a mentality of "servility") and possessed "a passionate hatred [for] everything that is known to him or her as American."[90]

In articles like these, the American press articulated the dominant racial narrative, in which Mexicans were racially inferior and therefore unworthy of full American citizenship. Despite the fact that Mexicans had been granted federal citizenship by the Treaty of Guadalupe Hidalgo, the dominant narrative defined them as racially inferior. Yet the dominant view did not go unchallenged. The story of how it was contested reveals a great deal about the racial politics of the statehood debate, as well as the larger dynamics of where Mexicans fit in the nation's racial order.

Ironically perhaps, it was a Euro-American lawyer and judge who traced his lineage to the Mayflower who led the fight to dislodge the dominant racial narrative. Lebaron Bradford Prince devised the progressive racial narrative as an express counter-narrative to the dominant view of New Mexico's race relations, and he articulated it in both the press and law. About a month after the virulently racist *New York Times* article appeared in 1882, Prince responded with a lengthy letter to the editor, published under the headline "The People of New Mexico and their Territory. The Hon. L. Bradford Prince finds Much to Admire in his New Neighbors—the Spaniards of the Territory and their Qualities as Citizens."[91] It is significant that Prince referred to Mexicans as "Spaniards" (although he did not always do so), an early indication of the popularization of this ethnic label among both Euro-American and Mexican elites (and later Mexican

Americans of all classes).[92] It suggests that the adoption of "Spanish" as an ethnic label for New Mexico's native Mexican population was the product of Euro-American racism associated so viscerally with the terms "Mexican" and "greaser," which had become interchangeable in the dominant narrative.

Writing twenty years later, on the eve of New Mexico's becoming a state in 1912, Prince characterized New Mexico as having three "different nationalities and forms of civilization—the Aboriginal and Pueblo, the Spanish and Mexican, and the American." What was remarkable about contemporary New Mexico, Prince continued, was that a (presumably Euro-American) visitor could

> in a single day visit an Indian pueblo exhibiting in unchanged form the customs of the intelligent natives of three and a half centuries ago; a Mexican town, where the architecture, the language and the habits of the people differ in no material respect from those which were brought from Spain in the days of Columbus, Cortez, and Coronado; and an American city or village, full of the nervous energy and the well-known characteristics of modern western life.[93]

Prince depicted Pueblo Indians and Mexican Americans as people trapped in their quaint pasts: Pueblo culture had remained static over three and a half centuries and Mexican American towns were no different than the Spanish villages of five hundred years earlier. Using an appellation that conflated ethnicity, race, and nationality, he portrayed "Americans" as having a dynamic culture able to adapt to technological and other changes denoted by the wave of "progress" washing over early twentieth-century America. In Prince's narrative, New Mexico's many non-Pueblo Indian populations remained invisible, victims of the American military assaults of the late nineteenth century and the reservation policy that segregated them out of view and out of the polity.

Despite a contrived avoidance of the concepts in the quotation, Prince was talking about race and racial difference. In the progressive narrative, New Mexico's complicated, lengthy history of racial conflict—between Pueblos and non-Pueblo Indians, between Mexicans and Pueblos, between Mexicans and non-Pueblo Indians, between Euro-Americans and Indians, between Euro-Americans and Mexicans—was erased from public consciousness. Instead, public memory was fixated on the notion of *cultural* difference unmediated by stark group-based inequality in the economic, social, and political realms. Most importantly, the progressive view of race assigned no blame; no person or group was responsible for social inequalities that increasingly matched racial lines, and thus no person or group could do anything to rectify a situation that was, after all, the result of an inevitable clash between a dynamic culture wedded to progress and the native static cultures hampered by their allegiance to ancient, outmoded traditions.

Prince played a central role in New Mexico politics beginning in 1879, when he accepted President Rutherford B. Hayes's appointment as Chief Justice of the Supreme Court of the Territory of New Mexico.[94] At this time, each of three justices of the territory's highest court served both as an appellate judge and as a trial judge, riding circuit among several counties. Prince's district included six counties and covered some one thousand miles. He quickly developed the reputation as the hardest-working territorial judge New Mexico had ever had,[95] disposing of 2,667 civil and criminal cases in the district court over three and a half years and, in his spare time, compiling New Mexico's statutes, which had not been revised since Kearny's compilation of 1846.[96] During his forty-three years in New Mexico (he died there in 1922), Prince served in each branch of government: in the judicial branch, as chief justice 1879–82; in the executive branch, as governor 1889–93; and in the legislative branch, as a member of the territorial council 1909–12.[97] Of the Euro-Americans appointed to positions in New Mexico—recall that the top positions in territorial government were appointees of the U.S. President—Prince had the most enduring impact. He was a central figure in politics, and his articulation of the progressive view of New Mexico race relations had a tremendous impact on the region. Historian Robert Larson, author of the most widely read text on New Mexico's battle for statehood, notes that Prince was called by many "The Father of New Mexico Statehood."[98]

There was little in Prince's background to have predicted his role in articulating a counter-narrative to the dominant view that New Mexico's Mexicans were not fit for self-governance. He grew up in a wealthy Long Island family, attended private colleges, and entered politics as a Republican. After the untimely death of his first wife, Prince married Mary Beardsley, "like himself of Mayflower and Revolutionary descent."[99] What a strange course of events that the Princes, scions of upper-class Eastern society, would end up hosting lavish parties at the rather humble governor's mansion in a former Mexican capital.[100]

Most commonly, Prince made his arguments in popular forums, but when the opportunity presented itself, he also utilized his varied legal roles. Such an opportunity arose in 1881, when a Euro-American convicted of first-degree murder asked the territorial supreme court to rule on whether Mexicans who could not speak English could serve as jurors in the territorial courts. Richard Romine had been convicted of the first-degree murder of fellow Euro-American Patrick Rafferty. According to eyewitness evidence, Romine had killed Rafferty with a hammer in 1877 in a mining camp in Grant County. Created by the territorial legislature in 1868 when silver was discovered there, Grant County was the only of New Mexico's fourteen counties to have a majority-Euro-American population. Undoubtedly because every potential juror there knew about the murder, Romine received permission to move his trial from Grant County to Doña Ana County. In so doing, he moved the case from a county where Euro-Americans made up 57 percent of the population to one where they comprised only 5 percent of the population.[101]

Represented by the most powerful lawyer and one of the richest men in the state, Thomas Catron, Romine argued that his conviction must be overturned because "the jurors who sat in the trial of this case were Mexicans, and none of them understood the English language, in which the proceedings at the trial were had."[102] Catron's brief drew heavily on an 1874 case in which the Texas Supreme Court had reversed a Euro-American defendant's conviction for murdering a Mexican man because of the presence of jurors who did not speak English.[103] The Texas decision was not binding on New Mexico's territorial supreme court, but Prince still might have chosen to rely on its reasoning to establish legal precedent in New Mexico. Alternatively, assuming Prince wanted to affirm Romine's conviction, he could have easily disposed of the appeal by telling Romine that he had gotten what he deserved, in that the racial and linguistic composition of his jury was a function of his earlier choice to move the case out of the only majority-Euro-American county in the territory.

Instead, writing one year before his letter to the editor of the *New York Times*, Prince used the case to launch the progressive view of New Mexico race relations. Prince's opinion in the *Romine* case offered two rationales for upholding the right of monolingual Spanish-speaking jurors to serve. The first was practical: there simply were not enough potential English-speaking jurors in the territory. If New Mexico was going to have jury trials, it would have Mexican American jurors, and, hence, it would have to provide simultaneous Spanish-English translation of trial proceedings. Prince wrote:

> We cannot shut our eyes to the peculiar circumstances of this territory, taken from the Republic of Mexico in 1846, and nearly all of whose inhabitants, in the years first succeeding the annexation, understood no English. Even at the present time the preponderance of Spanish speaking citizens is very large; and in certain counties the English speaking citizens possessing the qualification of jurors, can be counted by tens instead of hundreds. In at least three of the courts of the territory at the time of this trial below, it may be said without hesitation, that a sufficient number of English speaking jurors could not have been obtained to try any important case which had attracted public attention.[104]

But Prince went further, articulating a second rationale based on justice—a rationale that put him in the position of defending the civil rights of the native Mexican citizens of the region:

> [I]t would have been manifestly unjust to the great majority of the people of the territory, had such a requirement as language been made. Either they would have had to be tried in a language which they did not understand, or else a double system would necessarily have been established, including an English speaking jury for English defendants, and a Spanish speaking jury for Spanish defendants; and if the theory had been carried to its logical conclusion, an English speaking judge to address the English jury, and a Spanish speaking one to instruct the Spanish jury.[105]

Such a system was not inherently problematic—it all depended on how one perceived the relationship between New Mexico and the United States at the time of the American conquest and on how one imagined the future of that relationship. If one viewed New Mexico as a colonial possession that would exist in a permanent state of political disadvantage relative to the rest of the nation, then such a dual-language and, effectively, dual-race system was conceivable. If, instead, one viewed New Mexico as an annexed territory that would eventually join the Union as a state, then Prince was correct—a system of separate courts (divided by race and language) was unjust because it signaled a second-class citizenship. Moreover, Prince viewed the establishment of a criminal justice system—complete with jurors—as crucial to the statehood agenda: in order for New Mexico to achieve statehood, it had to look as much as possible like its neighbors to the east.[106]

More than a decade after he wrote the *Romine* opinion, Prince would articulate a more comprehensive and subtle vision of civil rights as inextricably linked to statehood. In essence, he argued that *territorial* citizenship was incommensurable with full American citizenship and civil rights. In an essay written for an audience of Euro-American elites on the East Coast and published in the *North American Review*, Prince wrote: "We insist that self-government is the normal condition and indeed an inherent right of American citizenship; that it is inseparable from any true idea of republican institutions. . . . A territorial condition, therefore, is an unnatural one, which deprives resident citizens of many of their dearest rights."[107] Although Prince spoke in general terms about New Mexico's "resident citizens," the Mexican majority was not far from his mind. One need only look to how Prince deployed a reconstructed version of New Mexico history to his rhetorical advantage. Prince saw the representation of history as crucial in the statehood debate, and he sought to control the framing of characters, events, and trajectory. In 1883 he was elected president of the New Mexico Historical Society and served in that position until he died in 1922.[108] He founded the Society for the Preservation of Spanish Antiquities.[109] He authored at least a half-dozen books on New Mexico history, including *Historical Sketches of New Mexico*, published in 1883, and *A Concise History of New Mexico*, published in 1912.

In an 1893 article written when he was governor, Prince argued that Americans should view the U.S.–Mexico War and the annexation of New Mexico as a kind of sacred covenant that required granting statehood to New Mexico. Prince conceived the United States as having "a special obligation . . . to the native people of New Mexico" because of the manner of military conquest in 1846 and the treaty that ended the war in 1848:

> When General Kearney [*sic*] made his peaceful entry into Santa Fe, he issued a formal proclamation . . . : "It is the wish and intention of the United States to provide for New Mexico a free government, with the least possible delay, similar to those in the United States." The people were satisfied with the assurances of the American commander, trusted the promises of the proclamation and offered no opposition to the occupation of the whole area of the Territory.[110]

Clearly, Prince misrepresented the facts to suit his rhetorical purposes. Following the bloodless conquest narrative, he portrays the military occupation as "peaceful." He also omits the revolts of 1847 and the American executions at Taos in order to portray the native Mexican and Indian residents of the region as welcoming, rather than resisting, the American occupation. In 1883, when Prince was writing, he found these rhetorical moves necessary in order to portray the native Mexican population as unfairly put upon by the continuing delay of statehood.[111]

A second tactic in Prince's arsenal was to confront directly the transparent racism of the dominant view of New Mexico race relations. Prince concedes that Congress would be well within its legitimate powers to deny statehood to a territory based on the "unsatisfactory character of the population" but suggests that this is connoted by insufficient education, patriotism, or adherence to the law.[112] Prince does not state outright but clearly implies that the dominant view's emphasis on race as a proxy for "unsatisfactory character" is illegitimate. Instead, he turns to demography with the assumption that Mexicans should be included as full-fledged citizens. He notes that the 1880 Census counted 153,076 New Mexicans, "without counting Indians on the reservations," and notes that the actual population, including Indians, is at least 180,000, making New Mexico considerably more populous than other recently admitted territories (including Idaho, Wyoming, Montana, and Nevada).[113]

It was not, however, only a matter of numbers. Prince also sought to repackage New Mexico in order to put its Spanish settlers on an equal footing with the Anglo setters of the original thirteen colonies. Rather than duck the question of the racial character of the "native" population, Prince sought to redefine it in mythic terms. He spoke of the mixture of "the solid and conservative native element of *Spanish* descent" as moderating "the energetic and enterprising, but sometimes over-zealous, Anglo-American[s] from the East."[114] In his telling of the myth, notice that the Pueblo and other indigenous elements drop out of the equation; they were not included in the territorial polity, and so would not be in the polity of the state-to-be. The finishing touch was to suggest that Mexicans and Euro-Americans were, after all, equally great colonial powers: "Our citizens are mainly the descendants of the two great nations which insisted on the rights of people in England under the Magna Carta and drove the Moors out of Spain that self-government should reign there. They are the children of the patriots who fought for the independence of the United States in 1776, and in Mexico from 1810–1821. Surely the sons of such sires must be capable of self-government!"[115]

The progressive view was embraced by a cadre of Euro-American elites in New Mexico beginning in the 1880s. Historian Porter Stratton argues that the racial attitudes of the Euro-American editors of New Mexico newspapers changed dramatically at this time in direct response to the rise of the dominant view in Congress and the national press, and that "as a result the entire territorial press sprang to the defense of the Spanish-Americans."[116] This was a considerable overstatement. In fact, Euro-American newspapermen in New Mexico were split between advocating the dominant and progressive views. If Stratton is correct, the majority embraced the progressive view, but a substantial minority, especially those based in the southeastern and southwestern quadrants, subscribed to the dominant view. In 1905, the Euro-American editor of a Santa Fe paper openly declared: "It has been demonstrated repeatedly that the Democrats of southeastern New Mexico, like their brethren in Texas, hate the early *white* settlers of Spanish descent in New Mexico."[117] The Euro-American leadership of southeastern Eddy County went so far as to institute an all-white primary in 1906, from which Mexican Americans were excluded, generating much criticism from Republican newspaper editors in central and northern New Mexico.[118]

Race and the Statehood Debate

The primary engine driving the cadre of Euro-Americans aligned behind the progressive view of race was gaining statehood for New Mexico.[119] Statehood would signal political legitimacy and, most importantly, would carry the promise of financial profit. Thomas Catron, New Mexico's most prominent lawyer and largest landowner, stated that New Mexico's land values would triple overnight with the granting of statehood.[120] He campaigned for statehood both nationally and within New Mexico and in 1912 became one of the new state's first two U.S. senators. Prince, who after resigning as chief justice of the territorial supreme court, had invested heavily in land and mining ventures,[121] also perceived his financial well-being as dependent on statehood.

Race was at the crux of the congressional debate over statehood for New Mexico, and so race figured prominently in the strategies of Prince,

Catron, and others. Prior to the final push for statehood in 1910–12, there were two major battles on this front that reveal the centrality of race and racism in the debate and illustrate the dominant view of race that Prince and company sought to dislodge.[122] The first occurred in 1875, when New Mexico and Colorado were both up for statehood. Advocates for New Mexico statehood argued that it should be treated on at least an equal footing with Colorado, since New Mexico had at least 100,000 residents compared to 65,000 in Colorado.[123] In both debates, the key questions concerned the interplay of race, nation, and citizenship.

The national press was generally outspoken in its opposition to statehood for New Mexico.[124] Larson describes the press overall (especially the *New York Times*) as extremely critical of New Mexico's bid for statehood but relatively more positive toward Colorado.[125] The *Cincinnati Commercial* may have been typical, opining in its editorial pages that New Mexico was composed of at least 80,000 people of "Mexican descent" who were "almost wholly ignorant" of English and who "are aliens to us in blood and language."[126] The editorial reasoned that statehood was unjustified because New Mexico had a population three-quarters of which was illiterate, a larger proportion than was illiterate in South Carolina and Mississippi, states where "blacks outnumber whites."[127] Similarly, during the House's consideration of the New Mexico statehood bill, New York Congressman Clarkson Potter argued that statehood should be denied on the grounds that a "very considerable portion of the population of the Territory [of New Mexico] do [*sic*] not speak the English language."[128]

Despite the racial and linguistic differences, New Mexico's and Colorado's electorates were similar in one respect: they were presumed to be majority-Republican. Debate on African American civil rights issues in the last weeks of the 43rd Congress colored the statehood proposals. Radical Republicans managed to push through a Civil Rights Act requiring racial equality in hotels, theaters, and on transportation (which eventually was ruled unconstitutional by the Supreme Court), and they managed to derail a Democratic proposal to allow governors in Alabama, Arkansas, Louisiana, and Mississippi to suspend the writ of habeas corpus.[129] As Larson has noted, these Republican victories only "increased the antagonism of Southern Democrats toward any Republican effort," including the admission of news states likely to be Republican.[130] In a highly partisan congressional debate that went into the early morning hours on the last day of the session, Colorado won statehood, while New Mexico lost and would have to wait another thirty-two years for admission.[131]

If southern Democrats were able to muster the votes to defeat New Mexico, why did Colorado squeak through? Larson posits that it was due to Colorado's Democratic nonvoting delegate to Congress (as compared to New Mexico's Republican Elkins), but the difference is better explained by the racial composition of the two territories in 1875. Colorado had a majority Euro-American electorate and a relatively small Indian population, whereas New Mexico had a majority-Mexican electorate and a large population of Pueblo and other Indians. Commenting on the 1875 vote, the *New York Times* enumerated "several good reasons why New-Mexico should not be admitted as a State," most of which dealt with the faults of its native Mexican population: "The average [Mexican] citizen gets on in about the same old way, never richer and never poorer, while the lower element, the men who hire out, are but little better off than slaves, receiving scant wages for hard work."[132] To put it bluntly, and the *New York Times* did, "*its people are not of us* ... the most numerous inhabitants are the joint offspring of [Mexican] Peons and Indians."[133]

In a later anti-statehood diatribe, the *New York Times* faulted both the Mexican elite ("the aristocrats, more or less descendants of the Spanish") and the Mexican masses ("the peon or slave").[134] For newspaper editors in New York, the Mexican elite and the Mexican masses were equally problematic. The Mexican masses were weak—and unworthy of state citizenship—because they were not free. At the same time, and perhaps because of their dependence on the peons, the Mexican elite was similarly unworthy of state citizenship because its members did not aspire to hard work and achievement. As it was put in the *New York Times*, "Indeed, it is an undeniable fact that New-Mexico has steadily gone backward since its annexation to the United States, as well as for hundreds of years before, and upon every hand are the ruins indicative of a greatness in population and industry—of which the Pilgrim Fathers were as ignorant as we of the present day."[135] In response to the deluge of criticism after the 1875 vote, Prince's pragmatic solution was to take on the task of battling this portrayal of New Mexico's Mexican elite (though not particularly that of the Mexican masses). His goal was to revive the Spanish conquest as a moment of greatness that extended into the present to rehabilitate Mexican elites of the late nineteenth century.

In 1902, New Mexico again seemed to be on the brink of admission to the Union, and, once again, the racial composition of its population proved the major stumbling block. This time, its fate was paired with those of Arizona and Oklahoma (the newly renamed Indian Territory);

the so-called Omnibus Statehood Bill proposed that Congress admit the three territories together. The bill passed the House on May 9, 1902, but was doomed to failure in the Senate, where opposition to the admission of New Mexico and Arizona was orchestrated by Senator Albert J. Beveridge of Indiana, who chaired the Senate's Committee on Territories.[136]

Beveridge's virulent opposition to New Mexico statehood must be understood in the larger context of his outspoken advocacy for the continuation of Manifest Destiny as a national policy at the turn of the century. The stage this time was the American war against Spain in 1898, settled the following year with the Treaty of Paris. Cuba won its independence from Spain, and the United States annexed Puerto Rico and the Philippines. In what seemed almost like a throwback to the slogans of fifty years earlier that had fueled the war with Mexico, Beveridge linked American exceptionalism to race and religion: "We will not renounce our part in the mission of our race, trustee, under God, of the civilization of the world. . . . He has marked us as His chosen people, henceforth, to lead in the regeneration of the world."[137] The racism that animated Beveridge's imperialist goals also fueled his opposition to making state citizens of New Mexico's Mexican majority. For him, the world was divided into those capable of self-government and those who had to be governed by others: "You who say the Declaration [of Independence] applies to all men, . . . how dare you deny its application to the American Indian? And if you deny it to the Indian at home, how dare you grant it to the Malay abroad? . . . [T]here are people in the world who do not understand any form of government . . . [and] must be governed."[138]

At the age of thirty-six and without having held any prior political office, Beveridge ran successfully for the Senate.[139] In an 1898 campaign speech, he said, "We are a conquering race, and we must obey our blood and occupy new markets, and, if necessary, new lands. . . . [The result will be] the disappearance of debased civilizations and decaying races before the higher civilization of the nobler and more virile types of men."[140] In Beveridge's eyes, America's great imperial aspiration was the Philippines, which he saw as the first step in expanding American markets to "the Orient." One of his first acts as U.S. Senator was to visit the "front lines" of this imperial project by going to the Philippines in May 1899. While there, he formulated his ideas about self-governance of natives in American colonies—ideas that would later find their parallel in his attitude toward New Mexico's natives.[141] In the Philippines, he advocated for a colonial government by a strong, federal administration under the slogan: "No self-government for peoples who have not yet learned the alphabet of liberty."[142]

Given his travel to and interest in the Philippines, Beveridge appeared well-suited in 1901 to chair the Senate's committee on U.S. territories.[143] Among his first acts as chairman was to block the Omnibus Statehood Bill, principally because of his opposition to statehood for New Mexico, though he also opposed admitting Arizona. Despite passage of the bill in the House,[144] Beveridge led the successful move to table the measure in the Senate. In the meantime, he implemented a strategy to permanently scuttle New Mexico and Arizona statehood (though he supported Oklahoma's admission).[145] Beveridge orchestrated a two-pronged strategy for opposing New Mexico's admission—both parts of which reflected the dominant narrative of race—a public relations campaign and an appeal to good government reform.

The first part of Beveridge's strategy was to conduct whistle-stop hearings in the three territories, with a subcommittee calling as witnesses census enumerators, educators, and judges. Before leaving Washington for the Southwest, he tried unsuccessfully to line up eastern witnesses who would maximize press interest in the hearings.[146] Relying on Beveridge's private correspondence, Larson shows that the Senate Republican contacted at least four editors of major newspapers with whom he was personally acquainted to generate interest in the hearings and, he hoped, opposition to statehood for New Mexico and Arizona.[147] The subcommittee spent the most time in New Mexico, confirmation that this territory was the primary target of Beveridge's campaign.[148] In hearings in Las Vegas, Santa Fe, Albuquerque, Las Cruces, and Carlsbad, Beveridge pounded the theme that New Mexico was not ready for admission because its population was still largely made up of Spanish-speaking Mexicans.[149] Based on the hearing transcripts, Beveridge appeared to relish calling non-English-speaking Mexican American witnesses to testify in Spanish about their jobs as justices of the peace, schoolteachers, and census enumerators. In Las Vegas and Santa Fe, roughly two-thirds of those testifying before the subcommittee had Spanish surnames.[150] In a 325-page report, the committee's focus was largely on race and language, with two-thirds of the witnesses from New Mexico testifying on these topics.[151] Based on a review of newspaper coverage of the whistle-stop hearings, Larson concludes that Beveridge largely succeeded in his public relations campaign.[152]

The second prong of Beveridge's strategy was to portray the Democratic proponents of New Mexico statehood as being unethically motivated by their own financial interests. For example, Democratic senator Matthew Quay of Pennsylvania, who sat on Beveridge's committee (though he was not a member of the whistle-stop subcommittee), was a strong advocate for the omnibus bill.[153] Beveridge argued that the only reason Quay supported statehood was because of his substantial railroad investments: "if the [New Mexico and Arizona] territories were admitted the bonds of the [rail]road could be sold 'for several points higher.'"[154] Beveridge specifically pushed this story about Quay's railroad investments to the press; the *Chicago Tribune* responded by promoting the view that statehood was supported by "a large syndicate engaged in building railroads in Arizona and New Mexico."[155]

At one level, Beveridge seems like the model of a good-government reformer,[156] but one need not read too much into his argument to see that this strategy, too, was fundamentally about race and fitness for self-government. The notion that supporters of statehood for New Mexico were unscrupulous politicians (especially Democratic politicians associated with machine or ring politics) went hand in hand with the view of New Mexico's electorate as consisting of "simple" Mexicans who could be readily fooled. For example, in a 1902 letter, Beveridge wrote that Arizona was poorly suited for statehood because it was no more than "a mining camp," but proffered a wholly different rationale for opposing statehood for New Mexico: it was "in a much worse state educationally and her senators will be dictated by certain interests."[157] Others before Beveridge had propagated the idea that "sharp" Euro-Americans had long taken advantage of "simple" Mexicans in New Mexico, citing land speculation as the chief example.[158] This story of political corruption, however, works only if one erases the agency of Mexican elites by portraying them as dupes of smarter, more skilled Euro-American politicians. In this way, a strategy of Beveridge's that might be seen as protective of Mexican interests is revealed to be wholly consistent with the dominant view of race in which Mexicans were believed to be inferior to Euro-Americans.

Given Beveridge's blatant efforts to manipulate the press, it is not surprising that turn-of-the-century newspaper cartoons generally portrayed New Mexico in a negative light. Like newspaper articles and editorials, cartoons in the popular press played an important role in the effort to spread the dominant view of race relations and to derail statehood for New Mexico.[159] Just after it became clear that Beveridge had succeeded in blocking statehood for Arizona and New Mexico in 1902, the *Brooklyn Eagle* ran "Whoa! Not So Fast!!!," in which Oklahoma, Arizona, and New Mexico were portrayed as passengers on a runaway stagecoach (labeled "Omnibus Statehood Bill"). [160] While Oklahoma was depicted as a harmless cowboy, Arizona and New Mexico were portrayed as, respectively, an Indian wearing a headdress and a Mexican wearing a sombrero.While the Oklahoma cowboy was shown tipping his hat (and without a weapon), both the Arizona Indian and the New Mexico Mexican were shown firing their pistols in a haphazard, dangerous fashion. The message was clear: Mexicans and Indians were too wild and irresponsible, and, until they could be tamed, they were unfit for state citizenship.

Four years later, Beveridge reluctantly supported a bill to combine the Arizona and New Mexico territories and admit them as a single state. Beveridge reasoned that combining them would lessen the negative effects of admitting a majority-Mexican state: "the Mexican population will be in the middle, masses of Americans to the east of them, masses of Americans to the west of them—a situation ideal for Americanizing within a few years every drop of the blood of Spain."[161] This proposal also spawned cartoons in the press. Showing that the dominant racial narrative was not exclusive to the East, Midwest, and South, in 1906 a Colorado newspaper ran a cartoon with the caption: "The Matchmaker: She's yours, young feller. Heaven bless you, my children." Historian Richard Melzer's analysis of the cartoon is compelling:

> The [Glenwood, Colorado] *Post* chose to portray New Mexico as a Hispanic (again), while characterizing Arizona as an attractive young Anglo woman dressed in western attire. Artists of this era regularly drew attractive young females in their cartoons to represent virtuous, coveted beings dependent on dominant males for their ultimate protection and well-being. In this instance, female Arizona [saying "Well, I never!"] strongly resisted the offer of matrimony (or joint statehood) to a hot-tempered and rather sinister looking New Mexico [saying "Carramba!"]. . . . Not even an offer to use the proposed state's "maiden name" (Arizona) made a difference to Arizonans who dreaded marriage to an alien fellow who could not even swear (no less otherwise communicate) in the nation's mother language.[162]

By 1910, when Beveridge's stamina to fight New Mexico statehood was waning against a seemingly inevitable tide, the senator began using his considerable power to push through special hurdles for New Mexico statehood.[163] These included requiring approval by both the executive and legislative branches after the state constitution was passed; substantially

reducing the amount of public land granted to the new state; and imposing requirements regarding the use of English in public schools and in all
government offices.[164] But Beveridge's efforts failed; in New Mexico, the
constitutional convention of 1910 put the final touches on a proposed
state constitution that declared that "children of Spanish descent" would
never be placed in segregated schools, among other pro–Mexican American provisions.[165]And in August 1911, President William H. Taft signed
the bill making New Mexico and Arizona states.[166]

Conclusion

During the late nineteenth and the early twentieth centuries, the dominant
and progressive views of race in New Mexico co-existed, vying for ascendancy, alternatingly embraced by Euro-American elites. Statehood per se
did not trigger a transition from the dominant to the progressive view, but
the years prior to and after statehood began to suggest the limits of the
dominant narrative's emphasis on the racial inferiority of the majority of
the new state's population. Under the dominant view, Indians essentially
were written out of the fabric of political life and citizenry, while Mexicans
were portrayed as unworthy of membership in the American political community; in this regard, the dominant racial narrative expressed a nostalgic
longing, rather than the new political reality. Buoyed by statehood and the
concomitant economic penetration of New Mexico, the progressive view of
race had largely supplanted the dominant narrative by the 1920s. By that
time, the myth of tricultural harmony had become a key trope in public
relations efforts to draw Euro-Americans from other states to New Mexico,
whether as temporary tourists or as permanent immigrants.[167]

Over the course of the early twentieth century, the progressive view of
race became entrenched as New Mexico's official racial mythology and still
resonates in today's public discourse. As cultural anthropologist Sylvia Rodríguez aptly puts it, "The enduring and endearing cliché of New Mexico
as a tourist mecca is tricultural harmony."[168] The myth of tricultural harmony embraces the three tenets of the progressive view of race first articulated by Prince. First, there is the emphasis on *cultural* difference, rather
than race, allowing New Mexicans to talk about race without talking about
race.[169] The reference to "tricultural" harmony alludes to the state's diverse
Indian tribes, to Mexican Americans, and to Euro-Americans. Second,
the theme of racial *harmony* is featured prominently, displacing the long,

complex history of inter-group conflict. Writing in 1969, a Euro-American historian embodied this tenet in describing contemporary views among New Mexico's "three cultures": "Three distinct cultures—Indian, Spanish, and Anglo—live peacefully and cooperatively in modern New Mexico."[170]

The third tenet is an implicit explanation of group-based inequality as rooted in cultural difference, not race per se. The economic dominance of the "future-oriented" culture (Euro-American) overwhelms the Mexican and Indian cultures stunted by their adherence to past traditions. Not until the rise of the Chicano civil rights movement of the 1970s, itself largely spawned from the black civil rights movement, was there a sustained (though ultimately unsuccessful) challenge to the progressive narrative of New Mexico race relations. For example, writing in 1968, historian Robert Larson began his book about statehood with this description of the U.S. Army's 1846 invasion of New Mexico: "For now the energetic, aggressive Anglo-American civilization would be grafted on the aged and somewhat lethargic Spanish and Indian ones."[171] Larson's statement embraces the progressive view of race, within which racial inequality is naturalized as merely a reflection of cultural difference. Only after the Chicano movement, with its emphasis on racial conflict and its demand for racial equality, did such a statement become unacceptably racist.

This chapter has explored the rise of the progressive view of race as a counter-narrative to the dominant view of race in New Mexico. Significantly, both the dominant and progressive narratives were *racist*: both assumed Euro-American racial superiority and Mexican and Indian racial inferiority. They differed in the degree to which they allowed the participation of Mexican Americans in American civic life. Under the dominant view, Mexican Americans were unfit for democratic self-government because they were of inferior racial stock; under the progressive view, they were considered a more benign presence in New Mexico. The progressive view invented a glorious Spanish past that erased the brutality of Spanish colonialism toward Indians. This claim that Mexican Americans were the heirs of European colonizers of the Indians qualified them for full citizenship, as represented by statehood. The next chapter turns to the dynamics of Mexican–Indian and Mexican–black relations in New Mexico as another window into the process of how Mexican Americans became a racial group. While this chapter has focused on how Euro-American elites negotiated the racial order in the shadow of double colonization in New Mexico, Chapter 3 focuses on how Mexican American elites alternatingly accommodated and contested their place in the new American racial order.

3

How a Fragile Claim to Whiteness Shaped Mexican Americans' Relations with Indians and African Americans

Writing his *Concise History of New Mexico* on the eve of the territory's long-awaited statehood provided Prince with the opportunity to document the progressive racial narrative. Anticipating that anti-Mexican naysayers would not end their criticisms of New Mexico's native population just because Congress had voted for statehood, Prince used history to attempt to create a myth of origin for the region. He placed the anniversary of Spanish settlement in New Mexico on a par with that of the Pilgrims' landing at Plymouth Rock: "This date, July 12, 1598, may be considered as the birthday of European settlement in New Mexico; and its anniversary should be celebrated in the southwest, as the date of the landing of the Pilgrim Fathers on Plymouth Rock, on December 21, 1620, is annually observed wherever the memory of the founders of New England is venerated."[1] Prince's plea for recognition of the initial European settlement—including his emphasis on the fact that it occurred twenty-two years prior to the settlement of New England—elevated the Spanish settlement of the Southwest to the level of the British settlement of the eastern seaboard. In linking the Spanish arrival in the Southwest with the British arrival in New England, Prince—himself a Mayflower descendant—sought to integrate the Southwest into the national mythology.

A second outcome of Prince's plea, however, was to widen the divide between New Mexico's Mexican and Pueblo Indian populations. Given his knowledge of New Mexico history, Prince was aware that Pueblo Indians would not want to celebrate the anniversary of their brutal conquest by the Spanish. Moreover, Prince's focus displaced the Pueblo's view of the central historical event in New Mexico as the Pueblo Revolt of 1680. His portrayal of nineteenth-century Mexican Americans—the majority of whom lived in New Mexico—as heirs to the Spanish conquest, and Pueblo Indians as victims of that conquest, served to place Mexican/Pueblo conflict at the center and move Euro-American/Pueblo and Euro-American/Mexican conflict to the margins. This mythmaking shored up Euro-Americans' position at the center of the racial order by positioning them as mediators between Mexicans and Pueblo Indians (viewing it horizontally). Significantly, the celebration of the Spanish conquest also shifted attention away from the more recent American conquest of the region. In doing so, it welcomed the collective memory loss about the alliance between Pueblos and Mexicans against the Americans, as well as the longer history of their alliance against nomadic Indian tribes.[2]

By the late nineteenth century, New Mexico's racial hierarchy consisted of four strata: white Euro-Americans at the top; Mexican Americans below them; then Pueblo Indians; and other Indians at the very bottom.[3] Mexicans occupied a pivotal position as a wedge group between Euro-Americans and Pueblo Indians (viewing the order vertically).This outcome was not inevitable. Under the liberalized racial policy adopted during the late Spanish and Mexican periods, it was argued that Mexicans and Pueblos were essentially one category of persons under the law—Mexican citizens. Some used this argument in the post-occupation era to assert that Pueblo Indians had rights to federal citizenship under the Treaty of Guadalupe Hidalgo as Mexican citizens.[4] The vertical structure placed heavy pressure on Mexicans, but it also afforded considerable opportunity to Mexicans as the buffer group. The horizontal structure, on the other hand, functioned largely to remove Euro-Americans from the zone of racial conflict, now presented as occurring between Mexicans and Indians.

This chapter explores these dynamics by focusing on Mexican elites, who proactively navigated the transition from the Spanish-Mexican racial order to the Anglo-American racial order. In her study of Hawaii, anthropologist Sally Merry has identified "the ambiguous and contradictory position of colonized elites" who responded to the American colonization there "with varying degrees of complicity, resistance, and accommodation."[5] The position of Mexican elites under American colonialism was equally fractured and complex. New Mexico's double colonization, as a region colonized first by the Spanish and then by the Americans, made the position of native elites especially tricky. At the time of the American invasion, Mexican elites in New Mexico included the small group of truly

Spanish settlers, but also comprised a much larger proportion of mestizos who had climbed higher on the ladder of social status by deploying the strategies for racial and social mobility described in the previous chapter. For the mostly mestizo elites, the two colonizations could not have been more different: in the first they were colonizers, the "settlers" who were the subjects of the colonial enterprise; in the second, they were the "natives," the objects experiencing the actions of the American colonizers.

This, in turn, meant that Mexicans elites likely had more reason to be hostile toward the American occupation; their situation, arguably, deteriorated more drastically with the occupation. In comparison, the Pueblo Indians may have had reason to welcome the American invasion because it disrupted Mexican elites' authority. At the same time, elite Mexicans' roles as the local legal, political, and religious authorities made them key targets for co-optation by the Americans. Mexican elites came to play key roles in the new political and legal regimes (roles from which Pueblos were excluded). If one of the central aims of the colonial project was to foster the transition to the authority of a new nation-state, the new sovereign had to make citizens out of some natives. Thus, some Mexicans, especially elites, were converted from opponents of the new state to participants who held some degree of citizenship, albeit second-class. Law played a fundamental role in this process, incorporating Mexican elites as legislators, jurors, and in various other capacities.

Legally White, Socially Non-White

The mixed Spanish, indigenous, and African ancestry of the Mexican people opened the door to questions about where they would fit in the American racial order. Although American attitudes were not homogeneous, a broad consensus existed among Euro-Americans that Mexicans were non-white precisely because they were racially mixed. For many Americans, it was the fact of Mexicans' "mongrel" status that most strongly signaled their racial inferiority. But the collective naturalization of Mexican citizens under the Treaty of Guadalupe Hidalgo suggested Mexicans had white status given that, at the time, naturalization was limited to white persons. Thus, Mexicans' collective naturalization in 1848 promoted a *legal* definition of Mexicans as "white." Tension around Mexican Americans' racial status arose because this legal whiteness contradicted the *social* definition of Mexicans as non-white. As a result, Mexican Americans came to occupy a position in the American racial hierarchy that was between white and non-white, or what I have termed "off-white."[6] My adoption of this term connotes Mexican Americans' in-between status, rather than their status as *more* white than non-white.

Given Euro-American attitudes about Mexicans in the nineteenth-century, as well as social relations between Euro-Americans and Mexicans in New Mexico, we can conclude that the racial subordination of Mexicans was pervasive. Euro-American immigrants to New Mexico after the American conquest probably shared racist ideas about the native Mexican and Indian populations similar to those articulated by Euro-American travelers, whose writings were widely published in the press. The evidence suggests these beliefs formed an enduring, if not static, feature of the social landscape, coloring interactions between Euro-Americans and their Mexican and Pueblo neighbors in all social realms in which they interacted. Although Mexican men and Euro-American men were both enfranchised in New Mexico, racist beliefs about Mexicans created a broad gulf between the two groups. Additionally, de facto segregation of these groups allowed for infrequent interaction that might have weakened Euro-Americans' racist beliefs.

During the Mexican period, the small number of Euro-American immigrants to the region assimilated into Mexican communities. They universally became fluent in Spanish (because it was a business necessity), and they sometimes converted to Catholicism and became naturalized Mexican citizens. A number of them formed households with Mexican or Indian women. After the American occupation, however, most of the towns to which Euro-Americans emigrated in significant numbers—including Las Vegas, Santa Fe, and Albuquerque—were characterized by residential segregation.[7] For example, Las Vegas, the county seat of San Miguel, was divided into separate, racially identifiable municipalities until the 1970s.[8] Most Euro-American immigrants to Las Vegas arrived in the area with the construction of the railroad in 1879; the 1870 and 1880 censuses show that almost all Euro-Americans in the county resided in "New Town" Las Vegas (later the town of East Las Vegas)—the area built up around the railroad yards, with a visibly American-style architecture still evident today. Mexican Americans in Las Vegas were instead concentrated in "Old Town" (later, West Las Vegas), which was structured around the Mexican-era plaza defined by traditional adobe structures. The vast majority of smaller New Mexico communities had few Euro-Americans, and in those with a more sizable Euro-American presence, Mexican Americans and Euro-Americans lived in separate areas (if not separate towns), attended separate churches, and so on.[9] While much of the social history of New Mexico communities in this era remains to be written, it is clear that Mexicans and Euro-Americans lived virtually segregated lives.

Neither did Mexican Americans and Euro-Americans interact with any frequency in the workplace. Euro-Americans were either elites (lawyers, for example) who infrequently interacted with Mexican peers,[10] or they were laborers who were intentionally separated from Mexican workers. Consider, for example, the employment records of the Atchison, Topeka, & Santa Fe Railroad as late as 1895. Thirty-five percent of its workforce had Spanish surnames (likely both Mexican and Pueblo, but it is unknown in what proportions), but of those 92 percent worked in the track maintenance department, which performed seasonal, unskilled, and physically demanding work.[11] That department, in turn, was among the most racially segregated (only 15 percent of its workers did not have Spanish surnames) and the lowest paid. Moreover, the railroad even paid workers in the same jobs different wages on the basis of race: white track layers (predominantly Irish immigrants in 1895) were paid a daily rate of $2.25, while Mexican American and Pueblo Indian track layers earned $1.00 to $1.25 daily.[12]

These conditions made it entirely feasible for Euro-Americans to live and work in New Mexico without learning Spanish, and, conversely, gave Mexican Americans little incentive to learn English.[13] Language thus became a significant barrier to inter-racial social interaction.[14] Indeed, the newer Euro-American immigrants' refusal to learn Spanish became an important symbol of their resistance to acculturating and accommodating to the region's Mexican majority. This can be seen as both a product and a cause of anti-Mexican racism on the part of Euro-Americans, for it meant that Euro-Americans' deep-seated prejudices were likely to go unchallenged by social interactions or friendships that crossed racial lines. The persistence of language barriers conspired to cement racial divisions that continued well into the twentieth century in many communities.

The status of Mexican elites became a crucial factor in the transition from the Spanish-Mexican to the Anglo-American racial order. Under the Spanish-Mexican order, some mestizos had been able to improve their social status, but under the Anglo-American order, they were often lumped together with lower-status Mexicans as racially inferior. The evidence reveals the emergence of two dynamics, sometimes in conflict with each other. All Mexicans were considered racially inferior to Euro-Americans, which promoted the formation of a collective, racialized identity among Mexican Americans. Yet the formal, largely legal system allowed some

Mexicans to claim white status. Mexican elites were better situated to exploit this avenue not because they were white (they were not), but because they were structurally situated to do so. As previously noted, a central goal of American colonialism was to co-opt elite Mexicans. An important psychological inducement for Mexican elites was allowing them to claim white status.[15] Mexicans received a collective psychological boost by being allowed to claim whiteness within the American context of white supremacy. This fundamentally changed the calculus of Mexican elites regarding American colonialism. Especially for Mexican American elites, whiteness operated as a palliative to soften the sting of changing from colonial subjects to colonial objects.

For the boost to be meaningful, however, Indians—specifically, Pueblo Indians—had to be excluded. The assertion that members of the Navajo, Apache, Comanche, Ute, and other nomadic and semi-nomadic tribes were not "white" was not controversial. From the Euro-American perspective, these Indian tribes looked like the Indian tribes they had been battling, slaughtering, and gradually pushing west from the time of the first New England settlements. New Mexico's Pueblo Indians, in contrast, puzzled Euro-Americans. They had lived for centuries in permanent settlements in which they had perfected farming in New Mexico's arid climate. In fact, they often fought together with Mexicans against the non-Pueblo tribes in New Mexico.[16] From the perspective of the American colonizers, Pueblo Indians and the mestizo Mexican masses must have seemed similar: they lived near each other (often in adjacent communities) in villages along rivers; they practiced variants of Roman Catholicism; their economies centered on subsistence agriculture and sheepherding; they used Spanish-language first and surnames; and, under the relatively recent Mexican independence, they were full citizens under the Mexican Constitution.[17] It was precisely the region's prior colonization by Spain that had produced these commonalities between Mexicans and Pueblo Indians.[18]

In this context, it served the interests of both Euro-Americans and those Mexicans who wanted to claim whiteness to differentiate Mexicans from Pueblo Indians. It was precisely the fragility of Mexican Americans' claim to whiteness that produced their moves to distance themselves from Pueblo Indians, African Americans, and other Indian groups. Mexicans' ability to claim whiteness as well as the inherent instability of that claim stemmed from their status as a racially mixed people. Precisely because of this mestizo heritage, Mexicans were able to stake out a tenuous claim to whiteness, drawing particularly on their European ancestry and culture (Spanish language, Catholic religion). But because of this thoroughly mixed background, and especially because the non-white ancestry dominated, Mexican Americans' claim to whiteness was both weak and conditional. Insecurities and uncertainties about their claim led Mexicans to distance themselves from Pueblo and other Indians and blacks.

Mexican American Elites: Power in the Law

Beginning in the 1870s, county courthouses in New Mexico served as both a central site for public gathering and the most visible arm of territorial government-in-action.[19] The district court convened twice a year in each county, making the county seat busy with newcomers who included the presiding judge and lawyers (all riding circuit in four to six counties), witnesses, and newspaper reporters. They also provided opportunities for local residents to earn money in roles such as bailiff and juror in the courtroom and outside it by operating restaurants, boarding houses, or otherwise meeting the needs of the visitors.[20] In every county seat, the courthouse would have been among the most imposing buildings. Newspapers in the largest towns covered trials and even the more mundane happenings of the courts when they were in session, increasing the courtroom audience still further. In some counties, civil and criminal litigation increased tremendously in the late 1870s—coinciding with the entrance of the railroad and increasing Euro-American immigration to New Mexico. For example, in San Miguel County, one of the territory's most populous counties in 1870, criminal prosecutions increased five-fold between 1876 and 1882 and civil lawsuits doubled during this time.[21] The litigation boom of the 1870s and 1880s drew even more attention to the county courthouse, enhancing its role as the focal point for American governance.

The use of Spanish in New Mexico courts was an important symbol of Mexican Americans' power. Even in the early twentieth century, most Mexican American witnesses still testified in Spanish in the county courts. Their testimony was translated into English by an official court interpreter, who was one of the essential officials riding circuit with the presiding judge, lawyers, and other court personnel.[22] Trials were simultaneously translated between English and Spanish; court interpreters translated the statements by the judge and lawyers into Spanish for the benefit of the majority-Mexican jurors, many (if not most) of whom spoke only Spanish. Interpreters translated witnesses' testimony in Spanish into English for the benefit of Euro-American judges and lawyers who spoke little or no Spanish. Translation was essential because the American system depended on laypersons, many of whom spoke only Spanish, to serve as jurors and witnesses. Furthermore, the centrality of the Spanish language in American courts was indicative of the ownership of cultural space. The appointment of an official court interpreter and the simultaneous two-way translation between Spanish and English conveyed the message that the courtroom was an institution in which Mexican Americans had substantial power.[23]

All judges and most lawyers were Euro-Americans, but in other respects the district courts in most New Mexico counties were dominated by Mexican Americans.[24] For example, the vast majority of county sheriffs (like other elected officials) were Mexican American.[25] Sheriffs called the court to order, collected fees (including bail), summoned jurors, made arrests, and jailed prisoners. To accomplish these tasks when court was in session, they appointed from four to six bailiffs to assist them. Bailiffs too were likely to be Mexican American in most counties, given the demographics of New Mexico. For instance, in San Miguel County in one period during the last quarter of the nineteenth century, all but two of sixty-one court bailiffs were Mexican American.[26] Bailiffs were paid $2 a day (the same rate as jurors), and some evidence suggests that Mexican American elites used these positions as a form of political patronage. Given the region's demographics, Mexican Americans (including significant numbers of women) also composed the vast majority of witnesses in the county courts.

Mexican American jurors played a special role in the court system. In criminal trials, two sets of jurors functioned as a check on other actors in the legal system: grand jurors, who issued indictments, and petit jurors, who decided guilt or innocence. Given that nine of twelve counties had a Euro-American population of less than 20 percent, we can reasonably infer that the majority of jurors in those counties were Mexican American. Mexican American grand jurors checked the authority of Euro-American prosecutors to decide whether or not to accept prosecutors' recommendations for indictment. (None of the twenty-one prosecutors who served during the territorial period was Mexican American.[27]) Mexican American petit jurors checked the authority of Euro-American judges, deciding the guilt or innocence of defendants and their punishment. Of fifty-nine supreme court justices appointed during the territorial period (who served as both trial and appellate judges), only one was a native New Mexican—Antonio José Otero.[28] Otero was among the first three judges appointed by Kearny in 1846, but there is no evidence that he ever presided over court proceedings.

The experience of one New Mexico county is illustrative. In San Miguel County, where Euro-Americans comprised 12 percent of the population in 1880, Mexican American jurors outnumbered Euro-American jurors four to one; 80 percent of grand jurors and 86 percent of petit jurors were Mexican men.[29] Higher status, wealthier Mexican Americans were more likely to serve as jurors, and especially as grand jurors, while lower status Mexican American laborers served regularly on petit juries as a form of political patronage.[30] Mexican Americans' participation as jurors probably occurred throughout New Mexico well into the twentieth century. At one level this is not surprising, since there simply were not enough Euro-American settlers for the legal system to function. If jury trials were to be held in nineteenth-century New Mexico, Mexican American jurors would be needed.

Perhaps the most extensive site for Mexican power in the legal system was the territorial legislature.[31] Mexican men comprised the majority of all such legislative bodies between 1848 and 1870, ranging from a low of 55 percent to a high of 95 percent of delegates or legislators.[32] Political scientist Carlos Ramirez has estimated that, over the entire territorial period, Mexican American legislators made up 66 percent of the upper house (council) and 75 percent of the lower house in the New Mexico legislature.[33] Mexican Americans were just as likely to hold leadership positions in the legislature during the territorial period: of twenty-one council presidents, only six were Euro-Americans; of thirty-two speakers of the house, thirteen were Euro-Americans.[34] Although Euro-Americans played important roles in the territorial legislature, it is reasonable to speak about legislation passed by these bodies as the acts of Mexican American elites.

One indication of the power of Mexican Americans in the legislature was the role of the Spanish language and of translation, both written and oral. During this time period and beyond, New Mexico legislatures and constitutional conventions were conducted in Spanish, translated into English, and the laws and constitutions that resulted from them were officially printed in both Spanish and English.[35] In this sense too, the laws and other actions of these bodies were the voice and will of Mexican elites, not of Euro-Americans and the various Indian peoples in New Mexico. Treating Mexican elites as agents with a powerful voice and role in creating their own destinies—even after the American conquest—is an important corrective to past historical scholarship.[36]

And yet there were significant limits to the power of majority-Mexican legislatures. First, unlike state governments and the federal system, in which the legislative branch was a co-equal check on the executive branch, in the New Mexico Territory, the executive branch was much stronger than the legislative branch by congressional design. Remember that the governor and other major positions in the territorial government were appointed directly by the U.S. president (subject to Senate confirmation). Ramirez's analysis has shown that, for all territorial offices, this translated into a racial gap—with the more powerful territorial officials overwhelmingly Euro-American.[37] Second, Congress reserved the right to veto any legislation enacted by the territorial legislature.[38] Significantly, Congress did not give itself the right to nullify the legislatures of all American territories, but only those of the New Mexico, Arizona, and Utah.[39] Despite these limitations, majority-Mexican legislatures still emerge as a powerful site for exploring the ways in which Mexican elites negotiated the new American regime. In the following sections I examine how the actions of the majority-Mexican American legislatures impacted other racially subordinated groups: Pueblo Indians, African Americans, and other Indians in New Mexico.

Mexican American Elites and Pueblo Indians

A central figure in New Mexico politics during both the Mexican and early American periods was Father Antonio José Martínez, who served as the Taos priest from 1826 to 1856. Martínez is a controversial figure whose legacy continues to be contested today. He is idolized by some Mexican Americans, who recently succeeded in having a statue in his honor placed in the Taos town plaza.[40] Euro-Americans, on the other hand, have long demonized Martínez, whether in historical, religious, or literary circles.[41] In her 1927 novel *Death Comes for the Archbishop*, Willa Cather portrayed Martínez as corrupt and arrogant—perhaps still the most potent of the tropes about him.[42]

Martínez was born in 1804 into one of the wealthiest families of the region.[43] As a young man, he took part in the ideological republican movement that spawned Mexico's independence from Spain and later served three terms in the new republic's legislature.[44] As a middle-aged man, he initially resisted the U.S. occupation. As early as 1843, Martínez published a manifesto warning of the encroachments of Euro-Americans and portending the future invasion of Mexico by the United States.[45] He harbored a special enmity for Charles Bent, the American governor assassinated in

1847.[46] Although he was not among those prosecuted for the revolt, Martínez is credited by some as one of its major organizers.[47] It is likely that he at least had an indirect leadership role through the large network of youths and young adults who were or had been under his tutelage at the only school in the Taos Valley during the Mexican period.[48] Later, Martínez served as a legislator in the American territorial period.

Martínez was a complex figure who in many ways epitomized the dilemmas of Mexican elites. On the one hand, he subscribed to the liberal ideology expressed in the Mexican constitution's proclamation that all Mexicans were equal under the law, without regard to their racial status, and he specifically sought to incorporate "civilized" Indians and mestizos into the Mexican polity. He worked closely with the Taos Pueblo community as their priest and, at times, advocate before various Spanish, Mexican, and American officials. At the same time, Martínez was an elite Mexican who owned Indian slaves and who has been accused of abusing the trust placed in him by Taos Pueblo Indians. In 1920, Taos Pueblo Governor Porfirio Mirabal charged that Martínez had reneged on a promise to work to obtain leniency for the Taos Pueblo men tried for the 1847 assassination of the first American governor. According to the governor's testimony, Martínez was given Taos Pueblo land in exchange for brokering leniency with the American officials, and, despite failing to do so, Martínez kept the land.[49]

Some challenge Mirabal's account, and we probably will never know whether the allegations are true.[50] Perhaps more significant than the truth of the accusations against and defenses on behalf of Martínez is the fact that partisans have continued the debate for so long—a contemporary testament to the allure of one of the most powerful figures in the first generation of Mexican Americans. Historian David Weber describes Martínez as "an oversized figure for his time and place and a contradictory one":

> a village priest of great intellectual gifts and ego; a moralist with illegitimate children; a populist whose broad humanitarian vision and efforts to achieve political and ecclesiastical reform were often offset by arrogance and intolerance; and an ardent Mexican nationalist who led the way toward making New Mexico part of the United States. Whatever his weaknesses, his strengths had made him the most important cultural force in New Mexico in the two decades prior to the Mexican war . . . and a key political figure in both the Mexican and American eras.[51]

Martínez's contradictory stance toward Indians (that he both owned Indian slaves and fought for Indian civil rights) reflected a long-standing janus-like quality in Mexican policy toward "civilized" Indians such as the Pueblo peoples of New Mexico. Despite the Mexican constitution's promise of equality, Mexican law in practice likely recognized differences among Pueblo Indians, mestizos, and other racial groups.[52] We do know, however, that one motive for granting greater citizenship rights was to facilitate the dispossession of Indian lands into Mexican hands.

Martínez's views also demonstrate the dilemma Mexican American elites faced with respect to the Pueblo Indians in the new American era. As the majority of legislators in the post-war period, Mexicans held in their hands the fate of Pueblo Indians, and their actions revealed a deep ambivalence. Martínez was involved in the all the early conventions and legislatures, frequently holding a leadership position. He was elected president of the first constitutional convention (organized in 1850 prior to congressional declaration of New Mexico as a federal territory). At that gathering, a majority-Mexican body proposed a state constitution for New Mexico that enfranchised Pueblo Indian men (along with Mexican and Euro-American men).[53] During the same meeting, Mexican elites denied the franchise to blacks and Afro-mestizos ("africanos o descendientes de africanos") and to non-Pueblo Indians ("indios bárbaros").[54]

Mexicans had multiple reasons for wanting to enfranchise Pueblo Indians. First, they had much in common culturally and otherwise. Second, they had been allies in the past, most recently in the anti-American revolt of 1847. Making political allies of Pueblo men, as voters, was a natural next step. Yet Mexican elites were hardly consistent in their regard for and treatment of Pueblo Indians. The majority-Mexican legislature in 1849 (operating unofficially, since New Mexico had not been given territorial status by Congress) limited the franchise to "free white male inhabitants," intending to exclude Pueblo Indians. As part of the Compromise of 1850 establishing New Mexico as a federal territory, Congress restricted the right of suffrage to "free white males."[55] Even after Congress and successive territorial legislatures had formally excluded them from the franchise, Pueblo men apparently voted in some elections. In the early years of the American occupation, according to one territorial supreme court justice, Pueblo Indians "not only voted, but held both civil and military offices. In many localities, they, by their numerical strength, controlled the political destinies of [towns and counties]."[56]

Indeed, Pueblo electoral participation spawned its own cycle of protest and politics. In 1853 a committee of the territorial legislature considered a complaint that more than one hundred Pueblo Indians had voted illegally. The contest at issue involved the most important elected position (for nonvoting delegate to Congress) and a racially polarizing campaign that pit a native, monolingual-Spanish priest, José Manuel Gallegos, against a Missouri politician, William Carr Lane, who had only recently set foot in New Mexico.[57] Gallegos won, but Lane contested the results, alleging in part that Pueblo men had voted illegally.[58] A committee of the territorial legislature was charged with deciding which law governed: the 1850 extension of voting rights to Pueblo men or Congress' 1850 restriction of the franchise to white males (including Mexicans, but excluding Pueblo Indians). Not surprisingly given that all their acts were subject to congressional nullification, the legislators followed the congressional mandate. In the end, even without the disputed Pueblo votes, Gallegos was declared the winner.[59]

During the early years of the American occupation, Mexican elites took a variety of stances toward Pueblo Indians—from working with Pueblo men to combat the American colonizers (in the Taos revolt) to disenfranchising them. These standpoints undoubtedly reflected deep material conflicts between the groups (as when Mexican settlers encroached on Pueblo lands). But they also reflected the efforts of Mexican elites to negotiate a more favorable position in the post-occupation racial order. Mexicans sought to differentiate themselves from Pueblos by claiming whiteness, and thus the rights of full citizenship reserved for white males in American society (including voting and holding office). In this way, Mexicans ensured their second-place position in a four-group racial hierarchy. What ultimately became an anti-Pueblo project of Mexican elites played into the hands of the American colonizers, who sought to divide Mexicans and Pueblos in order to disrupt a potentially powerful alliance among these native groups.

The dynamics of this strategy are illustrated by how the question of Pueblo Indian citizenship played out in the U.S. judicial, legislative, and executive branches. Pueblo Indians became part of the United States because they lived in the lands taken from Mexico and governed by the Treaty of Guadalupe Hidalgo. When the war ended a long period of contestation among (and sometimes within) the three branches ensued about the place of Pueblos Indians in the American polity. There were two central questions, both of which led ultimately to the question of how Pueblo lands would be treated and, specifically, whether they could be transferred to Mexican American and Euro-American buyers. The first question was whether Pueblo Indians were federal citizens, like Mexicans, under the Treaty of Guadalupe Hidalgo. The second was whether Pueblo Indians were *really* Indians, and thus subject to federal legislation such as the Trade and Intercourse Act of 1834 (which prohibited the sale of Indian lands).[60]

These issues were at the center of *United States v. Lucero*, a land dispute between Mexicans and Cochiti Pueblo, southwest of Santa Fe.[61] Mexicans had settled near Cochiti Pueblo and claimed ownership of land, against the Pueblo's assertion that the land in question was part of the Pueblo's collectively owned property. Perhaps at the Pueblo's request, U.S. Attorney Stephen B. Elkins initiated the case against the Mexicans under the Indian Trade and Intercourse Act of 1834, seeking to eject them from the land. The Mexican defendants hired several prominent lawyers, including Kirby Benedict, who recently had returned to private practice after serving seventeen years on the territorial supreme court.[62] Benedict's involvement itself testifies to the precedent-setting nature of the case and its potential impact on land sales. While we cannot know what kind of fee arrangement Benedict and his partners had with their Mexican clients, it was common for attorneys in land dispute cases to receive title to a portion of land as a fee.[63] As was true throughout the territorial period, New Mexico's judicial system consisted of a two-tiered federal court, with the same judges acting as trial judges and sitting *en banc* as an appellate court.[64] Thus, the trial judge acted also as an appellate judge, reviewing his own earlier ruling. In this case, Chief Justice John P. Slough, the trial judge who first decided the case, and Chief Justice John S. Watts, who wrote the appellate decision, sided with the Mexican defendants and against the U.S. attorney and Cochiti Pueblo.[65] That both judges knew the stakes were high and that the outcome would ripple well beyond these parties was evident from their written opinions.

Both opinions rested on the twin conclusions that Pueblo Indians held Mexican citizenship and so, under the Treaty of Guadalupe Hidalgo, became federal citizens of the United States, and thus occupied a distinctive position with respect to other Indians; and that Congress did not intend to treat Pueblos like other Indians. The first conclusion was grounded in Mexico's extension of citizenship rights to "civilized" Indians: "But as a race, we think it impossible to deny that, under the [Mexican] constitution and laws of [that] country, no distinction was made as to the rights of citizenship and the privileges belonging to it, between this [civilized Indian blood] and European or Spanish blood."[66]

The rulings on the second question embroiled the New Mexico judges in a multi-decade battle with Indian agents in the executive branch (who advocated treating Pueblos like other Indians), Congress (which in 1910 enacted legislation specifying that "Indian country" included Pueblo lands), and the U.S. Supreme Court (which ruled, first, to uphold *Lucero* and, later, to overrule it). [67] The *Lucero* opinion essentially argued that Congress did not intend to treat Pueblos like other Indians because it had, on the whole, not done so in the past. *Lucero* emphasized that Congress had not ratified treaties with any Pueblo nations, had not appointed Indian agents to the Pueblos, and had not specifically mentioned Pueblo Indians in legislation other than that confirming the titles of Spanish land grants to seventeen Pueblos in New Mexico.[68] Perhaps reflecting Watts's former status as a legislator (he had been New Mexico's congressional delegate), the opinion dared Congress to act if it saw things differently: "If such destiny is in store for a large number of the most law-abiding, sober, and industrious people of New Mexico, it must be the result of the direct legislation of [C]ongress or the mandate of the [S]upreme [C]ourt."[69] At one level, the *Lucero* opinion reflects a tension between Euro-American outsiders at the national level and Euro-American insiders (that is, those within New Mexico), who asserted a personal knowledge of Pueblo Indians and sought to vouch for their distinctiveness from other Indians.[70]

The New Mexico–based Euro-American judges, in the *Lucero* opinion, made two related rhetorical moves in reaching their conclusion that the Trade and Intercourse Act did not apply to Pueblo Indians (and, as a result, that their property could be bought and sold). First, as illustrated above, they portrayed Pueblo Indians in a positive light, emphasizing that they were citizens equal to the "one thousand best Americans" and "one thousand best Mexicans" in New Mexico in terms of their "virtue, honesty and industry."[71] The more dominant strand of this reasoning, however, was the drawing of a bright line between Pueblos as "civilized" and other Indians as "savage." The court repeatedly asserted that Congress had passed the 1834 legislation to govern the class of Indians who were "wandering savages, given to murder, robbery, and theft, living on the game of the mountains, the forest, and the plains, unaccustomed to the cultivation of the soil, and unwilling to follow the pursuits of civilized man."[72] In contrast, the court found the Pueblos to be "a peaceful, quiet, and industrious people, residing in villages for their protection against the wild Indians, and living by the cultivation of the soil."[73] The judges thus with one hand complimented Pueblo Indians and lifted them above nomadic Indians, while with the other they opened the door for Pueblo lands to be bought (with all that implied in an era of rampant land speculation) by Mexicans and Euro-Americans.

The *Lucero* court braided an additional strand into its racial narrative. Foreshadowing the progressive view later articulated by Prince, Chief Justice Watts signaled his admiration for "the true Spanish adventurers," whom, he emphasized, had begun colonizing Mexico (and what would become the American Southwest) long before "our timid forefathers, who peeped out into the wilderness from their colony of Plymouth."[74] Watts credited the Spanish colonizers with bringing "civilization" and, especially, the Catholic religion to the Pueblos, but simultaneously chastised them for their "cruelty," "cupidity," and "despotic rule" over the Pueblo Indians.[75] The final trope in their narrative was the juxtaposition of Spanish despotism with Pueblo victimhood, expressed as "this condition of domineering on the part of the Spaniards, and meek obedience on the part of the pueblo [*sic*] Indians."[76] A decade earlier, Chief Justice Benedict used a similar narrative when he sided with Acoma Pueblo and against Mexicans accused of encroaching on their lands. Calling Mexicans "the better-instructed and more civilized race," he admonished them for trying to take advantage of Pueblo Indians. He saw the role of the American courts as leveling the playing field: "It is gratifying to us to be the judicial agents . . . affirming the rights of Pueblo Indians."[77]

Read as a narrative about New Mexico's racial dynamics, the judicial opinion is rich with insights. The Euro-American judges anointed Pueblo Indians as "civilized," and therefore racially superior to non-Pueblo Indians, while they reinforced the divide between Pueblos and Mexicans, emphasizing the Spanish dominance over the former (rather than, for example, the mestizo character of the latter). At the same time, the representation of Mexicans as the descendants of *Spanish* ancestors (even within the context of the demonization of Spanish cruelty to Indians) reinforced the basis of Mexicans' claim to whiteness. Meanwhile the exclusion of Pueblo Indians from whiteness was taken for granted as inevitable. Thus, Mexicans were supposed to feel good about their position relative to Pueblo Indians, who were supposed to feel good relative to other Indians. They and everyone else, meanwhile, understood the devastating material impact of the *Lucero* decision, which allowed Pueblo lands to be freely alienated in the marketplace, thereby leading directly to the transfer of Pueblo lands to Mexicans and Euro-Americans.

From the vantage point of the American colonizers, the opinion represented and solidified a predictable divide-and-conquer strategy: by allowing Mexican men to claim white status (and therefore vote and hold elected office) while denying such opportunity to Pueblo Indian men, they achieved multiple goals. This strategy allowed for a civilian government (in the dark shadow of military rule) that could not have operated without the cooperation (and perhaps embrace of) natives, given the paucity of Euro-American settlers in the region prior to the occupation. Neither could it have functioned without the interruption of the mestizo Mexican/Pueblo Indian coalition that had resisted the American occupation at Taos and elsewhere. The judicial ruling furthered both goals, even while claiming to be magnanimous to all. Consider the racial positioning that occurred. Euro-Americans positioned themselves as racially generous toward Mexican Americans, *allowing* them to take a position under the white tent. Meanwhile, in contradiction to this formal legal proclamation, Euro-American writers, newspapermen, and politicians continued to mockingly denounce Mexicans as racially inferior and as unfit for self-government as state citizens. Mexicans mobilized their Indo-Hispano mestizo heritage in a way that emphasized their European roots (hence, whiteness), despite the fact that their racial stock, overall, was far more indigenous than European. Through strategies akin to those demanded under the Spanish-Mexican racial system, mestizos sought both to distance themselves from Pueblo Indians, with whom they shared much in common, and to deny and denigrate their own non-white background.

The *Lucero* case is part of a line of cases dealing with the status of Pueblo Indians that made it to the Supreme Court. In 1877, the Court sided with the New Mexico judges in finding that Taos Pueblo Indians were not "Indians" in the general sense of the word's usage in federal policy.[78] Quoting at length from the New Mexico court's ruling, the Supreme Court emphasized that the fact that Pueblo Indians had been citizens under the Mexican republic made them distinctive from other Indians. This led the Supreme Court to uphold the Pueblo Indian community-owned land grants (which Congress had earlier confirmed), even though, during this same period, Congress and the Court were reluctant to certify similar collectively-owned grants for Mexican communities. A provocative bifurcation had begun taking shape with American rule: Mexican Americans were allowed to claim white status and have many political rights, but they were losing their communally owned lands to the American property regime. At the same time, Pueblo Indians were defined as non-white and virtually excluded from the political system, while their community land grants were confirmed. This definition of Pueblo status continued until 1913 when the Supreme Court heard another case involving Pueblos, this time deciding that they should receive the federal protections of Indian status.[79]

Mexican American Elites and Blacks, Free and Enslaved

Miguel Antonio Otero was born into a wealthy ranching family in Valencia County, New Mexico, in 1829. His paternal grandfather was Antonio José Otero, whom Kearny had appointed as one of three judges during the early weeks of the U.S. Army's invasion of New Mexico. Some biographers claim Otero's parents were born in Spain,[80] but if this was the case, they were rarities in New Mexico. Ramón Gutiérrez's research into Catholic marriage records reveals that of 13,204 people legally married in New Mexico between 1693 (after the Pueblo Revolt resettlement) and 1846, a mere ten individuals listed their *parents'* birthplace as Spain.[81]

Otero was seventeen years old when the Americans invaded New Mexico, so he was among the first generation of Mexican Americans to come of age under American rule. He spoke English fluently, which at that time was rare even among Mexican elites. Otero attended college in St. Louis and New York, studied law in Missouri, and returned to New Mexico in his early twenties. He quickly mounted a political career, first as a representative of Valencia County in the 1852 and 1853 territorial legislature (where he was among the youngest members) and then as New Mexico's nonvoting delegate to Congress from 1855 to 1859 (winning election to two consecutive two-year terms).[82] Otero was an outspoken Democrat during his years as the nonvoting delegate to Congress, aligning himself politically and socially with southerners.[83]

During his third year in Washington, D.C., Otero married Mary Blackwood of Charleston, South Carolina, whose father was a slaveholder.[84] Otero and Blackwood went on to have several children, including Miguel Antonio Otero II, who in 1897 became the only Mexican American appointed as territorial governor. Otero's brother-in-law, William Blackwood, was appointed to the territorial supreme court.[85] In the years before the Civil War, Otero took a strong pro-slavery stand and used his influence to persuade New Mexico legislators to enact a slave code in 1859.[86] After secession, however, Otero was more circumspect about New Mexico joining the fledgling Confederacy. In an 1861 letter written early in the Lincoln administration and published in the *Santa Fe Weekly Gazette*, Otero seemed genuinely wrought over the question and ultimately recommended siding with California:

> If a dissolution of this country should take place, we of New Mexico will be expected to take sides with one of the two or three or four of the Republics into which it would be divided. What will be the determination of the people of New Mexico if such deplorable consequences should come to pass, I cannot say. My own opinion and my counsel to them would be, in that event, a union with the Pacific free states, west of the great prairies. If California and Oregon declare their independence of this Government I am for joining them.[87]

On the other hand, Otero may simply have been preserving his options with a Republican administration; Lincoln appointed him Secretary of the Territory in 1861.[88]

Whereas Mexicans and Pueblo Indians lived near each other, shared much in common culturally, and regularly competed with each other over material resources such as land and water, Mexicans had little interaction with African Americans. As discussed in the previous chapter, black slaves were taken to Mexico in large numbers during the Spanish colonial period, and their descendants became part of the racially mixed population that settled the northern frontier. Frontier dynamics as well as those that characterized the Spanish-Mexican racial order generally led to the "disappearance" of black Mexicans into the general mestizo population. The first American census, in 1850, recorded only twenty-two blacks in New Mexico; ten years later, there were sixty-four.[89] The census records did not distinguish, so we do not know whether New Mexico's blacks were slaves or free persons, but their small numbers suggest that New Mexico's legislative politics around slavery and the rights of free blacks were mostly about symbolic politics. The actions taken by Mexican elites regarding blacks did not reflect competition with them over resources; rather, they should be seen as primarily signifying other contemporary debates and an understandable preoccupation with Euro-Americans as an audience.

In the 1850s, New Mexico legislators switched from an anti-slavery to a pro-slavery position. The conventional interpretation is to link this shift from an anti-slavery to a pro-slavery position to the politics of statehood. From the end of the war in 1848 until 1911, when Congress finally recommended statehood for New Mexico and Arizona, a significant segment of elites (both Mexican and Euro-American, but probably predominantly Euro-American) had pushed almost continuously, within New Mexico and nationally, for statehood.[90] According to the standard explanation, New Mexico elites took an anti-slavery position when they felt it would improve their chances of being admitted to the Union, and then shifted to a pro-slavery position when they felt their odds improved as a slave state. The argument is rarely made with respect to the majority of legislators and convention delegates who were Mexican, but is instead attributed to Euro-American elites in New Mexico and in Congress. For example, the historian Loomis Ganaway claims that anti-black legislative acts "reflected the growing influence of southerners in territorial politics. During the next three or four years, their control was tightened by the alignment of Miguel Otero, territorial delegate from 1855–1861, with southern political leaders and institutions."[91] Ganaway's use of the passive voice to discuss Otero is consistent with his attribution of important political shifts in New Mexico politics to Euro-American political actors (in New Mexico and nationally) and to national issues. Other historians are not quite as extreme but share his general approach.[92]

Missing from this interpretation, however, is serious attention to how Mexican Americans themselves constructed their interests, in either symbolic or material terms. A recent exception is offered by New Mexico State Historian Estevan Rael-Gálvez, whose analysis takes seriously the interests and strategies of Mexican political elites. He argues that Mexican legislators enacted a slave code that legalized black chattel slavery in order to better protect their real interest in slavery—the enslavement of Indians taken captive from nomadic tribes and sold into Mexican households. Rael-Gálvez cites a letter written by Territorial Secretary Alexander Jackson (the likely author of New Mexico's 1859 Slave Code) in which he states, "We have assured the Mexicans that [passage of a slave code] would protect their own system of peonage."[93] Both the conventional interpretation related to statehood politics and Rael-Galvez's argument linking a pro-slavery position and Mexicans' interest in maintaining Indian slavery are important, but they do not exhaust the possible explanations.

Given the fragility of Mexican Americans' claim to whiteness, Mexican elites' actions regarding African Americans can credibly be seen as a means of distancing themselves from the group undeniably at the bottom of the

American racial order. At the time of the initial American occupation, Mexican Americans were well aware of Euro-Americans' presumptions of racial superiority and concomitant Mexican inferiority. In the following decade, Euro-Americans allowed Mexican elites to claim white status in the political sphere, while inequality remained entrenched in the social sphere. But the questions that plagued Congress and the rest of America at the outset and conclusion of the war with Mexico still lingered: Where do Mexicans fit? Are they more like blacks or Indians? Mexican elites, too, were well aware of these questions, and Euro-Americans' potential answers to them likely shaped their attitudes toward black slavery.

Early under American rule, majority-Mexican legislative bodies took anti-slavery positions. In the first constitutional convention (held in October 1848, only a few months after Congress had ratified the Treaty of Guadalupe Hidalgo), Father Martínez presided over thirteen delegates, ten of whom were Mexican.[94] They staunchly opposed slavery with the following resolution: "We do not desire to have domestic slavery within our borders; and, until the time shall arrive for admission into the union of states, we desire to be protected by Congress against the introduction of slaves into the territory."[95] In 1850, the proposed state constitution said that New Mexico would join the Union as a free state; in a popular vote on that constitution, 6,771 New Mexican men voted in favor, with only 39 against.[96] In the first postwar legislature (which met in 1848, after ratification of the Treaty of Guadalupe Hidalgo but well before Congress declared New Mexico a federal territory in 1850), a majority-Mexican legislature, with Father Martínez as president, banned slavery. This anti-slavery sentiment likely reflected Mexico's historic opposition to African slavery (recall that Mexico abolished slavery thirty-three years before the United States), as well as ongoing hostilities with Texas. For example, in the 1848 resolution to Congress, the clause immediately preceding the anti-slavery provision stated: "We respectfully but firmly protest against the dismemberment of our territory in favor of Texas or from any other cause."[97] Hostilities between New Mexico and Texas existed for decades (and still persist in some quarters), and some historians have credited animosity toward Texans as fueling Mexican Americans' anti-Confederacy position in the Civil War.[98]

Seen in this light, the early anti-slavery positions by the majority-Mexican conventions and legislatures could have been anticipated, but the shift to a pro-slavery position in the late 1850s would not have been. In 1857, the territorial legislature enacted a law severely restricting the rights of free blacks.[99] The heart of the law was a thirty-day restriction on the presence of free blacks and mulattos in New Mexico, with the first offense punishable by fine and imprisonment and increasing in severity to "hard labor" if the free black person refused to leave New Mexico. As if that restriction was not severe enough, the law required free blacks and mulattos already in New Mexico to "give bond for their good conduct and behavior . . . with two or more honorable securities."[100]

The law also banned marriage and cohabitation between black men and white women. We can presume that Mexican men would have intended to include Mexican women within the category of "white women."[101] The latter move is especially interesting given the widespread, historic marriage, cohabitation, and/or reproduction between Indians and Spanish descendants. In other words, "miscegenation" between Mexicans and Indians was widespread and at least implicitly condoned by the movement of descendants of Indian-Spanish unions into the general mestizo category. Yet the law specifically banned another kind of mestizo union: black/Mexican. Given the small numbers of identifiable blacks, it was feasible to prohibit black/white sexual unions in a way that would have been impossible for other inter-racial unions—further suggesting the symbolic aim of the Mexican American legislature.[102] Historian Neil Foley notes a different pattern in Texas. There a miscegenation law banned white/black marriage, and, as in New Mexico, Mexicans were legally defined as white. Yet Mexican/black marriages in Texas were rarely prosecuted because the stronger *social* definition of Mexicans as non-white superseded the legal definition. In other words, in Texas, "white" meant "white, not Mexican."[103]

In 1859, two years after the law targeting free blacks was passed, a nearly unanimous legislative body composed of thirty-four Mexicans and three Euro-Americans enacted a slave code.[104] Entitled "An Act to Provide for the Protection of Property in Slaves in this Territory," the law imposed stiff criminal penalties for stealing slaves, assisting slaves in escape, or otherwise inducing them to leave their masters. It also made it illegal for free persons to gamble with slaves, to sell or give them weapons, and to trade or do business with them. New Mexico's slave code included provisions for private individuals and public officials to deal with runaway slaves, constituting a mini-version of a fugitive slave law within the slave code. Like many slave codes of the era, the law imposed more severe sentences on slaves convicted of crimes than those provided for by the general penal code; for example, it imposed the penalty of hanging for the rape or attempted rape of a white woman by a slave or free black or mulatto. Like the black codes enacted two years earlier, the slave code banned marriage between "white persons" and blacks, free or slave (this time without regard to gender). In the first provision of its kind in New Mexico, the slave code prohibited blacks, free and slave, from testifying "against a free white person" in any court of law. While such laws were commonplace in the South and in California, New Mexico had not previously had racial restrictions on witnesses.[105]

Within a decade, then, Mexican elites went from supporting abolition to enacting a harsh and comprehensive slave code. They went from little concern for blacks, to enacting a "black code" that all but locked free blacks out of New Mexico. New Mexico's laws suddenly became as harsh as those of the southern states (in the case of the slave code) and "the early old northwest states" (Illinois, Indiana, Ohio) that enacted so-called black codes to deal with increases in their free black populations.[106] The irony here is that while Illinois, for example, enacted a black code in reaction to a 258 percent increase in its population of free blacks between 1820 and 1830,[107] New Mexico enacted its law when there were fewer than one hundred blacks in a geographic area that spanned all of present-day New Mexico and Arizona. Rather than being motivated by fear of being overrun by free blacks or competition over land or labor, something else was at work. The historical record makes it hard to avoid the conclusion that these harsh laws reflected the preoccupation with pushing Mexican Americans up the racial hierarchy and keeping blacks at the bottom. Both laws contained miscegenation clauses that protected the "white" daughters and sisters of Mexican elites (although the black code also punished those "white"/Mexican women who transgressed the color line). The slave code banned blacks' testimony against whites at a time when Mexican Americans dominated juries as enfranchised citizens. In these ways, the laws served to brighten the line between *Mexicans as whites* and blacks as nonwhites.

In 1856 the U.S. Supreme Court issued its infamous *Scott v. Sandford* opinion, deciding that neither free Negroes nor slaves had federal citizenship (which we will discuss further in the next chapter). According to historian Don Fehrenbacher, the public reaction to the case was divided into three streams:

> Most conspicuous by far was the roar of anger and defiance from antislavery voices throughout the North. . . . From southerners, in contrast, came expressions of satisfaction and renewed sectional confidence at this overdue vindication. . . . Meanwhile, northern Democrats and certain other conser-

vatives were . . . [relieved] at the settlement of a dangerous issue and [delivered] pious lectures on the duty of every citizen to accept the wise judgment of the Court.[108]

Otero, then New Mexico's congressional delegate, wrote a series of letters about the Court's decision. In a letter to territorial secretary Alexander Jackson in 1858, Otero wrote:

> I know that the laws of the United States, the Constitution, and the decision of the Supreme Court in the Dred Scott case, establishes property in slaves in the Territories, but I think something should be done on the part of our Legislature to protect it. You will perceive at once the advantages that will result from the passage of such a law for our Territory, and I expect you will take good care to procure its passage. Immediately after its passage, you will dispatch copies to all the principal newspapers in the Southern States for publication, and also a copy to the New York Herald "very quick."[109]

It is difficult to gauge reactions to the opinion at the time in New Mexico. My review of surviving newspapers of that time, for instance, did not uncover any mention of the opinion in the New Mexico press. But in a promotional letter written by five Mexican American lawmakers shortly after passage of the 1859 slave code, the decision surfaces as one of the factors that convinced New Mexico legislators of the need to act to support slavery.[110] That letter and Otero's letter provide support for the conventional analysis. A Supreme Court decision widely viewed as pro-South and pro-slavery signaled the direction of the political winds (and, in many scholars' opinions, was one of the catalysts for secession and the Civil War). Otero's letter speaks of benefits to New Mexico of siding with the South, which could be interpreted to mean the potential for Congress's grant of statehood as a slave state.

But the Supreme Court's opinion must have caused alarm to those in New Mexico who had been genuinely committed to an anti-slavery position. It was a resounding statement of the official exclusion of blacks (free and slave) from the polity and from all but the minimum sense of citizenship. In such a climate, we can imagine Mexican elites feeling they had to distinguish themselves from this pariah group and enacting the slave code to do just that. Both interpretations probably intersect to explain what motivated Mexican American elites to switch from an abolitionist to a pro-slavery position. We should not forget, however, the link between black slavery and Indian slavery that was identified by Rael-Gálvez.[111] The last sentence of the New Mexico slave code passed by the majority-Mexican legislature in 1859 made it clear that the law did not affect the question of Indian slavery: "[T]his act shall in no manner apply to relation[s] between masters and contracted servants in this Territory, but the word 'slave' shall only apply to the African race."[112] It is to the issue of Indian slavery that we now turn.

Mexican American Elites and Indian Slavery

In 1868, nearly three hundred New Mexicans were served with arrest warrants charging them with the crime of holding Indian slaves or peons. Six years earlier, Lincoln had issued the Emancipation Proclamation freeing all black slaves. In 1865, President Johnson issued the "Special Proclamation" seeking the same result with respect to Indians in New Mexico.[113] That presidential act and subsequent federal legislation in 1867 that made it illegal to own Indian slaves brought the nation's battle over slavery to New Mexico, except that now it was not principally in symbolic terms.

It was the 1867 law that led to the subpoena of three hundred persons to testify before a federal grand jury that would decide whether or not to issue indictments against them.[114] Among those charged were many prominent citizens, both Mexican American and Euro-American, including elected and appointed officials, priests, and merchants. Those testifying included Juan José Santistevan, who at the time was between stints as the elected probate judge of Taos County; later, he would preside over the Taos County Commission and serve in the territorial legislature.[115] Santistevan testified without shame and, apparently, without fear of indictment or conviction—since he implicated his mother as a fellow slaveholder (though she was not one of those initially charged). About the Indians in his own and his mother's households, he said:

> They are there of their own free will. I don't know that they are paid especially. . . . I know as long as I can remember that the Indians have been as servants, that campaigns have been made against Indian tribes [Navajos] and the captives brought back and sold into slavery by parties making a campaign. In this way most of the Indians held and now living in the territory were obtained. In years past the Pah Utahs [Paiutes] before the American conquest used to sell and trade their children to the citizens of New

Mexico as slaves. The descendants of these slaves or servants now live in the families of the people.[116]

In relatively few words, Santistevan succinctly catalogued the various justifications for Indian slavery. He presents the "custom" of holding Indian slaves as a product of military conflict and as historically rooted. And, like southern slaveholders, his justification of the practice ("they are here of their own free will") is belied by his own description (they were not paid, they were captured and sold into slavery). He speaks about the history and mechanics of slavery in a detached way (for example, Indian slaves "were obtained" rather than purchased by himself or his ancestors), as if he is not personally implicated. Moreover, Santistevan's description presents a system of slavery that includes intergenerational transmission of slave status—the children and grandchildren of the slaves originally purchased or traded remain as "slaves or servants" within the households of the original owners and their descendants.[117]

In the end, the grand jury refused to return indictments against any of those charged with Indian slavery. This is not surprising, given that the grand jury likely was composed mostly of Mexican American men who knew or knew of Santistevan.[118] If Santistevan's experience is any guide, there was no lasting stigma in being charged with this crime, in either the community of Mexican American elites to which he belonged or among Euro-American elites. In the decade following his indictment as a slaveholder, Santistevan played an active role as a layperson in the American court in Taos County. On four occasions, three different chief justices of the territorial supreme court (all Euro-American) appointed Santistevan as one of three lay jury commissioners, whose task was to select panelists of grand and petit jurors for the following court session. Chief justices, who also served as presiding judge riding circuit in the first judicial district that included Taos County, named Santistevan the interpreter to the grand jury seven times during the 1870s, a position for which he was paid $3 per day. During the September 1875 term of court, Chief Justice Joseph G. Palen selected Santistevan foreman of the grand jury.[119] In short, Santistevan was a model citizen—and an elite Mexican American who owned Indian slaves.

Consider the multiple, crosscutting ways in which the efforts by American officials to contain Indian slavery in New Mexico shaped relations among the various racial groups in the region. Begin with the parameters of Indian slavery.[120] Despite the formal prohibition of Indian slavery under Spanish law, enslavement of Indians by Spanish and mestizo settlers in New Mexico occurred throughout the Spanish colonial and Mexican periods, as well as the American period.[121] Gutiérrez describes slaves captured by Mexicans directly from nomadic tribes and those purchased from middleman captors (usually other nomadic tribes) as crucial to the frontier economy: "Slaves were a medium of exchange and were pieces of movable wealth."[122] Using a quantitative analysis of baptisms in New Mexico of nomadic Indians between 1700 and 1849, Gutiérrez shows that the number of Navajo, Apache, Ute, and Comanche Indians baptized correlated strongly with the number of deaths of Spanish/Mexican settlers, thereby revealing the links between Indian slavery and cyclical armed conflict between settlers and nomadic tribes.[123]

In a comprehensive study covering several centuries, historian James Brooks describes the complex political economy of exchange in people that included both captivity of Mexican settlers by nomadic and semi-nomadic tribes and captivity and enslavement of Indians by Mexicans.[124] This political economy was gradually transformed and eventually destroyed with the American conquest of the region.[125] The American campaign to subjugate nomadic Indians and the fight against Indian slavery intertwined to eventually cripple the latter, though not in ways that necessarily worked to Indians' advantage.[126] In the short term, the effect of the transition from Mexican to American sovereignty was to greatly increase hostilities between the non-Pueblo Indian tribes and both Americans and Mexicans. The pattern that Gutiérrez had identified in the Spanish colonial period continued with a vengeance: increased hostilities, now with the Americans, Mexicans, and Pueblos aligned together against the nomadic tribes, meant increased numbers of Indian captives. Using a slave census taken in 1865 by a U.S. Indian agent in southern Colorado and northern New Mexico, Rael-Gálvez concludes that the vast majority of Indian slaves were Navajo and that almost three-fifths had been sold to Mexican households by Mexican middlemen, while two-fifths were sold to Mexican households by members of other nomadic tribes.[127] Perhaps the most striking fact is that conflict with nomadic Indians increased dramatically in the first two decades of the American occupation, likely leading to a correspondingly dramatic increase in the number of Indian slaves held in mestizo households.

Even after the Civil War, when American military and civil officials were charged with eliminating Indian slavery and peonage from New Mexico, the evidence suggests that anti-slavery efforts sometimes resulted in the capture of more Indian prisoners who were then sold into slavery. For example, Kit Carson's First New Mexico Volunteers conducted campaigns against the Navajos ostensibly to curtail their raids and captive-taking, but Carson then rewarded his Mexican and Pueblo militiamen and Ute scouts with Navajo captives.[128] After emancipation and the Civil War, the U.S. government participated in the transfer of Indian captives *into* slavery in New Mexico. While anti-peonage initiatives were underway in Washington, the army was engaged in a war *against* the same peoples who were the objects of the peonage legislation (the nomadic tribes). At the federal level, a number of Reconstruction-era initiatives were directed at ending the so-called "custom" of Indian slavery in New Mexico. President Johnson's "Special Proclamation of 1865" extended the Emancipation Proclamation to Indian slaves in the federal territories.[129] In 1867, multiple congressional bills were introduced on the subject, culminating in the passage of the so-called Peon Law, whose purpose was "to abolish and forever prohibit the system of peonage in the Territory of New Mexico."[130] There is little evidence to suggest, however, that change resulted from either of these federal initiatives, as neither contained enforcement provisions.[131]

Indian slavery emerges, then, as a fertile site for examining the conflicts among and within racial groups—between Indian slaves and their Mexican American masters, between Mexican American and Euro-American elites, among Euro-American elites who differed sharply, and even as a dramatic status difference between Pueblos and other Indians in New Mexico.[132] Euro-Americans' efforts to dislodge Indian slavery in New Mexico can be read in multiple ways. Certainly, they are consistent with the principles of equality and liberty and also with the abolition of slavery and eventual emancipation of enslaved blacks after the Civil War. But Euro-Americans' advocacy of Indian slaves can also be read as an effort to further entrench American hegemony against the interests of Mexican American elites. Whether consciously or not, the war against Indian slavery also became a political war against Mexican American elites who held Indian slaves.

The fact that Euro-Americans charged with combatting Indian slavery themselves owned Indian slaves is telling. Returning to the 1868 prosecutions, most charged with holding Indian slaves were Mexican, but significant numbers of Euro-American men and Mexican women married to Euro-American men also were among those charged.[133] Writing almost contemporaneously and speaking of Euro-American elites in New Mexico, Hubert Howe Bancroft noted that "there were few military or civil officials who did not own captive slaves, and they were found even in the service of the Indian agents."[134] Lafayette Head, the former New Mexico territorial legislator and Indian agent charged specifically with identifying and liberating Indian slaves, held multiple Indian slaves in his southern Colorado household in the mid-1860s.[135] Indeed, Head justified his slaveholding in a manner that resonated with Santistevan's grand jury testimony: they "enjoy the full privilege of returning to their people whenever they have the inclination or disposition to do so."[136] Yet he ignored the fact that most of his slaves were acquired as children, who could not have known where or how to find their families or tribes.

For Mexican American elites, possession of Indian slaves marked them as both economically and racially privileged. While it is difficult to determine with accuracy, it appears that slaveholding occurred primarily in elite families. Brooks reports that American authorities identified 288 households in Taos County in 1868 as having Indian slaves or peons out of a total of 2,820 households in the county.[137] Extrapolating from these numbers, this would mean that about 10 percent of Taos County households included Indian slaves or peons—although Euro-Americans, due to their class status, may have been proportionally more likely than Mexicans to have Indian slaves.[138] Brooks also shows that, typically, households with Indian slaves included only one or two such persons: 87 percent of households with Indian slaves had only one slave and 85 percent of households with Indian peons held only one or two peons.[139] This provides another contrast with the South: in New Mexico, Indian slaves provided mostly household labor (perhaps because they were predominantly captive women and children), rather than labor designed to further large-scale capitalist enterprises in farming or mining, for example. Indian slaves were not limited to the very richest native New Mexican households, but their presence was an indication of wealth and, perhaps more so, past status under the Spanish and Mexican governments.

Within the context of American colonialism and the intensifying debates over black slavery, the ownership of Indian slaves may have become a different kind of status marker, one which together with wealth marked white racial privilege. From this perspective, Mexican elites' defense of the system of Indian slavery constituted resistance to American hegemony, but also capitulation to American white supremacy. One sees this in the strained dance between three sets of actors in the legal system: Mexican justices of the peace, Mexican legislators, and Euro-American judges. Over the course of the first two full decades of the American occupation of New Mexico, these three sets of actors engaged each other in a series of legal skirmishes that reveal the contestation and ultimate negotiation of a new racial order.

Often, these disputes entered the legal system at the level of justice of the peace courts, where Indian slaves complained of mistreatment by their Mexican masters or where Mexican slaveholders sought to regain control of an Indian slave who had been stolen or had run away. Because these forums were not courts of record, we have relatively little data about how these disputes typically proceeded. In what we can assume is a small number of cases (in no sense representative), however, the losing party in the justice of the peace court appealed to the district court, presided over by one of the territorial supreme court justices (appointed, you will recall, by the U.S. president); and, in an even smaller number of cases, the loser in this second litigation forum pursued an additional appeal to the territorial supreme court. The pattern in these appealed cases was for justices of the peace—who were overwhelmingly Mexican Americans during the 1850s and 1860s—to rule in favor of the Mexican slaveholders and for Euro-American judges to rule against them.[140]

Two additional patterns emerge in the Indian slavery context. First, majority-Mexican legislatures continually sought legislative solutions to what they perceived as an activist judiciary composed exclusively of Euro-Americans. They formalized the ownership of Indian slaves by other names—under the rubric of an expanding master-servant law, drawing heavily on Anglo-American common law traditions.[141] As Brooks notes, this meant that "after 1851, peonage and slavery became densely interwoven" and, he concludes, "virtually merged."[142] Even as this route was increasingly stymied by Euro-American judges, Rael-Gálvez has concluded that Mexican slaveholders turned to county probate courts to use the guardianship system essentially to disguise the master-slave relationship in the euphemistic language of family relationships.[143] By taking the guardianship route, Mexican slaveholders satisfied two goals: first, they established their forum as probate court (a forum controlled by elected Mexican American judges);[144] and second, they cloaked the practice of slavery in familial terms (saying, for example, that they were rescuing "orphaned" Indian children).[145]

Euro-American judges responded in two ways that substantially curtailed the power of Mexican American elites. First, they overturned or narrowly construed master-servant legislation in the interests of litigants who were Indian slaves.[146] Second, and more comprehensively, they sought over a period of decades to curtail the power of the justice of the peace courts, with the effect of gradually weakening these largely Mexican-controlled courts of first resort.[147] Eventually, Euro-American elites appealed to higher authority—not the U.S. Supreme Court, but the Congress, which, as the reader will recall, had the authority to nullify any act of the territorial legislature. Frustrated by unsuccessful attempts to use general slavery and peonage prohibitions to address Indian slavery in New Mexico, Congress in 1867 directly prohibited Indian slavery and the practice of Indian peonage.[148]

Although one may see these Euro-American judges and federal legislators as champions of civil rights—and, in particular, as advocates of the extension to Indians of recently won black civil rights—in order to fully understand the dynamics at work we must consider the constellation of racial groups, racial ideologies, and the emergent racial order. From the actions of Mexican elites in the first twenty-five years of American colonization, it is impossible to deny that they perceived it in their interest to defend the practice of Indian slavery. It also appears that Euro-Americans, especially judges, were increasingly critical of the practice euphemistically labeled "peonage." What do the debates between Mexican elites and Euro-Americans over Indian slavery reveal about the deeper, highly racialized conflict in this colonial moment?

The broader historic context is extremely important because, at this same point in time, the American military was engaged in its most intense "Indian wars" against the nomadic tribes in New Mexico.[149] The culmination was Kit Carson's forced march of eight thousand Navajo men, women, and children for more than three hundred miles, from their homeland to the Bosque Redondo Reservation, where they were held as captives from 1864 to 1868. Historian Richard White provides this description: "The 'Long Walk' became an event seared into the Navajo memory, a lasting reminder of the power and ruthlessness of the federal government. It would be four years before the Diné, as the Navajos call themselves, returned to their own country. . . . These were four years of humiliation, suffering, death, and near starvation."[150] In this context, consider what "choices" a hypothetical Navajo woman enslaved in a Mexican household would have had in 1868, the year of the indictment against Santistevan and the other slaveholders. The investigator described how he liberated the Indian slaves and peons in 1868:

Upon the examination of each [of the] persons charged as aforesaid and finding the charges true, I at once had the Indians so held as slaves brought before me, and informed them that under the laws of the United States and the holding of the Supreme Court of New Mexico thereunder, they were strictly and absolutely free to live where and work for whom they desired, and were at perfect liberty to go where and when they pleased ... that slavery could not exist in the United States and if they should prefer changing their homes, and go to the Navajo Country ... they could do so.[151]

As Rael-Gálvez has observed, had the hypothetical Navajo slave in a Mexican household sought emancipation and return to her people, she would have joined them at the Bosque Redondo prison camp.[152] To say this is not in any way to justify Indian slavery, but instead to highlight the disingenuousness of American liberation efforts.

Americans' actions regarding Indian slavery are better understood as part of a larger project of institution-building for the purpose of extending and preserving American material and ideological interests in this newest colony. From this perspective, the conflict between Mexican Americans and Euro-Americans over Indian slavery represented a power struggle between colonizer and native and between dominant (Euro-American) and subordinate (Mexican) racial groups. Mexican American elites attempted to resist American hegemony by holding onto one of their most valuable assets (even as their land holdings plummeted during the nineteenth century). At another level, Mexican American elites sought to maintain their honor and status, which under the Spanish and Mexican periods had been deeply connected to making raids, taking captives, and holding Indian slaves in their households. This tradition surely resonated with the transfer of power to the Americans, who, after all, understood both the traffic in human beings and its justification on the basis of racial inferiority. In the context of American racial hierarchy, then, we must also read Mexican American elites' fierce battle to maintain Indian slavery as an effort to legitimize (and, thus, fortify) their ever-tenuous claim to whiteness.

Conclusion

Racism and the ideology of white supremacy were bound up with colonialism in New Mexico. The American colonizers needed a native governing elite, both because they had insufficient numbers of Euro-American settlers in the region and in order to legitimize the military occupation. The latter was especially important given extensive Whig criticism of the war with Mexico and of imperialism more generally. Americans did not want to see themselves as a colonial power. One of the striking features of the standard American history of this period—of the U.S.–Mexico War and the subsequent annexation of more than half of Mexico's territory—is the sheer absence of colonialism as a topic or theme. In the national mythmaking constituted by this conventional history, this encounter of peoples is not presented as one of conquest and colonialism. Instead, most histories of U.S. imperialism begin in 1898, with the end of the Spanish–American War and the U.S. acquisition of Puerto Rico, Guam, and the Philippines and annexation of Hawaii.[153] But we cannot fully understand the *second* imperial moment of the 1890s without understanding what occurred in the *first* imperial moment in the 1840s, in what is today the American Southwest.

Even as American colonizers tapped a native elite to govern in a region with far more Euro-American soldiers than civilians, they also needed to keep Mexican Americans and Indians in their racial place. For Mexican Americans, as the native elite in the colony, the distinction between political and social equality became paramount, if not always openly discussed. Though Euro-American men ceded formal political equality to Mexican American men, this did not translate into social equality between Euro-Americans and Mexican Americans. An essential element of the colonial strategy hinged on breaking up the military alliance and cultural affinity between Mexican Americans and Pueblo Indians. The lure of whiteness proved an ideal tool. With it, the American colonizers could, in one move, co-opt Mexican Americans willing to trade on their mestizo, part-European heritage and divide Mexican Americans from their Pueblo neighbors.

The power of racism is ideological, achieving its apex when racially subordinated groups themselves help to reproduce racism. As historian George Lipsitz has noted, "Aggrieved communities of color have often curried favor with whites in order to make gains at each other's expense";[154] as examples he lists American Indians' ownership of black slaves, black soldiers' roles in the Indian wars, and Mexican American and Chinese efforts to claim "whiteness." I have shown how this worked by describing situations in which Mexican Americans gained the upper hand over non-white groups lower on the racial hierarchy, including Pueblo Indians, free and enslaved blacks, and nomadic Indians. Despite evidence of ambivalence in the law—both on the books and in action—during the early years of the American occupation, Mexican American men disenfranchised their Pueblo brothers so that they were virtually excluded from the new American polity in New Mexico. Acting in symbolic terms because of the small numbers of African Americans in the region, Mexican American elites sided with pro-slavery and scientific racism to enact draconian black and slave codes in the 1850s. At least partly in order to affirm their whiteness, Mexican American elites sought to continue the enslavement of nomadic Indians during the first twenty-five years of the American occupation.

Mexican Americans took up American racism by claiming whiteness and seeking to distance themselves from other non-white groups. But Mexican Americans paid a price for the legal fiction that they were "white," and, therefore, that their men were eligible to vote and hold office; they ultimately were co-opted by the American colonizers. By the end of the nineteenth century, we begin to see shifts in the political system reflective of Euro-Americans' ascendancy in the region and the end of the period of power sharing with Mexican American elites. In all of these contexts, the divisions between Mexican Americans and other subordinated groups gave tremendous power to the American colonizers, increasing divisions among potential allies in an anti-American campaign, legitimizing the American presence as "protector" of Indians, and entrenching the American legal system as a neutral, fair forum for dispute resolution and punishment.

At the same time, conquest was not a totalizing experience. At the edges of a system of co-optation and colonial authority, Mexican American elites exercised more self-determination than other non-white racial groups in New Mexico and, perhaps, anywhere in the United States at the time. Given their control of judicial forums such as the justice of the peace and probate courts, Mexican American men exercised considerable control over disputes among themselves, with Euro-American merchants and ranchers, and with members of various Indian communities. Although these victories were sometimes overruled by the Euro-American controlled district courts, Mexican Americans held the balance of power even in those forums, where they were the majority of grand jurors checking the power of Euro-American prosecutors and the majority of petit jurors checking the power of Euro-American judges.

Ultimately, Mexican Americans's claim to whiteness simultaneously ruptured and buttressed white supremacy. It ruptured, and therefore destabilized, white supremacy by exposing the fluid and flexible nature of the category "white." If Mexican Americans were sometimes considered white, or could sometimes persuade others that was so, what did it mean to be white? Might not other groups potentially assert rights based on claims to whiteness? The racial hierarchy was less stable when groups could proactively negotiate and transform their status within it.

Yet the ability of Mexican Americans to at times succeed in claiming whiteness led them into a perverse trap. To solidify their classification as white, they had to act like whites, especially with respect to non-white groups. Mexican American elites, in particular, acted in ways that shored up their whiteness, at the expense of every non-white group below them in the racial hierarchy. Intentionally or not, they became agents in the reproduction of racial subordination and contributed to the consolidation of a new version of white supremacy in the Southwest.

4

Manifest Destiny's Legacy
Race in America at the Turn of the Twentieth Century

This chapter elaborates on the three central themes of this book as they relate to the national scene: (1) the centrality of colonialism in constituting Mexican Americans as a racial group; (2) the important links between the experience of Mexican Americans and the broader patterns of racial formation and racial ideology in the United States; and (3) the crucial role of law in the social construction of race.

One of the major effects of the American colonization of Mexico was to transform property ownership and the regime of property law itself.[1] These effects of colonialism led to the loss of the land base on which both elite and lower status Mexicans had depended (in the latter case, for subsistence farming and ranching). Although some Mexicans either held onto their land or gained new opportunities for ownership under American rule,[2] the vast majority of land that previously had been owned collectively by Mexicans—via community land grants awarded by the Spanish or Mexican governments—came to be owned by the U.S. Government or by Euro-American individuals or corporations. The process by which this massive transfer of property occurred is illustrated with the story of one Mexican American community's forty-year legal struggle to retain its land. Their lawsuit eventually ended in failure in the U.S. Supreme Court in 1897.[3]

The formation of Mexican Americans as a racial group was closely linked to the broader evolution of the American racial order in the nineteenth century. This process worked in two directions: Manifest Destiny was an important factor driving broader changes in the racial order, and the larger racial order in turn shaped the particular trajectory of Mexican Americans. Usually, the Civil War and Reconstruction are viewed as the key events shaping the nineteenth-century racial order because they so fundamentally transformed the black experience. However, we cannot fully comprehend those events without understanding their links to the earlier conquest of northern Mexico. Manifest Destiny was a catalyst for the Civil War in that the acquisition of the vast Mexican Cession brought to a head the question of whether black slavery would be allowed to expand beyond the American South. Specifically, the question of the constitutionality of the Missouri Compromise—which had banned slavery in the northern section of the new lands, but allowed it in the southern section—gained urgency once the United States had taken control of more than one million square miles of Mexican territory. We explore these connections by examining the Supreme Court's 1857 ruling in the *Dred Scott* case,[4] as well as the ways in which the subordination of blacks and Mexican Americans was intertwined.

Manifest Destinies has developed a third theme centered around the law's role in the social construction of race and racial ideology. We continue that discussion by returning to the phenomenon of the legal definition of Mexican Americans as white. Whereas we previously examined legal whiteness in the context of the early processes that incorporated Mexicans into the United States—such as the collective grant of American citizenship to more than 115,000 Mexicans and the extension of the franchise to Mexican men in New Mexico, this chapter considers the later consolidation of the legal definition of Mexicans as white at the turn of the century. Using the context of a federal immigration case,[5] we explore the larger tapestry of racial ideology, the law, and the social construction of race. On the one hand, at this time, the one-drop rule for African Americans was coming into being: one drop of black ancestry made someone black. On the other hand, with respect to Mexican Americans, a kind of reverse one-drop rule was emerging: one drop of Spanish ancestry made someone white. At the end of the day, these very different racial ideologies worked together to entrench white supremacy and to facilitate the racial subordination of African Americans and Mexican Americans, even as they promoted a gulf between these two groups. Only by looking at the history of Mexican Americans alongside that of African Americans can we see the full arc of the American racial order as it existed at the outset of the twentieth century.

Colonialism and the Property Rights of Mexican Americans

Exactly a century after Spanish authorities had given their ancestors title to the community land grant known as San Miguel del Vado, Julian Sandoval, Gregorio Roybal, José Angel Dimas, Catarino Sena, Tomás Gonzáles, Juan Gallegos, and Román Gallegos petitioned the U.S. Court of Private Land Claims to ask for American recognition of their collective ownership of 315,000 acres in northeastern New Mexico.[6] In 1894 when they went before the court, these men were the elected representatives of more than a thousand families who lived on the grant started with thirteen families in 1794.[7] In 1846, on the eve of the U.S. invasion of New Mexico, Kearny delivered one of his rooftop speeches in San Miguel—the largest village located on the grant—promising to protect the civil, religious, and property rights of the native people. The San Miguel petitioners claimed collective ownership of more than 300,000 acres that included small, individually allotted plots of land for a house and subsistence farming, but most of which was used collectively for woodcutting, sheepherding, hunting, and the like.

The word "vado" means ford in Spanish, and as lawyer Malcolm Ebright has described it, the center of the San Miguel del Vado grant was "where the trail to the plains, used by *comancheros* [Comanche Indians] and *ciboleros* [buffalo hunters], crosses the Pecos River," thus giving the grant its name.[8] When Spanish authorities issued the grant in 1794, this region of New Spain was controlled not by the Spanish crown but by the Comanche Indians. The San Miguel grant was awarded at the apex of Comanche control of northeastern New Mexico, roughly a decade and a half after the peak of hostilities between the Comanches and the Mexican settlers and Pueblo Indian communities.[9] As folklore scholar Enrique La Madrid puts it,

> The Comanches had the future of the province in their hands. The economic and political hegemony they established on the southern plains was without parallel. . . . Better armed than the presidial soldiers, the militia, and the Pueblo [Indian] auxiliaries, it was within their power to have driven everyone from their homes and destroyed the province completely had they so desired.[10]

The Spanish strategy was to give community land grants to mestizo settlers and Pueblo Indian communities willing to live in areas like these, where Spanish authority was precarious at best.[11] When the Spanish returned to power in 1692 after the Pueblo Revolt, they could not continue to exploit the Pueblos on *encomiendas* (large agricultural production sites that depended on coerced Pueblo labor), but instead turned to a system that provided the various Pueblo communities with substantially more autonomy than prior to the revolt.[12] The new system hinged on increasing the number of mestizo settlements in the outlying regions, where they could be a buffer to potentially hostile Pueblo and other Indian communities. The grants were attractive to mestizo settlers seeking upward social mobility and, especially, to *genízaros*—the nomadic Indians who had joined, voluntarily or by force, mestizo communities. In exchange for land and the opportunity for social and ethnic mobility (as previously noted, over time and sometimes rapidly *genízaros* moved into the general mestizo population), the *genízaro* or mestizo grantees organized militias to defend against Indian attacks. Anthropologist Claire Farago notes that *genízaro* settlers "established themselves as an upwardly mobile social class consisting of farmers and artisans in Abiquiu, Carnuel, San Miguel del Vado, Belén, Tomé, and elsewhere."[13]

The five conditions attached to the San Miguel grant in 1794 reveal the challenges anticipated by both the grantors and the grantees.[14] First, unlike grants awarded by the Spanish and Mexican governments to individuals (sometimes as rewards for military service or political patronage), the San Miguel grant was awarded "in common" to fifty-two male heads of household and to all future settlers of the grant.[15] Private grants would have been unreasonable on New Mexico's eastern plains at this time, given the Comanches' control of the region. As legal scholar Placido Gómez has noted, community grants also reflected the melding of Spanish and indigenous systems of settlement in the arid northern territories of New Spain.[16] In this circumstance, community land grants had to be more extensive in regions like New Mexico, where they were centered in valleys (where narrow strips of land that attached to a water source could be allotted to individual families for a dwelling and a small farming plot), and the surrounding mountains could be used collectively for hunting, fishing, woodcutting, and grazing.[17]

The second condition of the original grant is equally revealing: the settlers had to agree to equip themselves with firearms and bows and arrows to defend the new settlement from Indian attacks. In 1794, the settlers mustered twenty-five firearms and an unrecorded number of bows and arrows to defend themselves.[18] The third condition was that the settlers build a fortified plaza, or town center; before this ambitious construction was completed, they were to reside at the largely vacant Pecos Pueblo.[19] By 1811 the settlers had built a church, and shortly thereafter the priest at Pecos Pueblo requested permission to move to the new church in San Miguel.[20] The fourth condition, read together with the first, clearly indicates the fact that the grantees collectively owned the vast majority of the land: individually owned land was strictly limited to allotments to the leader (*alcalde*) and to future leaders of the community. Similarly, the fifth condition emphasizes the point: all work, from building the plaza to digging and maintaining the *acequias* (irrigation canals), was to be done "by the community with that union which in their government they must preserve."[21] Read together, the grant conditions established a political community as much as they constituted a contract for property transfer from the crown to the settlers.

The surviving written records tell us relatively little about the original thirteen grantees or the fifty-two families listed as maintaining the grant a decade later. The 1805 families included thirteen male heads of household who were formally designated as *genízaros* (which probably means that there were other *genízaros* among the group, who were not officially designated as such).[22] According to historian Ramon Gutiérrez, *genízaros* made up a significant portion of the eighteenth-century settler population, and they were, as a class, at the bottom of New Mexico's racial hierarchy.[23] This provided them with strong incentive to participate in the high-risk but potentially high-yield investment as settlers in frontier regions still controlled by nomadic tribes. Anthropologist Paul Kraemer has estimated that marital ties and economic success (linked in some cases to settlement on a community grant) allowed many to transform their status from *genízaro* to mestizo settler in the late colonial period, when the San Miguel grant began.[24]

The San Miguel grant was one of more than 150 community land grants awarded in New Mexico by the Spanish or Mexican governments.[25] Although the federal government eventually certified many of these grants, it generally did so by confirming only the small, individually owned plots of land and rejecting the notion of communally owned property.[26] This is precisely what occurred in the case of the San Miguel grant—the petitioners claimed collective ownership of 315,000 acres, and the U.S. Court of Private Land Claims agreed with their claim, but the Supreme Court disagreed and confirmed a mere 5,000 acres.[27] The Court reasoned that the other 310,000 acres belonged to the sovereign—the Spanish government as the original grantors, the Mexican government when it controlled the region, and now the U.S. federal government. The result was that more than 300,000 acres now went into the "public domain," to be owned and operated by the federal government.

In this way, millions of acres of land in New Mexico were transferred from collective ownership by Mexican Americans to the federal government, which could do any number of things with the property. Some of this "public domain" land was distributed to individuals for farming or ranching enterprises (under the Donation Act, Homestead Act, and Desert Lands Acts, for instance, the government gave individual users 160 acres each); the federal government also sold land to private buyers.[28] But these uses of federal land—which, in the 1850s, 1860s, and 1870s in New Mexico accounted for only 1.2 million acres[29]—paled in comparison to another use of public domain land: the U.S. Forest Service. In the early 1900s, the U.S. government transferred approximately 13.6 million acres of land in New Mexico from the public domain to the Forest Service.[30] The massive Carson and Santa Fe National Forests in north central New Mexico, with a combined area of 2.4 million acres, are located on lands that came primarily from community land grants. Geographer Jake Kosek has described the effects of the transfer of lands from community ownership to the U.S. Forest Service:

> The creation of these federal lands, especially the national forests, amounted to an effective closure of the de facto commons of forest and pasture and the conversion of locally controlled and defined places into national "productive" spaces. This closure threatened not only access to resources but also the identity of indigenous Hispano communities whose national allegiance was tied more to Mexico or Spain than to the United States of America.[31]

To understand how this happened we must return to the peace treaty of 1848. With the end of the war, the United States gained sovereignty over Mexico's vast northern territory, but the U.S. government did not "own" the land. Over time, however, as more and more of the former Mexican lands went into the public domain, the federal government became the owner of a large portion (perhaps most) of the land ceded by Mexico.[32] Simultaneously with ownership, the federal government became a land *manager*, with all three branches participating: Congress created the laws to settle land claims in California and New Mexico, which then were implemented by the executive branch's Department of the Interior; when disputes arose, they were adjudicated by federal trial and appellate courts. For example, solely to administer land claims in the Mexican Cession, Congress created three novel mechanisms that involved intensive executive branch and judiciary roles, as well as ongoing congressional administration.

In 1851, in the wake of the California gold rush and the land speculation that accompanied it, Congress hurriedly passed the California Land Act.[33] Under the law, a board administered by the Department of the Interior heard claims, which could then be appealed directly to the federal district court and then to the U.S. Supreme Court (bypassing the federal circuit court). Remarkably, the legislation specified only a two-year window for filing claims, after which all land not claimed in this way would revert to the public domain.[34] In contrast, in the rest of the former Mexican territory, Congress established itself as the arbiter of land claims by instituting the cumbersome surveyor-general system.[35] Under this process, landowners in New Mexico filed claims with the federal surveyor general's office in New Mexico, then waited in a queue for their land to be surveyed; eventually, the surveyor general made a recommendation to Congress, which ultimately decided whether to certify the claim.[36] The entire process could take several decades, and there was no possibility of judicial review.

The differences in the two systems reflected two important facts. First, there was the differential strategic and economic value of California and New Mexico, as viewed by Euro-American elites, particularly those in Washington, D.C. Simply put, California was far more desirable than New Mexico to gold miners and land speculators alike. Second, there were notable differences in the racial composition of the two regions. Within months of the peace treaty's ratification, Euro-Americans outnumbered Mexicans in California, whereas in New Mexico Euro-Americans always remained a numerical minority. Land was both less desirable given these demographics and less easy to control given New Mexico's Mexican and Indian majority and its community of Mexican elites. In contrast to California's rapid adjudication, in New Mexico, 205 claims were filed with the surveyor general between 1854 and 1885; almost half of them (95) were left in limbo because Congress never formally acted on them.[37]

Congress recognized the failure of the surveyor-general system in 1891, when it created the Court of Private Land Claims to attempt to put to rest land claims in the Mexican Cession (other than California).[38] By then, land in New Mexico had become more desirable, not the least because there was now a steadily increasing stream of Euro-American immigrants to the region. Congress now took the unprecedented step of creating a specialized federal court to hear only land claims. This court operated without lay juries, and appeals from it went directly to the U.S. Supreme Court (bypassing *both* the federal trial court and the federal appeals court). As the last chapter showed, Mexican Americans dominated juries in most New Mexico counties (and at all court levels), yet by design in this legislation, majority-Mexican juries would have no role to play in the new land claims court. Both the creation of a specialized federal court and the automatic appeal to the Supreme Court reflected the congressional agenda to transfer as much land as possible, as quickly as possible, into the public domain.

The case of *United States v. Sandoval* has come to symbolize the failure of the U.S. government to adhere to the property rights provisions of the Treaty of Guadalupe Hidalgo.[39] Under Article VIII of the treaty, the United States pledged to respect the property rights of Mexico's citizens living in the ceded territory.[40] At the same time, contemporary events during the ratification process suggest reasons to conclude that the United States hoped to avoid this obligation whenever it saw fit. For one, upon recommendation from President Polk, the U.S. Senate refused to approve Article X of the treaty (as drafted by U.S. and Mexican diplomats and as ratified by the Mexican legislature), which would have even more directly governed grants of land awarded by the Spanish and Mexican sovereigns.[41] The language of the proposed but never ratified Article X was forceful in its assertion that Mexican property rights in the ceded territory would be protected under American law to the same extent that they would have been protected under Mexican law: "All grants of land made by the Mexican Government or by the competent authorities . . . shall be respected as valid, *to the same extent that the same grants would be valid, if the said territories had remained within the limits of Mexico.*"[42]

The Mexicans strenuously objected to the provision's removal and later demanded a diplomatic accord to attempt to restore some of its meaning in non-binding diplomatic clarifications.[43] The resulting Querétero Protocol, signed by diplomatic representatives of the two nations just prior to the treaty's formal ratification, contained the following statement about the excised Article X:

> The American Government, by suppressing the Xth article of the Treaty of Guadalupe Hidalgo did not in any way intend to annul the grants of lands made by Mexico in the ceded territories. These grants of land, notwith-

standing the suppression of the article of the Treaty, preserve the legal value which they may possess; and the grantees may cause their legitimate titles to be acknowledged before the American tribunals.[44]

The inclusion of Article X by the Mexicans, its removal by the Americans, and the Querétero Protocol suggest that there was a strong contemporary concern (later borne out) that Mexican landowners in the ceded territory might well lose their property in the wake of the transfer of sovereign control over the region. Seen in this light, we may wonder why it took so long for the Americans to dispossess the Mexicans of their land, rather than why the law allowed it to happen.[45] Ultimately, what is more surprising than the Supreme Court ruling against Julian Sandoval and his neighbors is that the legal procedures so blatantly constructed by Congress to increase federal land ownership in New Mexico sometimes proved susceptible to interim victories and delayed losses on the part of Mexican American land grant heirs.

The Sandoval lawsuit's path illustrates the consolidation of federal power (across all three branches of government) over the new "Western" lands of the United States. For twenty-two years, the Sandoval litigation wound its way through the surveyor-general process, resulting in an 1879 recommendation that Congress partially confirm the grant, but failing to result in any congressional action. When in 1891 Congress created a second process for adjudicating land grant claims in New Mexico, the Court of Private Land Claims, Sandoval and his neighbors appeared within a year to restate their claim in this new forum. Thus, the Sandoval litigation illustrates the two congressionally devised processes for settling land claims in New Mexico: the more legalistic, judicial process created by Congress (largely in response to intense criticism of the first process)[46] and the surveyor-general system it had instituted thirty-six years earlier. Just over a decade after the start of the American occupation, in 1859, the local justice of the peace in the village of San Miguel, Faustin Baca y Ortiz, filed a petition with the surveyor general, seeking recognition of the land as a community-owned grant.[47] It would take a staggering twenty years for the surveyor general to act on the San Miguel claim.

Finally, in 1879, Surveyor General Henry M. Atkinson recommended to Congress (via the Interior Secretary), that the San Miguel del Vado grant be confirmed as the *private* grant of Lorenzo Márquez and his heirs.[48] Although the petition had come from all the current residents of the grant, as a request for recognition of communal ownership, Atkinson reasoned that the fact that only Márquez, and not the fifty-one other original grantees, was listed in a 1794 document showed that "title vests solely in the grantee named."[49] Atkinson made this ruling despite the fact that subsequent documents, including those signed by Spanish authorities in 1798 and 1803, contained the names of all the original male heads of families (including Márquez). Atkinson's position paralleled that of other San Miguel heirs, led by Márquez, who argued that they privately owned the entire grant.[50] The evidence strongly suggests, though we cannot be certain, that Atkinson aimed to facilitate Márquez's private ownership of the grant, so that Márquez could in turn sell it to Euro-American land speculators.[51] In this respect, the case also illustrates the not infrequent dynamic of Mexican American complicity in the transfer of land out of *collective* ownership by Mexicans.

When Atkinson's recommendation reached Washington in 1879, Congress refused to confirm any additional grants in New Mexico. Allegations of fraud and rampant land speculation were offered as explanations, and no action was taken on the San Miguel petition.[52] Atkinson was viewed as a prime suspect and was accused of promoting his personal financial interests through his position as surveyor general.[53] By this time, it appears that the Márquez faction had sold their interests in the grant to Euro-American land speculators, who probably were heavily lobbying Atkinson. In 1885, President Grover Cleveland appointed a purportedly reform-oriented successor to Atkinson, George Julian. But Julian's public comments revealed contempt for New Mexico's native Mexican and Indian people that resonated with the dominant racial narrative. In 1887, just two years after he had been sent to New Mexico, he wrote in the *North American Review* that the territory needed more Euro-American settlers so that "an intelligent and enterprising population [would build] a temple of civilization ... [on] the ruins of the past."[54] Although he went to New Mexico as a self-proclaimed reformer, he seemed to offer an apology for men like Atkinson: "Official life in an old Mexican province, and *in the midst of an alien race*, offered few attractions to men of ambition and force."[55]

In 1886, Julian wrote to Congress to criticize Atkinson's recommendation. Under Mexican law, he said, the grant should be confirmed to the heirs of the fifty-two original settlers as well as all those settlers (and their heirs) residing on the grant in 1846, when the American occupation began (more than six hundred families).[56] The radical shift in recommendations by the two surveyors general probably made Congress even more reluctant to confirm or deny the San Miguel petition, and it would be more than a decade before the litigation was resolved. Was Julian a friend of Mexican Americans since he was supporting the community grant, rather than the notion of the grant as owned by the small number of heirs, as Atkinson had recommended?[57] To understand how the positions of both Atkinson and Julian were contrary to the interests of the majority of Mexican Americans (although Atkinson's position favored Mexican American land speculators), we must understand that Euro-American elites were deeply split on the question of land use and distribution. The Atkinson camp promoted property as an investment strategy and so welcomed the role played by land speculators in driving up prices. The Julian camp favored getting land into the public domain, with the hope that it eventually would go into the hands of yeoman farmers in the homesteading tradition.

Both groups supported Manifest Destiny in both its ideological and material senses, and neither supported following Spanish-Mexican property law to its natural limits because that meant upholding the concept of communally owned land. It was the public domain faction of Euro-American elites (those against land speculators) who won out in 1891, when Congress created the five-judge U.S. Court of Private Land Claims to resolve claims stemming from the territory gained after the Mexican War.[58] One of the principal criticisms of the surveyor-general system had been that it did not provide for judicial review and the associated legal protections of claimants.[59] The new system attempted to cure this defect by creating a new court from which the losing party could appeal directly to the Supreme Court. One of the most contentious issues was how the new process differed from that created by the California Land Act of 1851. Under the California law, land claims initially were heard by a presidentially appointed board, then appealed to the federal district court, then to the Supreme Court.[60]

The transition from the surveyor-general system to the land claims court was intensely resisted by the cadre of lawyers in New Mexico who most frequently had petitioned the surveyor general and who were themselves among the wealthiest landowners in New Mexico as a result of their legal work. (As noted, lawyers often were paid in the form of title to property.) Their recognized leader was Thomas B. Catron, who at this time was the largest individual landowner in New Mexico. According to 1910 tax rolls, Catron owned $200,000 in assets—more than six times the wealth of the next richest Euro-American serving at that time with Catron in the territorial legislature and more than ten times the wealth of the richest Mexican American legislator.[61]

Two days before the Court of Private Land Claims first met in Santa Fe, Catron convened an emergency meeting of the New Mexico Bar Association and garnered the attendance of the five newly appointed judges.[62] The bar association voted to recommend substantial amendments to the 1891 Act and selected a committee to present them to Congress, to be headed by Catron.[63] In the end, Catron decided to work with the new court. He was involved with the San Miguel del Vado grant as attorney to Levi P. Morton, who had purchased land from the Márquez faction and stood to lose it if the court adopted the community theory of the grant.[64] Morton and Catron nicely illustrate the land speculators' strategy. Morton was a former New York congressman (1879–81) and former vice president of the United States under President Benjamin Harrison (1889–93). When he appeared before the land claims and Supreme Court, Morton was governor of New York.[65] His financial agenda was to buy land and sell it quickly at a profit. As his attorney, Catron likely was paid in land—if he won.

By the time the case was heard by the Court of Private Land Claims in 1894, more than one thousand families lived in eight villages (as well as in many communities too small to be described as villages) on the San Miguel del Vado land grant.[66] A century after their ancestors had received the original grant, the grandchildren and great-grandchildren of the original grantees made the trip to Santa Fe to testify. The judges were Euro-Americans whose states of origin included Iowa, North Carolina, Kansas, Tennessee, and Colorado, and who very likely did not speak Spanish.[67] The transcript of examinations and cross-examinations of witnesses shows that most of the witnesses testified in Spanish, with an interpreter translating the attorneys' questions to the witnesses and the witnesses' responses to the judges and audience. Fifty-nine-year-old Celso Baca testified that his grandfather was an original grantee and that his wife's great-grandfather also was an original settler of the grant.[68] Eighty-year-old Mariano Barros, of La Cuesta, spoke about how each family on the grant had an area of a few acres to cultivate for their own subsistence, and about how the common areas of the grant were collectively used for grazing sheep, cutting timber, and other activities.[69]

Euro-American lawyer John Veeder represented the petitioners and explained to the court that the case involved "a community grant" in which each settler was given "a place for planting and his house," with the rest of the land "to be in common for all the people who resided upon the grant."[70] In a preview of his lone dissent, Judge William W. Murray, a Tennessee Democrat, interrupted Veeder: "Do you claim it as a town or corporation grant?" "We claim it as a *pueblo* grant," responded Veeder, "we call it a town grant or a community grant" (the Spanish word *pueblo* means town).[71] During the trial, Veeder objected repeatedly to the questioning of witnesses by U.S. Attorney Matthew Reynolds about *individual* parcels of the grant used for subsistence farming, reminding the court that these facts were irrelevant to the *community* claim before it.[72] In the end, the court voted four to one to confirm *collective* ownership of the grant by the descendants of the original fifty-two grantees and all others who had settled there prior to December 1848, when the Treaty of Guadalupe Hidalgo was assumed to have taken effect in New Mexico (that is, when word of its ratification would have reached New Mexico).[73]

Under the California land law, a parallel ruling appealed by the losing party would have gone to the federal district court and then, if again appealed, to the Supreme Court. But under the 1891 law, the U.S. attorney's appeal went straight to the Supreme Court. It reversed the ruling of the Court of Private Land Claims, deciding to confirm only the individually allotted portions of the grant, totaling about five thousand acres. Prior to a series of cases decided around this time, the Supreme Court had essentially deferred to federal judicial interpretation of the Treaty of Guadalupe Hidalgo as requiring that Spanish and Mexican legal principles be applied to land claims in the former Mexican territories.[74] The Court of Private Land Claims had relied on these prior rulings when it confirmed the San Miguel grant.

In an opinion written by Chief Justice Melville W. Fuller, the Supreme Court decided that the differences between the congressional acts that created the California land court in 1851 and the 1891 court revealed Congress's intent to make the 1891 law more stringent than the surveyor-general standard.[75] Under this reading of the case, "the sovereign retained fee title to all communal lands."[76] In other words, because the prior Spanish and Mexican sovereigns had retained control of the common lands in community grants, the United States, as the current sovereign, now did so as well. The argument flipped on its head the notion of a community grant as recognized under Spanish-Mexican jurisprudence. Instead of acknowledging that the vast majority of the grant (310,000 acres in this case) was collectively owned and operated, and that only a small portion of it (5,000 acres) was allocated to individuals for farming plots, they argued that the only valid portions of the grant were the individual allotments.

Yet it probably was this kind of outcome that Congress sought when it created the specialized court in 1891. In this respect, I differ with those who claim that cases like *Sandoval* violated the spirit of the peace treaty. From a realpolitik perspective, this was precisely the outcome envisioned by the United States when it started the war and negotiated the treaty—it just took Congress some time to get there. If Article X, as proposed by the Mexicans, had been included in the treaty, then it was precisely the shift in congressional legislation and judicial rulings that occurred in the 1890s that would have been prohibited (which is not to say the Court would not have been able to use other avenues to achieve its ends). With the ratification of the Treaty of Guadalupe Hidalgo in 1848, the United States gained sovereignty over the Southwest and West. But it was not until fifty years later that the federal government truly began to realize the fruits of Manifest Destiny as it gained ownership over the Mexican Cession lands.

The tens of thousands of Mexican Americans in New Mexico who lost their communally owned lands at this time and in this manner reacted in two ways. The loss of these lands required many of them who had been subsistence farmers and ranchers, living close to the land, to become wage-laborers who often had to migrate out of the region seasonally to earn a living.[77] Yet many Mexican Americans who lost their communal lands did not simply sit idly by but instead participated in a variety of political mobilizations closely linked to their status as a colonized, racially subordinated group. An early movement called Las Gorras Blancas (the White Caps), which directly challenged the transfer of lands, thrived in the late 1880s and early 1990s in and around the San Miguel del Vado land grant. Sociologist Phillip Gonzáles describes the movement thusly:

> Covering riders and horses with white sheets, armed bands of Hispanos rode at night, killing livestock, knocking down fences, and tearing out railroad tracks. The movement posed considerable threat to the order that the territorial administration sought to maintain. . . . The organization won political support and influence in San Miguel and nearby counties.[78]

Though short-lived, Las Gorras Blancas demonstrates that some Mexican Americans, conscious of their status as a colonized people, became radicalized as a result of the loss of their community land grants.

Manifest Destiny as a Catalyst for the Civil War

Manifest Destiny was central to the larger nineteenth-century processes that restructured the American racial order. This section explores the connections between the conquest of northern Mexico and the Civil War that began just over a decade after the U.S.–Mexico War concluded. The role of Manifest Destiny as a catalyst for the Civil War remains almost entirely unrecognized. Yet a careful review of the historical record reveals that U.S. conquest of the expansive territory that had belonged to Mexico brought to a head the question of whether slavery would expand beyond the South, a question decided by the Supreme Court in the *Dred Scott* case. Understanding the connections between the two elucidates the similarities and differences between the racial subordination faced by Mexican Americans and that faced by African Americans.

The question of whether slavery would be legal in the newly acquired territories west of the original thirteen colonies arose almost with the birth of the nation, but it grew more acute as the federal government annexed ever-larger parcels of land, culminating in the Mexican Cession of 1848.[79] In perhaps the preeminent historical analysis of the *Dred Scott* case, Don Fehrenbacher identifies three important moments in this early history: Congress's prohibition of slavery in the Northwest Ordinance of 1787, which established federal administrative authority over the trans-Appalachian west; Congress's silence on slavery in the 1804 annexation of the Louisiana Territory; and, Congress's so-called Missouri Compromise of 1819–20. The Missouri Compromise actually consisted of three separate congressional actions, bundled together to accumulate sufficient numbers of votes for passage: (1) Missouri joined the Union as a slave state; (2) Maine joined as a free state; and, (3) slavery was prohibited in the remainder of the Missouri Territory (what remained of the Louisiana cession, after removing the states of Missouri and Louisiana and the Arkansas Territory) north of the 36th parallel but allowed south of that line.[80]

This national compromise did not last long; debates about slavery arose again in the context of various efforts to annex Texas. First in 1837 and again in 1844, northerners blocked the admission of Texas on the slavery question.[81] Southerners got the upper hand in 1845, and Texas was admitted as a state where slavery was legal. That result certainly pleased Euro-American settlers in Texas (both legal and illegal immigrants), who had for years advocated for Texas independence largely in order to protect the right to hold black slaves in the face of Mexico's anti-slavery laws. In

August 1846, when President Polk initially sought congressional funding to pursue negotiations with Mexico over the question of Texas's southern boundary, Congressman David Wilmot, a Pennsylvania Whig, attached an amendment to provide that slavery would be banned in any additional lands obtained from Mexico.[82] Whigs viewed Polk's efforts as the first step toward a war with Mexico, which itself, they believed, was a thin guise for acquiring more territory in which to expand slavery.[83] The so-called Wilmot Proviso passed the House in 1846, but did not make it to the Senate; in 1847, the House again endorsed the Wilmot Proviso, but it failed in the Senate.[84]

When Congress debated the ratification of the Treaty of Guadalupe Hidalgo in early 1848, the question of whether slavery would be allowed in the newly ceded territories figured prominently. During the presidential campaign later that year, Polk argued that the Missouri Compromise should be extended west to the Pacific Ocean—that slavery would be allowed south of the 36th parallel, but not north of it.[85] No agreement was reached until almost two years later, with the "Compromise of 1850." This congressional action consisted of a series of votes taken in the summer of 1850, each bearing on slavery.[86] First, Congress admitted California as a free state. Second, Congress designated the remainder of the Mexican Cession as the Utah and New Mexico territories, without specifying any policy on slavery in them. Third, Congress settled the question of the boundary between Texas and New Mexico, putting it considerably further east than Texas had wanted, but providing Texas monetary compensation for doing so.[87] Finally, it included a strengthened Fugitive Slave Act, demanded by southern slaveholders to protect against the increasing threat of slaves escaping to jurisdictions where slavery was illegal.[88]

With the 1850 actions, an earlier shift in federal policy on slavery in the territories became institutionalized. Congress began its regulation of newly annexed lands in 1787 with a prohibition on slavery in the Northwest Ordinance; by 1850, however, Congress had adopted the position euphemistically referred to as "nonintervention" in the territories. The positive gloss on nonintervention was that popular sovereignty in each territory would be allowed to run its course to decide whether or not to legalize slavery. But the reality was that nonintervention meant a victory for white slaveholders, who were free to settle in the new territories with their slaves knowing their "private property" would be respected.[89] At the same time, the enhanced fugitive slave law gave federal officials—from U.S. marshals to federal judges—a greater role in protecting the rights of slaveholders in all the states and territories. All in all, the increased rancor of the congressional debates about slavery in Texas, California, New Mexico, and the other far western territories revealed a federal legislature increasingly unlikely to resolve the slavery question, making judicial intervention almost inevitable.[90]

The Supreme Court finally did speak to the question of slavery in the territories in 1857, when it decided *Scott v. Sandford.*[91] Most narrowly, Scott's lawsuit involved his right as a slave to sue in federal court. Then and now, only certain types of cases can be brought in federal court, as a court of limited rather than general jurisdiction. Scott alleged that his case was appropriate for federal court due to the parties' diversity of citizenship—he, as the plaintiff, and Dr. Sanford, as defendant, were citizens of different states, Missouri and New York, respectively.[92] The substance of Scott's suit for freedom was that, because he had lived for substantial periods in states and territories where slavery was illegal, he was now free. Scott's travels were an integral part of his theory of the case, but they also reveal another layer of connection between Manifest Destiny and the Civil War, one typically neglected in historical accounts.

At around age thirty, Scott was purchased for $500 by Dr. John Emerson from the estate of Peter Blow.[93] When Emerson entered the military service as a surgeon in 1834, he took Scott with him from Missouri to Fort Armstrong, Illinois (about two hundred miles north of St. Louis). While at Fort Armstrong, Emerson took up land speculation, purchasing multiple lots in both Illinois and what would become Iowa; he directed Scott to build a log cabin on one lot in order to improve his claim. In 1836, Emerson was transferred to Fort Snelling (in the Wisconsin Territory) and again took Scott with him.[94] While at Fort Snelling, Scott married Harriet, the young female slave of the Indian agent stationed at the fort.[95] Emerson left Fort Snelling in 1837, but Scott and his family remained there, as he had been hired out to other officers. About a year later, Emerson, now living at Fort Jessup in the Louisiana Territory, sent for Scott, who traveled (unescorted) with his family by steamboat to join Emerson in St. Louis.

Once again, Emerson was transferred, and he returned with his own family and with his slaves, the Scotts, to Fort Snelling. When in 1840 Emerson was transferred to Florida where the Seminole War was in progress, Mrs. Emerson took their slaves with her to her family home in St. Louis.

In early 1843, Emerson died, and, perhaps to earn extra income, Emerson's widow rented Scott to her brother-in-law, Captain Bainbridge. Scott accompanied Bainbridge to army posts in Florida, the Louisiana Territory, and Texas.[96] From 1844 to 1846, Bainbridge served under General Taylor's command on the Texas border with Mexico, accompanied by Scott. At the very moment when the United States declared war against Mexico, Scott was with the U.S. Army in Texas. It was upon his return from Texas that Scott initiated his first suit for freedom, also claiming emancipation for his wife and two daughters.[97]

The Supreme Court might have dispensed with Scott's case in any number of ways in order to avoid reaching the merits of the larger claims as they related to the freedom of a slave who had lived in free territory.[98] In a sweeping decision, however, Chief Justice Roger B. Taney ruled that blacks, whether they were free or enslaved, stood outside the American polity: they were not citizens nor did they have the privilege of suing in federal court.[99] The *Dred Scott* case is considered a precursor to the Civil War, which erupted only a few years later.[100] As significant as the ruling on black exclusion from citizenship was, an equally important aspect of the case—and arguably one that was a more important catalyst for the Civil War—was the Court's ruling that the Missouri Compromise of 1850 was unconstitutional.

When a Supreme Court dominated by southerners heard Scott's case in 1857, it was poised to reach well beyond the narrow confines of the dispute between Scott and Sanford. Taney wanted desperately to reach the question of whether Scott had become free by virtue of his owner taking him into free territory under the Missouri Compromise, and hence the issue of Congress's power to prohibit slavery in the territories.[101] Like most white southerners, Chief Justice Taney perceived the question of slavery in the territories as central to the larger goal of maintaining slavery in the nation.[102] Fehrenbacher identifies the dilemma faced by Taney: "In short, while the power to prohibit slavery in the territories must be nullified, the power to protect [slavery] must be not only affirmed but converted into an obligation."[103] Taney accomplished this goal by way of a three-part argument: (1) the federal government had no power to govern new territories (other than a limited, temporary power to govern them until they were to be admitted as states);[104] (2) this limited governing power meant that the federal government was also limited in its regulation of the rights of "citizens" of the territories, including those Americans who had migrated from states to territories;[105] and (3) as a result, the federal government

(Congress, in this case) could not in any way restrict the property rights of citizens of the territories, making the prohibition of slavery north of the 36th parallel unconstitutional.[106]

The American colonization of northern Mexico brought to a head the question of whether slavery would expand beyond the South. It pointedly raised the issue of whether white slaveholders would be allowed to share equally in the profits of imperialism. If white slaveholders could not take their property in slaves with them into the vast new territory, then, according to Taney's view of the world, they were not equal beneficiaries of America's imperial enterprise. Relative to white Americans who did not own slaves, they would be held to second-class citizenship if the Missouri Compromise was enforced. Ironically, Taney's view of the case may have inadvertently led him to expand the rights of Mexican American citizens in the territories.

As one of the pillars for his argument about black inferiority, Taney pointed to the categorical exclusion of non-whites from the ability to become naturalized American citizens.[107] In doing so, however, he ignored the recent act of "collective naturalization" of more than 115,000 Mexicans under the Treaty of Guadalupe Hidalgo. Most of the Mexicans living in the vast region ceded by Mexico after the war were racially mixed and very likely would have been considered non-white by Taney and his brethren. The Mexican War had ended less than a decade before the Supreme Court decided the *Dred Scott* case, and the Taney Court already had decided several cases involving the peace treaty and the war.[108] Taney's omission of Mexicans' questionable racial status produced two outcomes. At least as a formal legal matter, it effectively ranked the nation's brand-new Mexican American citizens above African Americans in the U.S. racial hierarchy.[109] In so doing, Taney perhaps inadvertently expanded the rights of those Mexican Americans who held only federal (but not state) citizenship, such as Mexicans in New Mexico.

In invalidating the Missouri Compromise, the Court emphasized that the ban on slavery south of the 36th latitude violated the due process rights of slaveholders who had migrated or who might immigrate to the new territories. Taney framed the Missouri Compromise as a law that discriminated against territorial citizens, who by virtue of their migration west no longer held state citizenship:

> It is a total absence of power everywhere within the dominion of the United States, and *places the citizens of a Territory*, so far as these [property and

liberty] rights are concerned, *on the same footing with citizens of the States*, and guards them as firmly and plainly against any inroads which the General [i.e., federal] Government might attempt, under the plea of implied or incidental powers.[110]

As legal scholar Ediberto Román has noted, Taney's interest was in protecting the rights of white "settler citizens" to the federal territories, not the rights of territorial citizens per se.[111] While Taney's interest clearly was in protecting the property rights of white, slaveholding newcomers to the territories, the opinion applied to all "citizens" of all federal territories— including Mexican Americans who held only federal citizenship in New Mexico.

Implicit in Taney's logic was that the United States should not hold territories unless they would eventually become states.[112] From this vantage point, the western territories all were temporary territories: American citizens residing there might for awhile be only federal citizens, but once the territory achieved statehood, they would hold both state and federal citizenship. Under the Treaty of Guadalupe Hidalgo, Mexicans in the federal territories were similarly situated to white settler citizens in that they held federal but not state citizenship (though the settler citizens had formerly held state citizenship).[113] The case arguably enhanced the rights of Mexican Americans living in federal territories. That may not at all have been the Court's goal. But Taney was so determined to invalidate the Missouri Compromise that he was willing to open the door to an expansion of the rights of the newly incorporated Mexican Americans—or at least he did not expressly reject the implication.

Racial stratification in the nineteenth century was closely linked to questions of citizenship and inclusion in the polity.[114] Membership in nonwhite racial groups corresponded to degrees of exclusion from citizenship (understood as having both state and federal elements), the ability to become a naturalized citizen, and enfranchisement for men of color. Moreover, these more strictly legal dimensions of citizenship corresponded to racial groups' more general level of inclusion and belonging in American society.[115] For instance, over the course of the nineteenth century, white Euro-American men greatly improved their citizenship position with the lifting of property and other (non-racial) restrictions on the franchise. By the end of the century, white men and women who emigrated from Europe had full access to American naturalization and held (or could hold) both state and federal citizenship, and white men generally held federal and state political rights without regard to property ownership.[116] Each non-white racial group faced a different mix of formal and informal barriers to equality.

A mixed picture emerged for African Americans, as their fortunes shifted greatly over the course of the half-century before 1900. Under the Supreme Court's ruling in *Scott v. Sandford*, neither free nor enslaved blacks possessed federal citizenship, which meant virtual exclusion from the American polity. Even in the northern states where slavery was banned, blacks did not hold equal civil rights. According to political scientist Rogers Smith, in most northern states, blacks possessed legal rights (such as the right to property, liberty, and to sue in court), but they did not have full political rights (such as voting and running for office).[117] With the enactment of the Civil War Amendments to the Constitution, however, African Americans received full federal citizenship and African American men received the right to vote. And, in 1870, Congress amended the naturalization laws to allow immigrants of African descent to become American citizens.[118] But with the Supreme Court's 1896 ruling in *Plessy v. Ferguson*, the limits on African Americans' inclusion in American society reappeared in a more familiar form.[119] The Court's distinction between political rights and social rights legitimated state and local efforts to further white supremacy by segregating blacks from whites in all facets of American life. (We will return to this case later in this chapter.) By the turn of the century, despite the Civil War and the amendments to the Constitution, black racial status reflected the paradigmatic instance of racial inferiority and subordination in the United States.

American Indians' racial status can be understood as more ambiguous. Indians certainly were viewed as non-white and as racially inferior.[120] Moreover, status as a member of an Indian tribe was, over the course of the nineteenth century, an impediment to U.S. citizenship.[121] Racial status as Indian, tribal membership status, as well as local contexts interacted to determine the extent to which Indians, individually or as part of particular tribes, participated as state citizens.[122] The Chinese faced different roadblocks to citizenship than either blacks or Indians. Actively recruited from thousands of miles to be laborers, they could not become citizens no matter how long they had lived in the United States. After Congress passed the Chinese Exclusion Act of 1882, Chinese laborers were barred from entering the United States.[123] The Chinese were viewed as racial others and were largely excluded from political rights and from even being part of society.[124]

Compared to these groups, the citizenship status of Mexican Americans might well have been enviable. Under the Treaty of Guadalupe Hidalgo, Mexicans held American citizenship—more legalistic than real, second-class yet still desired citizenship. Mexicans gained this "collective naturalization" at a time in American history when only white immigrants could naturalize. As a result, the treaty's citizenship provisions can be read as conferring white legal status on Mexicans. In California and Texas, some Mexican American men possessed state and federal citizenship and participated as fully enfranchised members of the polity. But state lawmakers in both states also made sure that not *all* Mexican American men did. Whiteness was defined locally, by law and custom. Frequently, local practices and institutions excluded Mexican Americans from full rights. This likely fell more harshly on the majority of Mexican Americans who were predominantly indigenous and of lower economic status.

For Mexicans in New Mexico, who substantially outnumbered Euro-Americans, the mechanisms blocking full inclusion varied. New Mexico's Mexican Americans were excluded from full rights via the limitations of *federal* citizenship and the subordinate status of federal territories as compared to states. Nonetheless, Mexican American men in New Mexico, and some in California and Texas, participated on an equal footing with Euro-American men in terms of formal political rights. Moreover, the rights of Mexican Americans as *federal* citizens living in a federal territory were arguably strengthened by *Scott v. Sandford*, the same Supreme Court case that so unequivocally excluded both free and enslaved blacks from the polity. The logic of the Court's ruling in that case was to enlarge the scope of citizenship rights of non-blacks living in the federal territories. The unintended consequence was that the rights of Mexican American citizens in the federal territories also were expanded. This meaning of the *Dred Scott* case, however, was never tested in the legal system since there was so little time between the Court's decision and the Civil War.

Race, Law, and Contrasting "One-Drop" Rules

As legal scholar Ian Haney López has noted, one of the first laws passed by Congress after it ratified the Constitution was to limit naturalization to "free white persons," meaning that only white immigrants to the United States could become citizens.[125] In the wake of the Civil War, amid the passage of the Reconstruction Amendments to the Constitution, Congress amended the law to allow white persons as well as "persons of African nativity or African descent" to become American citizens.[126] In 1848, more than 115,000 Mexicans were *collectively* naturalized under the Treaty of Guadalupe Hidalgo. We have explored the resulting paradox—that the collective grant of American citizenship in some senses conferred legal whiteness on Mexicans as a group with a distinctly non-white history. Now we turn our attention to the fates of Mexicans who sought U.S. naturalization after 1848. Were Mexicans to be allowed to become American citizens, given that naturalization was limited to whites until 1870 and after that to whites and blacks only?

Two caveats are in order. First, the two-thousand-plus-mile U.S.–Mexico border was more symbolic than real in the late nineteenth and early twentieth centuries.[127] Substantial numbers of Mexican nationals crossed the porous border without any difficulty whatsoever, as did Americans entering Mexico.[128] Historian George Sánchez has described the social construction of the border, arguing that procedures to regulate Mexican immigration did not become institutionalized until the 1940s.[129] Prior to that time, Mexicans entered the United States freely and blended into Mexican American communities, in many cases without perceiving formal naturalization as necessary or desirable.

Second, naturalization occurred at the local level and very rarely resulted in the kinds of court records studied by legal scholars (typically, appellate decisions).[130] As a result, we cannot with confidence know how Mexicans who sought naturalization fared in these various jurisdictions. We do know that, at least in particular contexts, the federal law limiting naturalization to blacks and whites often made little difference. In my research on nineteenth-century New Mexico courts, for example, I routinely came across uncontroversial instances of the court's naturalization of Mexican nationals as American citizens. But we cannot extrapolate from New Mexico to other parts of the country; in other places, formal racial restrictions likely were used to prevent certain classes of Mexicans from becoming U.S. citizens.

The only precedent-setting legal case involving a Mexican seeking American naturalization is *In re Rodriguez*, decided by a federal judge in Texas in 1897. The essential logic of *Rodriguez* was that Mexicans were *white enough*, despite not being truly white. The case emphasized the prior collective naturalization of Mexican citizens in 1848 as setting the precedent for finding that Mexicans are white persons, given that the law then limited naturalization to white persons. But the social context probably was more important in determining the outcome of the case. Largely because of the exclusion of Chinese workers from the American labor market beginning in 1882, the United States, and especially certain industries in the Southwest and West, faced a labor shortage.[131] For more than two decades, Japanese immigrants filled this void, but when that flow was cut off in 1907, Mexican immigrants were recruited to replace them.[132] In the early decades of the twentieth century, Mexican immigrants became the workforce of choice for a wide range of agricultural and industrial sectors of the U.S. economy.[133]

Judge Thomas Sheldon Maxey began his opinion in *Rodriguez* by acknowledging "the delicacy and gravity of the question" presented, a candid admission about the delicate racial issue presented in the case and its likely broader impact.[134] We can only speculate as to how Maxey's own experience, as a native of Mississippi and veteran of the Confederate Army, may have influenced his estimation of the importance of the case or his resolution of it.[135] His requests for additional briefing may indicate that he was disturbed by the degree to which local politicians and the press had inserted themselves into the case. According to historian Arnoldo De León, Euro-American politicians in San Antonio openly sought it out as a "test case," hoping they could block any widespread Mexican naturalization in order to stem the rising numbers of Mexican American voters.[136] In any event, Maxey ruled in Rodríguez's favor, against the interests of the Euro-Americans seeking to have Mexicans declared unfit for naturalization because they were not white.

Rodríguez had lived in San Antonio, Texas, for ten years prior to his application for citizenship; the court records do not indicate where in Mexico he was born. According to Judge Maxey, Rodríguez was illiterate in English (we do not know whether he was literate in Spanish);[137] the record does not say, but it seems that Rodríguez testified in English. Maxey described Rodríguez as "lamentably ignorant" and as "a very good man, peaceable and industrious, of good moral character, and law abiding."[138] Rodríguez's racial phenotype and ancestry are discussed in some detail in the case. Rodríguez testified that he was a "pure-blooded Mexican," which carries with it great irony given the mestizo racial character of the Mexican people as part Spanish, African, and indigenous.[139] Maxey interpreted Rodríguez's statement to mean he did not have ancestral "relation to the Aztecs or original races of Mexico."[140] Yet Maxey and other Euro-Americans present in court viewed him as "looking Mexican," meaning having dark skin and Indian features.[141]

The opinion suggests that Maxey was quite perplexed with the case. He acknowledged, on the one hand, that "if the strict scientific classification of the anthropologist should be adopted, *he would probably not be classed as white*. It is certain he is not an African, or a person of African descent."[142] But he rejected the idea that social-scientific views of race were the appropriate measure.[143] He similarly rejected the idea that Mexicans were non-white because they were racially similar to American Indians, saying forcefully that "the dissimilarity [between Mexicans and American Indians] is so pronounced."[144] Instead, Maxey's strategy ultimately was to emphasize the laws that gave Mexicans political rights, suggesting that these laws had earlier conferred white status on Mexicans.[145] Maxey suggested that his choice to treat Mexicans as "white" for purposes of the naturalization law was natural and legally inevitable.[146] But he reached this conclusion by ignoring law and custom that indicated, with at least equal force, that Mexicans were anything but white.

Consider two of the laws upon which Maxey relied—the 1836 constitution of the Republic of Texas and the 1845 Texas state constitution. The 1836 document conferred citizenship on all men *except "Africans and their descendants" and "Indians,"* thereby including Mexicans by default.[147] When Congress voted to annex Texas as a state in 1845, it incorporated the former Mexican citizens who were at that time citizens of Texas. Both instances elide the vigorous, ongoing debate at the time about Mexicans' racial status. For example, in the context of the implementation of these provisions, some Mexicans were deemed not *white enough*—or too Indian and/or too black—to become Texas citizens.[148] Similarly, while the Treaty of Guadalupe Hidalgo did not itself contain racial restrictions, racial prerequisites were included in the constitutions of several states carved from the Mexican Cession lands, as well as in the federal legislation creating the New Mexico Territory.[149]

Rodriguez is perhaps surprising in that, as historian Mae Ngai puts it, "Mexicans were thus deemed to be white for purposes of naturalization, an unintended consequence of conquest."[150] The case becomes less startling if one pays close attention to the larger forces swirling around immigration—the cutting off of Chinese immigration in 1882 and Japanese immigration in 1907, and the reform of immigration law that followed in later decades. The exclusion of Chinese and Japanese laborers created a labor shortage that Mexicans were filling at the time *Rodriguez* was decided. Euro-American elites were divided on how to confront this new reality. No doubt influenced by the racism and xenophobia that had driven out Asians, some wanted to prevent Mexicans from voting and in any sense becoming Mexican *American* (like the San Antonio politicians who objected to Rodríguez's naturalization application). Others wanted the United States to remain attractive for Mexican workers.

In 1917, Congress passed a major immigration bill that consolidated the anti-Chinese efforts into a virtual ban on immigration from *any* Asian country (creating the so-called Asiatic barred zone).[151] In the same law, Congress created the first exception for temporary Mexican workers—sojourners who would be allowed into the United States as contract laborers for a limited period of time. Actively recruited by employers and U.S. government agents, more than 400,000 Mexicans entered the United States in this fashion to work in the 1920s.[152] For these workers, naturalization was not an option; the United States invited them only as temporary workers and did not give them the choice to become permanent citizens. If the 1917 immigration law permitted some Mexicans the opportunity for short-term economic improvement, it also constituted a huge exception to the naturalization opportunities created by *Rodriguez*.[153]

We have explored the significant wedge that whiteness constituted between Mexican Americans and Pueblo Indians. By allowing Mexican Americans legal whiteness while denying it to Pueblo Indians, American colonizers strengthened their position and disrupted a potential alliance between two native groups. In the larger American racial order, what effect did granting Mexicans legal whiteness—in cases like *Rodriguez*—have on African Americans and on Mexican/black relations? The formal "white-enough-to-naturalize" status afforded by *Rodriguez* encouraged many Mexican Americans to further distance themselves from blacks and other non-white groups. In this context, any group or person seeking equality appreciated the extent to which it paid to be perceived as white (or white enough) under the law. For many Mexican Americans, that meant distinguishing themselves from blacks, but also from Indians, the Chinese, and the Japanese, depending on the region. In this way, New Mexico's racial order came to influence the evolving national racial order.

Indeed, by the turn of the century, we can perceive mutually reinforcing racial logics involving blacks and Mexican Americans. For blacks, the turn of the century signaled the beginning of the entrenchment of the one-drop rule: one drop of African ancestry was sufficient to confer black status, and black status signified a host of legal and social disabilities. For Mexican Americans, a kind of reverse one-drop rule was in play: one drop of European ancestry (Spanish in this case) was sufficient to confer some modicum of white status, and thus a host of corresponding legal rights.[154] The silence in American public discourse about the reverse one-drop rule as it governed Mexican Americans is significant. To talk openly about the way the one-drop rule operated for Mexicans would have exposed the tensions and contradictions in the racial order. In this respect, collective silence about the reverse one-drop rule for Mexicans helped perpetuate the subordination of blacks, even as it promoted Mexican Americans' permanent insecurity as "off-white."

Another result of this dynamic was to view American race relations as involving white-over-black subordination, to the exclusion of the subordination by whites of other non-white groups. This perhaps allowed for the more total subordination of blacks. Intermediate racial groups like Mexican Americans were bought off with honorary white status and so became complicit in policing the one-drop rule for African Americans. Finally, Mexican access to the white category promised an easier path into legal whiteness for other groups. If Mexicans had been admitted, how long could whiteness be foreclosed to groups like the Irish, Italians, and Jews?[155]

When, instead of ignoring it, we examine closely the reverse one-drop rule, the American racial system seems far more fluid and malleable than typically portrayed. Instead of seeing a racial system that has hard, closed categories (such as the one-drop rule operating to define blackness), we begin to see the contours of an American racial system in which mobility occurs. Identifying Mexicans' trajectory as off-white allows us to see with more clarity the movement of other off-white groups into the white category in the early and middle twentieth century. Americans (scholars included) have tended to avoid identifying these patterns by classifying them under the "ethnic" or "immigrant" rubric, rather than by seeing them as about race. This tendency is misplaced and has prevented us from fully understanding American racial dynamics. A common rhetorical move has been to characterize dynamics involving African Americans as "racial" and those involving Mexican Americans as "ethnic" (or as "immigrant"). Yet the dynamics involving Mexicans tell us a great deal about the American *racial* order. And by continuing to uncritically reproduce the standard account of race in the United States, we may inadvertently reinforce white supremacy.

The *Rodriguez* case was decided in 1897, a year after the Supreme Court's infamous *Plessy v. Ferguson* opinion.[156] While Mexican Americans had experienced de facto segregation in the West (and would continue to do so until the 1960s in some places), blacks experienced a heightened level of legalized (de jure) segregation after *Plessy*. The case helped entrench the hypo-descent rule for blacks, but, before *Plessy*, it was not at all inevitable that the one-drop rule would become dominant in the United States. In fact, for centuries before then, there had been many definitions of black status vying for supremacy. The American revolutionary generation defined someone as black only if one or more of their grandparents was black.[157] Between 1850 and 1920, the census identified not only blacks in the United States but also mulattos, suggesting that the government viewed black/non-black mixing as substantial enough to be counted.[158] The 1890 census, the one that preceded *Plessy*, actually counted quadroons and octoroons, in addition to blacks and mulattos.[159] Not until the 1920s and 1930s did the hypo-descent rule hastened by *Plessy* become consolidated as the American rule for defining black status.[160]

In part, it was the instability and variety of definitions of blackness that led to Mr. Homer Plessy's case. Plessy was seven-eighths white and one-eighth black and was phenotypically white.[161] Yet, under various Louisiana definitions of race in its Jim Crow laws, Plessy's legal identity varied, despite the fact that he self-identified as black and participated fully in black community life (in other words, Plessy did not seek to "pass" for white). As legal scholar Cheryl Harris has observed, it was precisely Plessy's appearance as white that made him an ideal candidate for the test case that would challenge Louisiana's mandate that railway cars provide separate cars for whites and "colored persons."[162] It is telling that for Plessy's case to receive the court's review, a deal had to be struck between his civil rights attorneys and the Louisiana and Nashville Railroad to arrest him for violating state law. Without the deal, train personnel, like others in his day-to-day interactions, may well have assumed he was white and accordingly *not* challenged his selection of a seat in the white car.

Plessy's lawyers made a number of arguments designed to expose the fallacies of Jim Crow laws. They argued that the laws were unenforceable—in the first instance, by those people who decided who was in the wrong railway car, for example, and also by appellate courts deciding whether the law had been correctly applied—because racial mixture in Louisiana's population sometimes made it impossible to visibly ascertain an individual's race and to definitively prove a person's racial status in court.[163] Since segregation laws could not be enforced consistently (and often were enforced in contradictory ways), Plessy's attorneys argued, the Court should look for the underlying purpose of the law and, on that basis, find it unconstitutional. Plessy's brief made the point this way: "Why not count everyone as white in whom is visible any trace of white blood? There is but one reason to wit, the domination of the white race."[164]

The Supreme Court majority largely ignored these issues (though Justice Harlan, dissenting, did not). They did so because the mere fact of debating them would have loosened the boundaries of racial categories, thereby disrupting the myth of race as fixed and stable. The majority's one concession to Plessy's powerful arguments was, in the penultimate paragraph of its opinion, to acknowledge the variety of existing definitions that determined who was black:

> It is true that the question of the proportion of colored blood necessary to constitute a colored person, as distinguished from a white person, is one upon which there is a difference of opinion in the different states; some holding that any visible admixture of black blood stamps the person as belonging to the colored race; others, that it depends upon the preponderance of blood; and still others, that the predominance of white blood must only be in the proportion of three-fourths. But these are questions to be determined under the laws of each state, and are not properly put in issue in this case.[165]

In the end, the Court's ruling fueled the most extreme definition: the hypo-descent rule under which any visible proportion of African ancestry, however slight, marks a person as black.

Although cases like *Plessy* contributed to American ideas that race was immutable and fixed, the reality was that race was more fluid. A powerful example comes from the Senate's 1902 debates on the Omnibus Statehood Bill (see Chapter 2), which sought to admit Oklahoma, New Mexico, and Arizona as new states. The racial composition of each of the proposed states was a major topic of floor debate. Senator Matthew S. Quay of Pennsylvania used official census numbers to estimate the *non-Indian* population of New Mexico at just under 200,000.[166] But Indiana senator Albert Beveridge, who as we know from earlier discussions strenuously opposed New Mexico statehood, said emphatically, "There is no ground for [the] assumption [that Mexicans are white]."[167] Beveridge was supported by senators Knute Nelson of Mississippi and Eugene Hale of Maine, among others, who refused to countenance the census's inclusion of Mexicans in the white category. Mexicans had been "white enough" to be collectively naturalized in 1848 and to be counted as white in 1897 under the naturalization laws, but, here, U.S. senators decided they were not white enough to warrant the full citizenship statehood would have provided.

These conversations in 1902 suggest that fluidity has been an enduring quality of American racial dynamics (especially in the construction of racial categories), rather than a feature unique to Mexican Americans. A similar conversation to the one involving New Mexico arose soon thereafter, when Congress took up the proposed state of Oklahoma, to be formed largely from the Indian Territory. The very senators who, by refusing to include Mexican Americans in the "white" category, argued that New Mexico's white population was too small to warrant the territory's admission as a state now argued that Oklahoma should be admitted because the number of "pure Indians" there was very small. Senator Nelson argued that, of Oklahoma's 87,000 Indians enrolled in tribes, "a very small part are pure Indians and a very large portion of them are *practically white men.*" Senator Hale supported admission of Oklahoma because it possessed "just as pure and clean a white population as exists in Indiana or Pennsylvania or Maine." Senator Beveridge made a parallel argument about the Indian Territory, saying, "Only a very small number, to wit 87,000 [of 400,000 persons] at most, are classed as Indians, and of those who are classed as Indians *a very large number are pure white men,* so far as blood is concerned, *quite as white as we are.*"[168]

By this point, the direction of the conversation had begun to seriously bother Senator Benjamin Tillman of South Carolina. He asked, indignantly,

> How [have] white men as pure blooded as he or I . . . gotten the right to all that Indian land, and how [is it] that the 87,000 Indians, so called, are nearly all white people? Some stealing has been done somewhere, or something, and I should like to know how it happened. *I know a bleaching process is going on over there; but still that does not make them as pure white men as he and I, because I do not think either of us could be suspected of having anything else but Caucasian blood in our veins."* (emphasis added)

Tillman's annoyance reveals the American racial order as, at once, fluid and rigid. Like the Mexican and Latin American process of "whitening" described earlier, he acknowledged "a bleaching process" in the United States. In the same breath, he embraced the primacy of blood purity, which invokes a more inflexible racial hierarchy and categorization. Senator Beveridge's response to Tillman was to say that white men had become

Indians by marriage and by adoption into tribes. But a more accurate and honest approach would have acknowledged that, despite the presence of Indians in the region, it should be admitted as a state because the Indians there would be dominated by whites.[169] The Indians in the proposed state of Oklahoma did not then pose a threat to political domination by Euro-American men; in stark contrast, New Mexico's Mexican men did, as the majority of those to be enfranchised in the proposed state.

This conversation in Congress belies the claim that American racial categories were perceived and employed by social actors, even one hundred years ago, as immutable and fixed. American racial dynamics were and are often seen as the mirror opposite of Latin American race relations on this point. While Spanish-Mexican categories are viewed as flexible, American categories are viewed as historically fixed. In reality, the Spanish-Mexican system regularly produced racial dynamics that were harder than they appeared to be, while the Anglo-American system regularly produced dynamics that were more malleable than they appeared to be.[170] Of course, the United States actually includes both models of race relations. By virtue of Manifest Destiny and the conquest of northern Mexico, the United States inherited the Spanish-Mexican racial order. Over time, the national racial order evolved to include substantial elements of the Southwest's racial order.

Epilogue

As I was nearing completion of this book, one morning over breakfast my ten-year-old son asked, "Mom, are we white?" From the habit formed of reading too many parenting books, I took a deep breath and then probed for more information (thinking to myself, Is he asking what I think he is asking?). After acknowledging that his was a big question, I asked him to tell me more about what he was interested in finding out. "Well, back when there was slavery, were Mexicans white or black?" I began my answer by saying the question was complicated and one that people disagreed about. I told him that Mexican Americans had ancestors who were Indian, African, and Spanish, but they were primarily indigenous. I said that I did not believe we were white. He responded with another question—"Then why don't we say whites, blacks, and browns?"—and then was quickly off to get ready for school. Thinking more about my son's question, at least part of his dilemma comes from the continuing tendency in popular culture (including elementary school social studies) to see American history, from slavery to the civil rights movement, in black and white terms. My son was struggling with how to reconcile that standard story with the complexity he knew existed.

Manifest Destinies has focused on how race evolved in the larger historical context, as well as how race and racial ideology organized social life and, particularly, how they shaped relations among racial groups. In this epilogue, I consider the contemporary relevance of Mexican Americans' history. At least a small slice of that relevance concerns the twenty-first-century legacy of Mexican Americans' history as off-white—sometimes defined as *legally* white, almost always defined as *socially* non-white. Unlike other off-white groups that moved definitively into the white category within decades after their initial arrival in the United States (for example, Jews, the Irish, Italians), Mexican Americans, as a group, have continued to be off-white, neither definitively white or definitively non-white.[1]

Remarkably, after more than 160 years, Mexican Americans still are insecure in their collective claim to white racial identity, and, in the early twenty-first century, may be further than ever from becoming white, or, to put it another way, they may be permanently off-white. At least by some indicia, there has been a growing rejection of white status among Mexican Americans, even as some of them continue to embrace whiteness as a route to social equality in the United States. In a sense, this is predictable given the history explored in this book. One of the effects of Mexican Americans' existence as socially non-white has been the adoption of a non-white racial identity that has been both assigned by the dominant society and asserted by group members themselves.[2] At the same time, Mexican Americans occasionally, and particularly in legal contexts, have been treated as white. It is not so surprising, then, that Mexican Americans have at times embraced both a white and a non-white racial identity, both collectively and individually.

To explore the contemporary manifestations of this dynamic I examine how Mexican Americans have responded to official census questions regarding their racial identity.[3] Census questions and responses to them are a fascinating way to explore racial identity. The Census Bureau stands in for the nation-state and for the government's conception of racial and ethnic categories. The historical evolution of census categories offers an example of the social construction of race.[4] Moreover, the decadal enumeration of the American population serves symbolic purposes. The very act of counting the nation and dividing that count into particular categories has been an act of defining who we are and who we aspire to be as a nation.[5]

The process of defining the nation in this way, at least since 1970 and perhaps before, has become implicated in interest group and electoral politics. For example, President Lyndon B. Johnson created the Inter-Agency Committee on Mexican American Affairs, which early in the Nixon administration morphed into the Cabinet Committee on Opportunities for Spanish-Speaking People.[6] These events at the national level stemmed from the larger context of the civil rights movement, as well as partisan estimations about the potential value of the Mexican American electorate.[7] At around the same time, and partly in response to the criticism that Mexican Americans had been undercounted in 1970, the Census Bureau formed an advisory committee to explore how to better identify Spanish-speaking people in the 1980 census.[8] The majority of the nineteen committee members were Mexican Americans (including leaders of the major civil rights organizations), and they recommended use of "Hispanic" as a term to include Mexican Americans, Puerto Ricans, Cuban Americans, and other Americans with origins in Latin American countries.[9]

As has been widely noted in the media, in 2004 Latinos (14 percent of the U.S. population) surpassed blacks (13 percent) as the largest minority group in the United States.[10] Hispanics are the fastest growing ethno-racial group in the United States: between 1990 and 2000, the Hispanic population increased by almost 60 percent, while the overall population increased by 13 percent in the same period.[11] The Hispanic group will continue to grow at a high rate because it is a relatively young population: whereas 15 percent of whites are sixty-five years old or older, only 5 percent of Hispanics are in that age group; 34 percent of Hispanics are under eighteen years old, compared to 20 percent of whites.[12] Of the nation's 41.3 million Latinos, nearly 60 percent are Mexican American, nearly 10 percent are Puerto Rican, and less than 4 percent are Cuban American; almost all of the remaining 25 percent come from six additional countries in the Caribbean and Central and South America.[13] As might be expected given these points of origin, the population is regionally concentrated, with 75 percent of Cubans living in the South, 60 percent of Puerto Ricans living in the Northeast, and just over half of all Mexican Americans living in the West.[14] More than 160 years after its invasion by the United States, New Mexico continues to have the highest proportion of Hispanics of any state (43 percent), followed by California and Texas (both at 35 percent).[15]

How the Census Bureau has counted Mexican Americans has varied considerably over the past 160 years.[16] Between 1850 and 1920, Mexican Americans were not distinguished as a separate group in the census; they were counted in the white category. Inconsistently asked and inconsistently phrased questions pertaining to foreign birth, foreign parentage, language usage, and Spanish surname were used in the mid-1900s as proxies for counting Mexican Americans. Consistently unreliable estimates of the Mexican American population resulted. Foreign birth and foreign parentage, for example, failed to include the descendants of those Mexican Americans who lived in the Mexican Cession. Spanish surname was especially problematic, as it was both over- and underinclusive of Mexican Americans. One 1970s study found that reliance on Spanish surname resulted in overcounting Mexican Americans by about one-third and undercounting them by about one-third; in other words, Hispanics who did not have Spanish surnames (by virtue of intermarriage) were undercounted, while non-Hispanics whose names were mistaken as Spanish were included in the total.[17] If this study was correct, Spanish surname might have resulted in the correct estimate overall, but not the identification of the right people.

The pattern of counting Mexican Americans as "white" changed in 1930 when, for the first and only time, "Mexican" appeared as a separate *racial* category.[18] The designation of Mexicans as a racial group coincided with the Great Depression and with increased economic competition between whites and Mexicans, both native-born and immigrant.[19] The economic climate fomented anti-Mexican racism, violence, and government hostility, including mass deportation (to Mexico). More than 400,000 Mexican-origin persons, including many American citizens were rounded up by police and deported during this period.[20] In Los Angeles, fully one-third of the Mexican American population returned to Mexico in the 1930s, either forcibly or voluntarily (in anticipation of the round-ups).[21] In northern New Mexico, where economic opportunities did not lure substantial numbers of Mexican immigrants until recently, Mexican Americans "remember being loaded in trucks and taken by train and truckload and dumped as 'Mexican citizens'" across the U.S.–Mexico border in the 1930s.[22]

The racist, violent events of the 1930s were a sharp reminder to Mexican Americans of their marginal status. Although they were formally U.S. citizens, their Mexican American racial status kept them in a second-class position. Mexican American elites responded to the outrages of the 1930s by pressuring the Census Bureau to reclassify Mexican Americans as white.[23] Given the 1930 debacle, the Census Bureau felt constrained in counting directly the Mexican American population. Instead, in 1940 and 1950, it unsuccessfully utilized the already mentioned proxies. The 1960 census experimented with the category "*white* persons of Spanish surname" but only in the states of Arizona, California, Colorado, New Mexico, and Texas, where 90 percent of Latinos in the United States (virtually all Mexican Americans) then lived.[24]

By 1970, it was obvious that a separate question was needed to identify Hispanics—foreign birth, language, surname, and other proxies had become increasingly problematic, given the preponderance of U.S.-born Hispanics, increasing patterns of intermarriage (making surname a less reliable indicator), and cultural assimilation that included the transition from Spanish- to English-language dominance. The addition of a specific question about "Spanish-speaking people" on the long-form questionnaire in 1970 was the direct result of political pressure from the U.S. Inter-Agency Committee on Mexican American Affairs.[25] In 1976, as noted previously, the "Census Advisory Committee on the Spanish-Origin Population for the 1980 Census" recommended the adoption of the pan-ethnic label "Hispanic." In this way, the current census policies about Latinos' racial and ethnic status reflect both the state's construction of race and ethnicity as well as the efforts of Latino powerbrokers to negotiate the spaces between white, off-white, and non-white racial categories.

Today the Census Bureau intentionally treats Latinos as an ethnic group, rather than as a racial group.[26] Since 1980, people living in the United States have been asked to identify themselves as a member of a racial group and, in a separate question, as Hispanic or non-Hispanic.[27] The Hispanic ethnicity question (which in 1990 followed the race question but in 2000 preceded it) asks, "Is this person Spanish/Hispanic/Latino?" and provides five possible choices: no; Mexican American; Puerto Rican; Cuban; and other Spanish/Hispanic/Latino (then asking for specific subgroup identification).[28] In 2000, the race question directed respondents to choose one or more of the following options: white; black; American Indian or Alaskan Native; one of ten Asian categories; or "some other race."[29] Ninety-nine percent of those who identified themselves as Hispanic selected only one racial category, and the Census officially reports that "among Hispanics, 92 percent were White."[30]

The reality, however, is considerably more complicated and may well reflect Mexican Americans' history as off-white. When answering the race question, Latinos select "some other race" in substantial proportions, rejecting white, black, Indian, or Asian racial identification. In 2000, 42 percent of Hispanics preferred "some other race," while 48 percent selected white, 4 percent selected black, and 1 percent selected American Indian.[31] Latinos' preference for "some other race" is all the more striking because, combining all non-Hispanics, only one percent of people selected "some other race."[32] Moreover, this makes all the more perverse the Census Bureau's disregard for this preference by folding those persons who chose "some other race" into those who selected "white" as their race.

To explore why such a large number of Latinos are unwilling to identify as white, black, Indian, or Asian, we must return to a variation of the debate that preoccupied the nation in the mid-1800s: where do Mexican Americans—and now Hispanics—fit in the national racial order? Consciously or not, Latinos are engaging in a debate about this question when they identify themselves racially, as they do on the census questionnaire. The debate is both descriptive and normative—it is about how they see themselves and how they perceive others as seeing them, and it is very much about their desire to belong in the national community. In the context of debates over immigration and citizenship in Europe, sociologist Rogers Brubaker has said,

> The politics of citizenship today is first and foremost a politics of nationhood. As such, it is a *politics of identity*, not a *politics of interest* (in the restricted, materialist sense). It pivots more on self-understanding than on self-interest. The "interests" informing the politics of citizenship are "ideal" rather than material. The central question is not "who gets what?" but rather "who is what?"[33]

Similarly for Mexican Americans today (and perhaps since 1848), the politics of identity are about who they are racially and who they are in terms of their long and complex history in the United States.

The tendency of Hispanics to identify themselves as "other" is not a fleeting phenomenon, but has existed since 1980—or since the beginning of modern census practices allowing self-identification (as opposed to identification by a census enumerator) and the inclusion of a question regarding Hispanic identity.[34] In 1980, 40 percent of Hispanics selected "other" rather than black, white, or Indian as their race.[35] In 1990, the number of Hispanics who selected "other" was about the same as those who selected "some other race" in 2000 (44 percent in 1990, 47 percent in 2000),[36] suggesting that the different wording of the question and the different order of the race and Hispanic identity questions did not influence choices.[37] These data show that, over time, the proportion of Hispanics who reject white racial identification is rising (during the same three decades, the proportion of Hispanics choosing "white" has decreased from 64 to 48 percent).[38]

What does it mean that Hispanics—60 percent of whom are Mexican Americans—divided their responses to the race question between white (48 percent) and "some other race" (42 percent)? Four explanations appear most consistently in the literature.[39] One explanation implicitly validates the 50 percent of Latinos who selected "white" as choosing the "correct" answer and labels those Latinos who selected "some other race" as ignorant or confused. I include in this category those who are generally critical of the census approach to race, such as sociologist Nathan Glazer, a long-time critic of race-based government policy. "Do the American people in general know? If they do not—and it is hardly likely they are fully briefed on the legislation and regulations and politics and the pressures that have made the census form, with respect to race and Hispanicity, what it is today—what are they to conclude?"[40] How would Glazer respond to the fact that virtually all of the non-Hispanics who responded to the race question in 2000 seemed to have no trouble selecting a category? A variant of this explanation targets Hispanics specifically: because they are recent immigrants to the United States, it implies, they must be confused about how race works here and so they erroneously select "some other race."[41] This explanation would seem to be the one adopted by the Census Bureau itself given how it collapses "some other race" into "white" responses.

A second explanation can be considered a hybrid of the "they're confused" explanation. According to this explanation, the fact that the majority of Hispanics selected the "white" race category shows that Hispanics are, collectively, white in American society.[42] Under this explanation, appropriately little weight is given to the fact that almost half of Hispanics selected "some other race" (since it reflects their racial confusion, it need not be taken seriously). However, the ubiquity of the phrase "non-Hispanic whites" in both the media and social science to distinguish "real whites" from Latinos suggests that who is and is not white is considerably more contested than this explanation would lead one to believe. A third theory posits that the census responses accurately reflect a Latino population that is racially bifurcated, roughly half (truly) white and the other half (truly) non-white.[43]

Both the second and third explanations, then, take Hispanics' census responses at face value—that is, they assume that respondents intended their responses as literal reflections of their perception of their racial status in the United States. Several researchers, however, have instead posited a fourth interpretation—that Hispanics' racial self-identification is highly symbolic of other dynamics, including their experiences of racial and economic discrimination in the United States, their general level of inclusion in or exclusion from the nation, and their different view of race as influenced by the Spanish-Mexican racial legacy described in Chapter 2.[44] In a two-year study convened by the National Academies, sociologists Marta Tienda and Faith Mitchell found strong support for this explanation, concluding that Latinos see themselves as a separate race:

> [Hispanics'] choice of "some other race" on the census forms reflects more than four centuries of *mestizaje*, or racial miscegenation, in Latin America and the Caribbean, as well as the differing conceptions of race noted above. Hispanics may also mark "some other race" simply because they do not see themselves as fitting under any of the categories provided by the Census

Bureau. . . . Thus, their rejection of the [Office of Management and Budget] racial classification by checking "some other race" on the census questionnaire reflected their lived experience rather than a statistical artifact or measurement error.[45]

If responses to the racial identity question reflect genuine differences in how Latinos see themselves in the nation, we should expect to see significant differences among Latino groups according to national origin. As noted, 90 percent of Hispanics overall divide their racial identity between "white" (48 percent) and "some other race" (42 percent).[46] One finds interesting patterns when comparing racial identification with national origin. Ninety percent of Hispanics identify as Mexican origin (60 percent) or as from one of eight other Latin American countries: Puerto Rico, Cuba, the Dominican Republic, El Salvador, Guatemala, Colombia, Peru, and Ecuador.[47] Among these groups, self-identification as white versus "some other race" varies widely, ranging from a low of 28 percent for Dominicans to a high of 88 percent for Cuban Americans.[48] It is not the case that large numbers of national-origin subgroups identify as black—those numbers range from 11 percent for Dominicans (the highest of any Hispanic subgroup), to 7 percent for Puerto Ricans, to 4 percent for Cubans, to mention just three subgroups where we might expect to see a larger black identification.[49]

We can distinguish two tiers of Hispanics, in terms of their racial self-identification.[50] The first, relatively small group embraces white racial identity at rates approaching 90 percent. Cubans and those who trace their origins to Argentina fall into this category, identifying as white 88 and 89 percent of the time, respectively. Hispanics who emigrated from or whose family origins are in Chile or Venezuela come close: 77 and 76 percent of them, respectively, identify as white. The second tier includes those subgroups whose members self-identify as white at rates between 28 and 52 percent. The two largest Latino groups fall into this category—Mexican Americans (50 percent) and Puerto Ricans (52 percent), together 70 percent of all Latinos. Central Americans (Guatemalans, Hondurans, and Salvadorans) identify as white in percentages ranging from 41 to 49 percent. Dominicans, as mentioned above, are the Hispanic subgroup least likely to identify as white, at 28 percent. If we take these same groups and explore the proportion selecting "some other race," we see the mirror image. Cubans, for instance, selected "some other race" only 7 percent of the time. In contrast, 39 percent of Puerto Ricans and 47 percent of Mexican Americans preferred "some other race." Central Americans selected "some other race" in percentages ranging from 43 to 57, and 59 percent of Dominicans preferred "some other race."

It should not surprise us that almost as many Mexican Americans opt for the "some other race" option as for white. Both choices seem reasonably to be a product of Mexican Americans' peculiar history as off-white— as sometimes legally white and almost always socially non-white. Given their history, it is predictable that many Mexican Americans would seek to formally identify themselves as racially white. *Manifest Destinies* has described Mexican Americans' long history of utilizing whiteness (or claims to be white) to combat discrimination and racial subordination. On the one hand, claiming whiteness is a way of blunting the full impact of racial discrimination. Like others in American society, Mexican Americans also have internalized anti-black racism such that "white" could reflect "I'm *not* black."[51] Sociologist Joan W. Moore, one of the authors of the landmark 1970 study *The Mexican American People: The Nation's Second Largest Minority*, recalls that, in the late 1960s, "many Mexican Americans rejected the term 'minority' and its implied association with black America."[52] Given their historic legacy as off-white, it should not surprise us that substantial numbers of Mexican Americans would today continue to identify as white.

That same history has influenced many Mexican Americans to reject a view of race as black and white but to view themselves as non-white. Mexican Americans' origins in this country as a colonized group, like Puerto Ricans, also contribute to their identification as non-white outsiders. Certainly the collective memory of events in the twentieth century that dramatically reinforced Mexican Americans' second-class citizenship (such as the deportations of Mexican American citizens in the 1930s) may continue to haunt present generations. Mexican Americans participated disproportionately in World War II, and returning veterans formed the first "civil rights" organizations as we have come to understand that term.[53] Inspired by the black civil rights movement, the Chicano student movement of the 1970s led many Mexican Americans to expressly reject a white identity in favor of a non-white identity. Part of the Chicano movement's rhetoric was to embrace—rather than denigrate—Mexicans' indigenous ancestry as part of the embrace of an oppositional, non-white identity.[54]

Given this history, Mexican Americans' selection of "some other race" may reflect their recognition of a racial heritage that includes white, black, and Indian ancestry, as well as an affirmative rejection of white identity as a political statement. Certainly, Cuban Americans have little in common with this history, and that may account for their identification as white 90 percent of the time. Rather than a history as a conquered people, Cubans initially came to the United States as voluntary immigrants only fifty years ago. Most fled Cuba in the wake of the 1959 socialist revolution led by Fidel Castro in "the silk stocking exodus," invoking their status as the most affluent members of Cuban society.[55] Cubans entered American society during the midst of the civil rights movement, when the racial order was transitioning to one of formal equality and anti-discrimination policy that was mandated by law and they benefited accordingly. Sociologists Stephen Cornell and Douglas Hartmann have noted the dramatic differences in government policy aimed at Cuban and Mexican immigrants (including those Mexican immigrants who came to the United States at exactly the same time as the first Cuban immigrants).[56] For example, in 1960, the U.S. government established the Cuban Refugee Program to help Cubans find jobs and housing, learn English, and generally adjust to a new society. No such effort was made on behalf of Mexican Americans as a group. Today, U.S.-born Cuban Americans have a *higher* median income than non-Hispanic whites.[57]

Recent empirical research lends support to my hypothesis about how current Mexican American racial identity—as divided between white and "some other race"—reflects the group's historic legacy as off-white. In a study focusing on native-born Latinos (not only Mexican Americans), demographer Sonya Tafoya compared "white Hispanics" (that is, those who identified as both Hispanic and white on the census) and "some other race Hispanics" (those who identified as Hispanic and selected "some other race"). She found that white Hispanics had significantly higher incomes, were twice as likely to consider themselves Republicans, and were considerably less likely to believe that Hispanics experience significant discrimination in the United States.[58] She posits that native-born Hispanics' racial identification depends on their degree of inclusion in the American polity and economic success: to the extent that Latinos feel politically excluded and economically marginalized, they will opt for "some other race."[59]

Tafoya's study dealt generally with Latinos, and she did not provide national-origin break-downs. However, she reported significant differences in racial identification between native-born Mexican Americans who live in Texas and those who live elsewhere. While about half of Mexican Americans generally identify as white, two-thirds of Mexican Americans in Texas do so.[60] As Tafoya puts it, Texas "is the only state where a large

Latino population was caught up both in Southern-style racial segregation and then the civil rights struggle to undo it."[61] In another study comparing Mexican Americans in Los Angeles and San Antonio, Texans were found to be more likely to identify as white but also more likely to speak Spanish, marry other Mexicans, and live in Mexican neighborhoods.[62] These studies offer tentative support for my hypothesis about the continuing legacy of Mexican Americans' off-white status. Texas Mexicans identify as white not because they live white lives, but precisely because the opposite is true: they are embedded in Mexican American neighborhoods, speak Spanish, and probably experience continuing racism because of those facts. In this context, their claims to whiteness are defensive.

Sociologists Edward Telles and Vilma Ortíz have recently completed a study of Mexican Americans that is methodologically unprecedented. They followed subjects longitudinally (they were interviewed initially in the late 1960s and then again in the late 1990s) and considered the direct effects of generational status by collecting data on immigrants (first-generation Americans), their children, grandchildren, and great-grandchildren.[63] Whereas surveys have found very low levels of ethnic identity among the grandchildren and great-grandchildren of European immigrants, Telles and Ortiz found persistently high rates of ethnic identity even among the great-grandchildren of Mexican immigrants.[64] Based on their National Academies research, Tienda and Mitchell agree, concluding that Hispanics are increasingly viewing themselves in racial terms, "in strong contrast to the experience of earlier immigrant groups from southern and Eastern Europe, whose social acceptance and cultural assimilation in the United States involved self-identification as white."[65]

The presence of large numbers of immigrants complicates the picture for Latinos. On the one hand, a high proportion of relatively uneducated immigrants depresses Latino averages for educational attainment, income, and wealth acquisition.[66] On the other hand, the so-called immigrant paradox may inflate Latino gains, especially in the area of education. The children and grandchildren of Mexican immigrants outperform third- and fourth-generation Mexican Americans on a host of educational attainment indices.[67] Telles and Ortíz found support for the immigrant paradox in their research tracking Mexican American families in Los Angeles and San Antonio over time. They concluded that Mexican children who were themselves immigrants and second-generation Mexican Americans (the children of immigrants born in the United States) had education performance levels comparable to those of first- and second-generation Italian

Americans in the past, but for Mexican Americans in the third-generation and beyond "educational assimilation is abruptly halted and slightly reversed."[68]

Mexican Americans who reject white identification in favor of "some other race" may be doing so as a reaction to the high and persistent levels of discrimination they perceive.[69] But this oppositional racial identification is by no means limited to native-born Hispanics. In fact, among Latinos overall, those born outside the United States were more likely to select "some other race" than native-born Latinos (46 compared to 40 percent).[70] Other surveys have shown that the children of immigrants are more likely to identify as white than their immigrant parents.[71] This has implications for Latinos, the majority of whom today are either immigrants or the children of immigrants. There are significant class differences among Latino immigrants, with most immigrants from Cuba (pre-1980) and South American countries having a middle-class profile when they emigrate, in contrast to Mexican, Central American, and most Caribbean immigrants, who come to the United States without substantial capital, whether monetary or human (education and skills).

The data suggest that this class bifurcation among immigrants may correspond to the degree to which they identify as white versus "some other race." Salvadorans and Guatemalans were two of the national-origin subgroups who selected "some other race" at levels above 50 percent. Most of them came to the United States in the 1980s in the midst of civil wars in their countries, arriving with low levels of education, and they may have substantially more indigenous ancestry than other Latino immigrants. Moreover, Central Americans initially settled in California during a period of intense anti-immigrant and anti-minority political mobilization. In the 1990s, Californians passed the anti-immigrant Proposition 187, the anti–affirmative action Proposition 209, and the anti–bilingual education Proposition 227. It was not a climate in which these new immigrants felt welcomed as "white" Americans.

In Los Angeles, Central American immigrants settled in majority-black south Los Angeles County, and during the riots of 1992 they were arrested at higher rates than blacks.[72] In the long-questionnaire sample of the 2000 Census, 49 percent of Central Americans selected "some other race," 39 percent white, and 5 percent black.[73] The latter may well reflect their material and symbolic affinity with blacks. Finally, Latinos who are immigrants are considerably more likely than native-born Latinos to report discrimination as a major problem.[74] These data suggest that the infusion of immigrants into the Mexican American population is not likely to temper the effects of their historic racial discrimination and colonial experience in the United States. If anything, the current anti-immigrant climate and the mass mobilizations by immigrants in 2006 and 2007 may fuel greater political participation.[75]

My son's question speaks to the malleability of racial identity in the United States, and also to its grounding in history. It reveals at once his sense of the burden of race for black people, but also his awareness of his (and other Mexican Americans') interactions with white people. It reflects his desire, conscious or not, to make a place for himself in the national racial fabric. In that sense, it is perhaps parallel to Mexican Americans' collective struggle, over more than a century and a half, to find their place in the nation.

Notes

Notes to the Introduction

1. For studies of the nation's early multiracial history, see Almaguer, *Racial Fault Lines*; Takaki, *A Different Mirror*; Zinn, *A People's History*.

2. See, generally, Williams, *The American Indian in Western Legal Thought*. For analyses of the complexity of Indians' status as a racial group and as members of sovereign nations in the contemporary context, see Goldberg, "Descent into Race"; Valencia-Weber, "Racial Equality."

3. See, generally, Hing, *Making and Remaking Asian America*; McClain, *In Search of Equality*; Takaki, *Strangers from a Different Shore*; Yamamoto et al., *Race, Rights and Reparations*.

4. Sánchez, *Becoming Mexican American*, 50.

5. In 1965, President Lyndon B. Johnson signed into law a major immigration reform bill that lifted many long-standing race-based restrictions on immigration, thereby opening the door to legal immigration from Asian and Latin American countries. Ngai, *Impossible Subjects*, 259–62.

6. These estimates are based on the number of Mexican-origin persons compared to the number of persons born in Mexico reported in the 1970 and 2000 censuses; the Census Bureau did not directly report these figures.

7. I might just as easily use the term "off-black" to describe Mexican Americans' in-between status. Employing the term "off-white," however, invites focus on Mexicans' striving (but rarely succeeding) for white status and equality with whites.

8. Cornell and Hartmann, *Ethnicity and Race*, xvii.

9. Ibid., 25.

10. Ibid., xvii.

11. On the social construction of race, see, generally, Cornell and Hartmann, *Ethnicity and Race*; Frankenberg, *White Women, Race Matters*; Haney López, *White by Law*; Omi and Winant, *Racial Formation*.

12. For book-length studies, see Allen, *The Invention of the White Race*; Brodkin, *How Jews Became White Folks*; Fine et al., *Off White*; Foley, *The White Scourge*; Frankenberg, *White Women, Race Matters*; Ignatiev, *How the Irish Became White*; Jacobson, *Whiteness of a Different Color*; Lipsitz, *The Possessive Investment in Whiteness*; Roediger, *The Wages of Whiteness*.

13. Jacobson, *Whiteness of a Different Color*, 4.

14. Foley, *The White Scourge*, 7.

15. "To many Americans then and since, the 'manifest destiny' years stand out as a happy interregnum between more troubled times: the expansion during the mid-1840s followed the economic distress touched off by the Panic of 1837 and preceded the tumultuous sectional strife of the 1850s that climaxed in the Civil War." Hietala, *Manifest Design*, 10.

16. Horsman, *Race and Manifest Destiny*, 1–2; see also Gutiérrez, "Significant to Whom?" 68 (referring to "the cluster of racist and nationalist ideas collectively known as Manifest Destiny"); Cartwright, "Reconsidering Race and Manifest Destiny," 292.

17. See Francaviglia, "The Geographic and Cartographic Legacy"; Zoraida Vásquez, "Causes of the War." As early as 1835, and several times between then and 1846, U.S. presidents attempted to purchase Alta California from Mexico. Smith, *The War with Mexico*, 324; see also Fehrenbacher, *A Basic History of California*, 24, 27.

18. Treaty of Guadalupe Hidalgo, 9 U.S. Statutes 922 (1848). For a history of the peace treaty, see Griswold del Castillo, *The Treaty of Guadalupe Hidalgo*. On the size of the Mexican Cession, see Historical Abstracts of the U.S., 428 ("Territorial Expansion and Land and Water Area of the U.S.: 1790–1970"); Brack, *Mexico Views Manifest Destiny*, 2; Fehrenbacher, *Era of Expansion*, 135, 138. I include Texas in the Mexican Cession since Mexico did not relinquish its claims to Texas until the ratification of the peace treaty. Fehrenbacher, *Era of Expansion*, 138; Brack, *Mexico Views Manifest Destiny*, 135. The United States added another 45,000 square miles of Mexican territory in 1853 with the Gadsden Purchase. 10 Stat. 1031 (1853).

19. As this region was defined by Spain and later Mexico, it included all or part of Arizona, Colorado, Kansas, Nevada, New Mexico, Oklahoma, Texas, Utah, and Wyoming. See Beck and Haase, *Historical Atlas*, Map 19 (Boundaries of New Mexico During the Spanish and Mexican Periods).

20. Whereas an estimated 75,000 Mexicans lived in New Mexico in 1850, 23,000 lived in Texas and only 14,000 in California. Martínez, "On the Size of the Chicano Population," 49, 54–55. In the most comprehensive demographic analysis of the region, historian Oscar Martínez considers a range of census and other population estimates to conclude that the American census data underestimated the Mexican population in New Mexico by about 20 percent, and in California by 40 percent. He estimates that at mid-century, there were 7,800 to 14,300 Mexicans in California and 13,900 to 23,200 in Texas (excluding Indians). Ibid. Other estimates of New Mexico's Mexican population prior to the American occupation range from a low of 60,000 (Lamar) to a high of 160,000 (Weber). See Lamar, *The Far Southwest*, 92; Weber, ed., *Foreigners in Their Native Land*, 140.

21. New Mexico remains the U.S. state with the largest proportion of Hispan-

ics (43 percent). "Race and Hispanic Origin," 7. Congress carved out three additional federal territories that eventually became states from New Mexico in the 1860s: Colorado (1861), Arizona (1863), and Nevada (1861). Beck and Haase, *Historical Atlas,* Map 32 (Division of New Mexico).

22. Technically, Texas's 23,000 Mexicans who became U.S. citizens in 1845 by virtue of Texas statehood might be considered the first Mexican Americans. However, since Mexico did not concede its claims to Texas until 1848, in the peace treaty, I include Texas Mexicans in the general category of Mexicans who became Mexican Americans in 1848. For a history of Mexican Americans in Texas, see Montejano, *Anglos and Mexicans in the Making of Texas.*

23. A Mexican official visiting Texas in 1834 estimated that American immigrants outnumbered Mexican settlers 4 to 1 (and that an additional 2,000 black slaves were owned by the Americans—about half the total Mexican population in Texas). Weber, ed., *Foreigners in Their Native Land,* 89; see also Foley, *The White Scourge,* 18; Langum, *Law and Community,* 4.

24. Before the outbreak of war, there were fewer than 700 Euro-Americans living in Alta California; after gold was discovered in 1849, 10,000 miners entered the state. In that year, California's non-Indian population climbed from 20,000 to 100,000 (the vast majority Euro-American). Fehrenbacher, *A Basic History of California,* 27, 33–34.

25. Lamar, *The Far Southwest,* 92. There is reason to believe these numbers underestimate New Mexico's Indian population, given its diversity and geographic dispersion.

26. Legal scholar Ediberto Román makes this point in the following way: "The importance of an influx of white settler citizens into a nonstate territory should not be underestimated because their presence underscores the early American expansionist ideology that nonwhite, non-European peoples were inherently foreign—and thus inferior—and could not therefore constitute a populace prepared for the Anglo-Saxon notions of democracy and civilization that were appropriate for achieving statehood." Roman, *The Other American Colonies,* 25.

27. Hawaii became the fiftieth U.S. state in 1959; New Mexico became a state in 1912, sixty-four years after the war ended (only Arizona had to wait as long). The following other states were admitted in part or in full out of the Mexican Cession in the year indicated: Kansas, 1861; Nevada, 1864; Colorado, 1876; Wyoming, 1890; Utah, 1896; Oklahoma, 1907; Arizona, 1912. On the American colonization of Hawaii, see Merry, *Colonizing Hawaii.*

28. As sociologist David Montejano put it in his landmark study of race in Texas, "A commitment to history meant, among other things, portraying the possibilities that human actors have at any particular moment, understanding their society as they did, and preserving the integrity of situations and events as much as possible. A commitment to sociology, on the other hand, meant teasing out patterns and sequences from a number of unique cases and moments in order to

arrive at some general conclusions about society and social life." Montejano, *Anglos and Mexicans in the Making of Texas*, 318.

29. For some prominent examples of the exceptionalism thesis, see Acuña, *Occupied America*; Gómez Quiñones, *Chicano Politics*; McWilliams, *North from Mexico*.

30. This was brought home to me when an accomplished scholar expressed surprise that I was discussing a legal case from Texas in a book about New Mexico. For accounts of similar reactions to a study comparing the American economic penetration of New Mexico and Texas, see Reséndez, *Changing National Identities*, 8.

31. I have done local studies in the past. See Gómez, "Race, Colonialism, and Criminal Law."

32. On the controversy over ethnic labels, ethnic identity, and the Mexican American population, see Gómez, "The Birth of the 'Hispanic' Generation"; Gonzáles, "The Political Construction of Latino Nomenclatures"; Oboler, *Ethnic Labels, Latino Lives*; Padilla, *Latino Ethnic Consciousness*.

NOTES TO CHAPTER 1

1. Wheeler Peak, in the Sangre de Cristo mountain range, is 13,160 feet above sea level. *Webster's New Geographical Dictionary*, 1332.

2. Tórrez, "The New Mexican 'Revolt,'" 12. Former New Mexico State Historian Robert Tórrez's unpublished writing on the 1847 trials is the most thoroughly researched, drawing on government documents, newspapers, church records, and secondary literature. What we know about these events remains sketchy, partly because, as the saying goes, history is written by the victors.

3. Garrard, *Wah-to-Yah*, 195–96. The hanging scaffold was built to be seen from near and far, and an eyewitness described the rooftops as "covered with women and children," but noted that "no men were near; a few afar off stood moodily looking on."

4. The eyewitness was Lewis Garrard, a young American adventure-seeker who inadvertently ended up in New Mexico at the outset of the U.S.–Mexico War. He kept a diary of his travels that was first published in 1850. Garrard, *Wah-to-Yah*, 196–98.

5. For accounts of Bent's assassination, see Keleher, *Turmoil in New Mexico*, 116–18 n. 24; Lamar, *The Far Southwest*, 60–61; Weber, ed., *Foreigners in Their Native Land*, 98.

6. Sociologist David Montejano notes the simultaneous presence of "a popular and romanticized awareness of southwestern history" and the "absence of a sociological memory" about the Southwest. Montejano, *Anglos and Mexicans*, 2.

7. Limerick, *The Legacy of Conquest*, 27.

8. Brubaker, *Citizenship and Nationhood*, 182.

9. Weber, ed., *Foreigners in their Native Land*, 89; Foley, *The White Scourge*, 12.

10. See, for example, Merk, *Manifest Destiny*, 151–52 (quoting editorials in the *Louisville Democrat* and *Washington Union*).

11. During the early 1830s in Mexico, there were frequent expressions of concern about immigration policies, with fear that the plan to settle Mexico's northeastern region with American immigrants would backfire. For a general discussion, see Zoraida Vázquez, 28–37.

12. Foley, *The White Scourge*, 18; see also White, *"It's Your Misfortune,"* 65.

13. Acclaimed Mexican historian Josefina Zoraida Vázquez notes that most of the American settlers in Texas were southerners and that "for the most part, they were racists and slave owners, who were uneasy with Mexican abolitionism from the outset." Zoraida Vázquez, *México al Tiempo de su Guerra con Los Estados Unidos*, 29 (author's translation).

14. Ibid.

15. From 1850 to 1860, Texas's population of slaves grew from 58,000 to 180,000. Koch, "Federal Indian Policy."

16. Horsman, *Race and Manifest Destiny*, 213 (emphasis added); see also Eisenhower, *So Far from God*, xviv.

17. Horsman, *Race and Manifest Destiny*, 215.

18. Ibid.

19. For an analysis explaining how "the far-flung boundaries of Texas" today came to exist, see Montejano, *Anglos and Mexicans*, 16–19.

20. Johannsen, *To the Halls of the Montezumas*, 7; Brack, *Mexico Views Manifest Destiny*, 115–17.

21. The declaration passed 174 to 14 in the House (with 20 abstentions), despite John Quincy Adams leading the anti-war faction. The Senate endorsed the declaration on May 13, with 40 votes in favor and only 2 against (with 3 abstentions). Bauer, *The Mexican War*, 68–69.

22. As quoted in Horsman, *Race and Manifest Destiny*, 236–37.

23. Johannsen, *To the Halls of the Montezumas*, 12; see also Fehrenbacher, *The Era of Expansion*, 132.

24. Fehrenbacher, *The Era of Expansion*, 134.

25. See ibid., 133 (regarding California); Bauer, *The Mexican War*, 106 (regarding Mexico's eastern coast).

26. Fehrenbacher, *The Era of Expansion*, 132.

27. Johannsen, *To the Halls of the Montezumas*, 12.

28. Ibid., 115.

29. Ibid., 116.

30. Ibid., 12.

31. DeVoto, *The Year of Decision*, 207. In promotional literature today, West Point acknowledges the central role of the U.S.–Mexico War in allowing the

academy to achieve national recognition. Http://www.usma/edu/history/asp, last accessed July 20, 2006.

32. Http://www.siadapp.dior.whs.mil/personnel/CASUALTY/WCPRINCIPAL. pdf, last accessed July 28, 2006; see also Fehrenbacher, *The Era of Expansion*, 133.

33. Johannsen, *To the Halls of the Montezumas*, 25–26; see also Smith, *The War with Mexico*, 286.

34. Johannsen, *To the Halls of the Montezumas*, 13 (noting that volunteer units went so far as to *elect* their commanding officers).

35. Ibid., 58.

36. Streeby, "American Sensations," 13.

37. Foos, *A Short, Offhand, Killing Affair*, 13.

38. Kearny's troops were accompanied by a thousand mules carrying supplies and, on about the last half of their trip, by four hundred civilian wagon trains heading to New Mexico on their annual Santa Fe Trail caravan. Bancroft, *History of the Pacific States*, 409; Bauer, *The Mexican War*, 130.

39. On these facets of the war, see Bauer, *The Mexican War*, 164–231; Smith, *The War with Mexico*, 333–44. Both Bancroft's and Smith's studies of the war have been frequently criticized by contemporary scholars because of their anti-Mexican bias. Yet both remain important sources due to their heavy reliance on primary documents, including some no longer available.

40. Marcy, who was in direct and constant communication with Polk, made this statement in a July 9, 1846, letter to Kearny. President's Message of 1846, 7.

41. Marcy's June 3, 1846, letter to Kearny further emphasized the necessity of getting to California before the winter storms so that the Sierra Madres would be passable. President's Message of 1846, 5–6.

42. In the June 3 letter, Marcy promised Kearny the promotion, and he later made good on that promise, as shown by subsequent communications from Marcy to "General Kearny." President's Message of 1846, 5–6, 13.

43. Kearny made this claim in an August 22, 1846, letter to Marcy. President's Message of 1846, 21.

44. Bancroft, *History of the Pacific States*, 416. The view that the American conquest of New Mexico was accomplished without violence largely remains dominant in both academic and popular histories. See Eisenhower, *So Far from God*, 209–10; Lamar, *The Far Southwest*, 55 (reporting that Kearny "had taken New Mexico without firing a shot") and recent tourist brochures in New Mexico (New Mexico Department of Tourism, Official 2004 Brochure, 26).

45. Durán, "'We Come as Friends,'" 43–47.

46. President's Message of 1846, 17–18, 20–21; see also Bancroft, *History of the Pacific States*, 415–16; Bauer, *The Mexican War*, 134.

47. The Americans were worried that priests might play a central role in leading resistance to the invasion, given their prominence in Mexican politics and government. In a July 9 letter, Marcy provided Kearny with a tutorial on the his-

tory of Catholic clergy in Mexican politics and, particularly, in the Mexican independence movement. President's Message of 1846, 7–9.

48. Ibid. The administration's plan for California was the same, with Marcy emphasizing "the great importance that the good will of the people towards the United States should be cultivated. This is to be done by liberal and kind treatment. They should be made to feel we come as deliverers." President's Message of 1846, 11–12.

49. Kearny explained his homage to Marcy in a September 16, 1846, letter. President's Message of 1846, 25.

50. President's Message of 1846, 5–6.

51. Ibid., 21.

52. Kearny informed Marcy of these appointments on the day he made them, September 22, 1846, but the administration in Washington did not receive them until November 23, due to the length of time it took mail to reach Washington from Santa Fe. President's Message of 1846, 26–27.

53. See Bauer, *The Mexican War*, 135; for the most detailed secondary account of the congressional inquiry, see Thomas, "A History of Military Government," 106–13.

54. For example, in a November 3, 1846, letter, Kearny was warned not to overstep his authority in California (as he had in New Mexico): "You will not, however, formally declare the province to be annexed. Permanent incorporation of the territory must depend on the government [i.e., Congress] of the United States." President's Message of 1846, 15. Kearny was again warned, in a January 1847 letter from Marcy (which Kearny likely did not receive before late February), that, in New Mexico, he had gone "beyond the line designated by the President" in promulgating laws and courts. President's Message of 1848, 13–14.

55. President's Message of 1846, 26–27.

56. Ibid., 27–73. For additional background on the 115-page Kearny Code, see Bancroft, *History of the Pacific States*, 425–26 n. 22. According to Bancroft, the Kearny Code was compiled by three soldiers: Colonel Doniphan (who was a trained lawyer), Captain Henry L. Waldo (a volunteer who was fluent in Spanish), and Willard P. Hall (who was elected to Congress while serving in the U.S.–Mexico War).

57. Thomas, "A History of Military Government."

58. Bent, Magoffin, and other merchants played significant roles in the invasion—so much so that historian Howard Lamar has labeled the American invasion of New Mexico "the conquest of merchants." Lamar, *The Far Southwest*, 52–56; see also Bancroft, *History of the Pacific States*, 409.

59. Ignacia Jaramillo was married to Jose Rafael Luna in 1829 and was widowed sometime in the 1830s. No church records show she married Bent, although they lived together and had children together (who were baptized under their mother's surname, another indication she and Bent were not married). E-mail

communication from archivist Samuel Sisneros to the author based on his review of church records at the New Mexico State Records Center and Archives, January 2007.

60. Bancroft, *History of the Pacific States*, 410, 415.

61. Marcy's communications with Kearny suggest a secret plot (warning Kearny that, if the press were to learn the facts, the administration would "disavow" any knowledge of it), perhaps an allusion to Magoffin's mission. President's Message of 1846, 5–7; see also Bancroft, *History of the Pacific States*, 411–13; Durán, "'We Come as Friends,'" 47.

62. Historian Myra Ellen Jenkins concludes that Polk's administration knew "from the beginning that the occupation [of New Mexico] must be carried out as peaceably as possible, and the inhabitants of the region so treated that a large occupying force would not need to be left behind when the main body of troops pushed on [to California]." Jenkins, "Rebellion against America," 2.

63. President's Message of 1846, 7–9.

64. Ibid.

65. Ibid.

66. Ibid., 24–25.

67. Durán, "'We Come as Friends,'" 48–49; see also Twitchell, *History of the Military Occupation*, 122.

68. *New Orleans Daily Delta*, March 5, 1847.

69. Bancroft, *History of the Pacific States*, 430 n. 25 (quoting Bent's December 26, 1846, report).

70. Twitchell, *Military Occupation of New Mexico*, 298, 314.

71. *New Orleans Daily Delta*, March 5, 1847.

72. As quoted in Horsman, *Race and Manifest Destiny*, 232.

73. *New Orleans Daily Picayune*, June 23, 1847.

74. See González, *Refusing the Favor*, 50–54; Langum, "California Women."

75. González, *Refusing the Favor*, 72–74, 113–14.

76. Cutts, *The Conquest of California*, 218–20 (quoting Bent letter of January 5, 1847).

77. As an elderly woman, Scheurich gave this account of her father's murder to L. Bradford Prince, who, in addition to considering himself a historian of New Mexico, was chief justice of the territorial supreme court and governor of the territory. (Prince's career is discussed in the next chapter.) The original statement was transcribed by Prince to retain Scheurich's colloquial pronunciation. I have adjusted the text to standard spelling and grammar. The oral statement totals two pages of typed text. It is the only surviving eyewitness account of the events, although, as noted, it was recorded many decades after the events occurred.

78. Report on Discovery of Conspiracy, 8–13.

79. Bancroft, *History of the Pacific States*, 432 n. 28.

80. Report on Discovery of Conspiracy, 8–13.

81. Lawrence Waldo was the brother of Captain Henry Waldo, who had been a member of the team that drafted the "Kearny Code." Lawrence Waldo's son eventually served as a justice of the territorial supreme court in New Mexico. Revealing his loyalties, Twitchell dedicated his book *History of the Military Occupation of the Territory of New Mexico* to Lawrence L. Waldo, whom he described as "a martyr to the march of American progress and civilization."

82. Report on Discovery of Conspiracy, 8–13.

83. *New Orleans Daily Delta*, April 7, 1847. At least one anti-war newspaper used the Taos uprising to criticize the Polk administration for sending troops prematurely to California and while leaving others behind in New Mexico spread too thin over a vast, populated region. *New York Herald*, March 18, 1847.

84. Bancroft, *History of the Pacific States*, 432. See, generally, Jenkins, "Rebellion against American Occupation"; Twitchell, *History of the Military Occupation*.

85. Cutts, *The Conquest of California*, 222–23.

86. Unless otherwise noted, I have relied on Price's official report of February 15, 1847, which was reproduced in the U.S. Congress's "Report on the Discovery of Conspiracy by Governor Bent." Price's report is in the form of a letter he wrote to the Adjutant General of the Army in Washington, D.C., and posted from "Headquarters Army in New Mexico." It begins as follows: "Sir: I have the honor to submit to you a short account of the recent revolution in this territory, and a detailed report of the operations of the forces under my command consequent upon the rebellion." The Price report was widely reprinted in the press, including in two newspapers I have examined for their coverage of these events (*New Orleans Daily Delta*, April 29, 1847, and *New York Herald*, April 21, 1847).

87. Price's men included Charles St. Vrain's company of sixty-seven volunteers, seven of whom were Spanish-surnamed. See also Bancroft, *History of the Pacific States*, 433; Tórrez, "The New Mexican 'Revolt,'" 6.

88. One newspaper described soldiers returning from New Mexico to St. Louis as looking "more like icicles of the [N]orth [P]ole than human beings." *New Orleans Daily Delta*, February 10, 1847.

89. Price reported that thirty-six of the enemy were killed. Report on Discovery, 8–13.

90. *New York Herald*, April 8, 1847; *New York Herald*, April 11, 1847.

91. *New Orleans Daily Delta*, April 6, 1847.

92. Price reported that "many of the men were frost-bitten, and all were very much jaded with the exertion necessary to travel over unbeaten roads." Report on Discovery, 8–13.

93. Tórrez, "The New Mexican 'Revolt,'" 7.

94. Garrard, *Wah-to-Yah*, 187–88.

95. Price notes, in minimalist style, only that "Tomas was shot by a private while in the guard-room" at Taos. Historian Robert Tórrez writes that Romero

was killed by "a nervous guard while allegedly trying to escape," but does not provide further documentation. Tórrez, "The New Mexican 'Revolt,'" 8.

96. *New York Herald,* April 18, 1847; Tórrez, "The New Mexican 'Revolt,'" 8; Garrard, *Wah-to-Yah,* 187.

97. Tórrez, "The New Mexican 'Revolt,'" 8.

98. Tórrez puts the number of executions resulting from trials for the January attack on Bent as between fifteen and twenty-one. Tórrez, "The New Mexican 'Revolt,'" 2. The *New Orleans Daily Delta,* an important source of coverage of the war given Louisiana's relative proximity to Mexico, reported at various times that eleven or twelve men were executed. *New Orleans Daily Delta,* May 26, 1847; *New Orleans Daily Delta,* June 11, 1847.

99. Frank Blair, the man whom Kearny had appointed "U.S. District Attorney" for New Mexico, was the prosecutor. He reported seeking indictments against seventy-nine native men on charges of Bent's murder and treason, twenty-nine of whom were jailed and tried in Santa Fe and fifty of whom were jailed and tried in Taos. President's Message, 1848, 26–27.

100. The local *alcaldes* of the Spanish-Mexican system can be thought of as akin to local justices of the peace in the Anglo-American system. And, indeed, in "the Kearny Code" of laws, the Spanish word *alcalde* was translated as "justice of the peace." Rev. N.M. Stat. 126, chap. XXI, §14 (1865); see also Lamar, *The Far Southwest,* 85 (noting that most of Kearny's justice of the peace appointments were *alcaldes* previously serving under Mexican authority). Both historically performed a diverse range of duties: adjudicating criminal and civil cases; handling formal claims as well as informal disputes among neighbors and family members; playing leadership roles such as forming militias and overseeing elections. On the historic role of justices of the peace in the United States, see Steinberg, *The Transformation of Criminal Justice,* 254, n. 13; Kadish, ed., *Encyclopedia of Crime and Justice,* 414–15; Wunder, *Inferior Courts, Superior Justice,* xv, 9. Historian Howard Lamar describes the New Mexico *alcaldes* as acting "as a justice of the peace, a mayor, a probate judge, and sometimes as a militia captain." Lamar, *The Far Southwest,* 31. For additional descriptions of the *alcalde* system, see González, *Refusing the Favor,* 19–27, 36–37; Gutiérrez, *When Jesus Came,* 100; Reichard, "'Justice Is God's Law.'"

101. Reichard, "'Justice Is God's Law,'" 8.

102. When a villager took a complaint to the *alcalde,* the latter called witnesses immediately and crafted a resolution on the spot. The perceived informality and case-by-case settlement of disputes engendered disdain among Euro-American merchants, who prior to the war with Mexico relied on these courts to settle commercial disputes in New Mexico and California. Gregg, *Commerce of the Prairies,* 159, 164–65. See also, generally, Langum, *Law and Community.* Regarding Gregg's diary of his days in northern Mexico as a trader, it is difficult to draw unbiased assessments of the *alcalde* system given his frequent losses in the forum, his lan-

guage and other cultural barriers, and his racism toward Mexicans (which is readily apparent in his diary). Writing more than a century later, Lamar's assessment was similarly biased; he described merchant Charles Bent (later appointed civil governor by Kearny) as being wary of *alcalde* courts because "there was no jury system nor any common law to use as a guide in criminal or property disputes. Appeals to the governor faced the same hazards of family influence and personal caprice" (citing an 1845 note by Bent to himself). Lamar, *The Far Southwest*, 46.

103. As Lawrence Friedman reminds us in his epic history of American criminal justice, we must remain mindful of the myriad diversity of the criminal courts, which not only varied from state to state, but also according to the nature of the crime and the level of court. At the same time, "The roles of judge and jury, the rhythm of witness and cross-examination—these have remained fundamentally unaltered. There were, no doubt, some local variations, local trial customs, local differences in codes of criminal procedure, nuances of selecting and charging a jury, and in carrying on a trial. The details tend to be, as we said, obscure." Friedman, *Crime and Punishment*, 235–37.

104. For example, in New York County in 1900, an average of 300 people were indicted monthly by the grand jury of 23 men. Over the course of that year, the 12 grand juries returned indictments on 3,674 cases out of 4,473 people arrested. Friedman, *Crime and Punishment*, 242.

105. For example, under a later-enacted New Mexico statute, it was the jury's prerogative to assess punishment after it reached a guilty verdict (sometimes choosing from among legislatively enacted options). Revised N.M. Stat. Chap. LII, §14, 1865.

106. Friedman, *Crime and Punishment*, 242 (discussing petit jurors specifically). In my research on San Miguel County, New Mexico, some thirty years after the initial American occupation, however, I found that Mexican jurors outnumbered Euro-American jurors four to one; Mexican men were 80 percent of grand jurors and 86 percent of petit jurors. Wealthier Mexicans were more likely to serve as grand jurors, while laborers served regularly on petit juries as a form of political patronage. Gómez, "Race, Colonialism and Criminal Law," 1165–66, 1168–71. Preliminary research on two other New Mexico counties—Taos and Doña Ana—shows that Mexican men dominated grand and petit juries in the 1860s and 1870s.

107. Friedman, *Crime and Punishment*, 245. No state provided indigent defendants with free lawyers until the late nineteenth century. Ibid.

108. Friedman and Percival, *The Roots of Justice*, 40.

109. Friedman, *Crime and Punishment*, 245. In one New Mexico jurisdiction in the 1880s, the length of trials, from jury selection to a jury verdict, ranged from a few hours to several days. See, generally, Gómez, "Race, Colonialism and Criminal Law."

110. Friedman, *Crime and Punishment*, 256. Although we do not have any

systematic data from which to draw conclusions, the limited data on nineteenth-century appeals tells us that appellate courts were much more likely to reverse convictions than they are today. For example, in 1893 the Texas appellate court reversed 61 cases and affirmed 110 convictions. Friedman, *Crime and Punishment*, 257.

111. Friedman, *Crime and Punishment*, 248–49; see also ibid., 245–47.

112. *Santa Fe Weekly Press*, November 26, 1870.

113. Grassham, "Charles H. Beaubien."

114. Lamar, *The Far Southwest*, 57.

115. One of the names is illegible, making it unclear how many Spanish-surnamed jurors there were. The Spanish-surnamed grand jurors included surnames still common in northern New Mexico: Ortíz, Martínez, Sánchez, Martin, Vigil, Cordova, Romero, Medina, and Váldez. One of the grand jurors was the brother of Father Antonio José Martínez, one of the most influential men in the region (about whom we will hear more in later chapters). Weber, *On the Edge of Empire*, 77.

116. Garrard, *Wah-to-Yah*, 181.

117. Ibid.

118. Under the legal theory of accomplice liability, one is liable for a crime when one assists the person who actually commits the crime. The liability of the accomplice is "derivative in nature," stemming from the legal responsibility of the person who committed the offense. Dressler, *Understanding Criminal Law*, 460. The problem in the Taos trials for the prosecutor seeking to apply this crime theory to Bent's murder is that he probably did not know who actually killed Bent.

119. In court records, the presiding judge and clerk referred to these defendants as "the five Indians." Since Pueblo Indians had long been baptized with Spanish names, it is not possible to know which defendants were Taos Pueblo or Mexican, unless there were specific references such as this in the record.

120. See, generally, Cheetham, "The First Term of the American Court."

121. Garrard, *Wah-To-Yah*, 172.

122. Cheetham, "The First Term of the American Court," 24.

123. Garrard, *Wah-To-Yah*, 172.

124. Thomas, "A History of Military Government," 122.

125. President's Message of 1848.

126. Tórrez, "The New Mexican 'Revolt,'" 10.

127. Sentence of Antonio Maria Trujillo. History File #166, Taos Treason File, New Mexico State Records Center and Archives; see also Tórrez, "The New Mexican 'Revolt,'" 9.

128. See President's Message of 1848.

129. Tórrez, "The New Mexican 'Revolt,'" 10.

130. President's Message of 1848, 24–25.

131. Ibid., 31–33; see also *New Orleans Daily Delta*, June 11, 1847.

132. For a sampling of congressional criticism, see Thomas, "A History of Military Government," 106–12.

133. *Fleming v. Page*, 50 U.S. 603 (1850).

134. Ibid., 615–616 (emphasis added).

135. Kettner, *The Development of American Citizenship*, 181.

136. Tórrez, "Crime and Punishment," 3.

137. Conversation with Gloria Cordova on August 2, 2006. Cordova is an eighth-generation descendant of Juan Antonio Abán Cordova, who participated in the rebellion against the Americans.

138. The leading text on New Mexico's path from territorial status to statehood is Larson, *New Mexico's Quest for Statehood*.

139. See Horsman, *Race and Manifest Destiny*, 11–12.

140. For example, Horsman reports that "Secretary of State James Buchanan had a particularly low opinion of Mexican character and talents and for much of the war balked at the idea of annexing territory that contained any large numbers of Mexicans." Horsman, *Race and Manifest Destiny*, 232; see also Merk, *Manifest Destiny*, 151–52 (quoting editorials in the *Louisville Democrat* and the *Washington Union*).

141. As quoted Horsman, *Race and Manifest Destiny*, 241.

142. Griswold del Castillo, *The Treaty of Guadalupe Hidalgo*, 44. Under Article II, Section 2 of the U.S. Constitution, the President is authorized to negotiate treaties with foreign nations; treaties must then be approved by two-thirds or more of the Senate; after Senate approval, the President ratifies treaties. Government Accountability Office Report, 29 n. 7.

143. Texas senator Sam Houston succeeded in moving the Senate to conduct its deliberations of the Treaty in secret. Griswold del Castillo, *The Treaty of Guadalupe Hidalgo*, 44–46.

144. The boundary-setting function of the treaty was important because, up until this point, Mexico and the United States had disputed Texas's southern boundary. Larson, *New Mexico's Quest for Statehood*, 46.

145. Griswold del Castillo, *The Treaty of Guadalupe Hidalgo*, 46–53.

146. As originally proposed, Article IX read, in part: "The Mexicans [in the ceded territory] . . . shall be incorporated into the Union of the United States *as soon as possible.* . . . With respect to political rights, their condition shall be on an equality with that of the inhabitants of the other territories of the United States." Griswold del Castillo, *The Treaty of Guadalupe Hidalgo*, 46 (emphasis added).

147. Ibid. (emphasis added).

148. Ibid., 50 (quoting a pamphlet entitled "Observations on the Treaty of Guadalupe Hidalgo," authored by Mexican senator Manuel Crescencio Rejón, who led the opposition to ratification). In the end, the Mexicans ratified the treaty by a vote of fifty-one to thirty-five in the lower chamber and thirty-three to four in the upper chamber. Ibid., 53.

149. Ibid., 33, 62–72.

150. Historian Samuel Sisneros has done the most thorough research to date. See Sisneros, "Los Emigrantes Nuevomexicanos"; see also Bancroft, *History of the Pacific States*, 472; Twitchell, *History of the Military Occupation*, 290.

151. Griswold del Castillo estimates that two thousand Mexican men took this route, but he does not provide sources for his conclusion. Griswold del Castillo, *The Treaty of Guadalupe Hidalgo*, 65. Although figures are difficult to come by, it appears that many Mexicans living in New Mexico exercised this option. Twitchell reports that "a large number" took this option and that that number included "many names of prominent men." Twitchell, *History of the Military Occupation*, 65.

152. Twitchell, *History of the Military Occupation*, 291 n. 216; see also Davis, *El Gringo*, 331–32.

153. For a discussion of the relationship between state and federal citizenship generally, see Kettner, *The Development of American Citizenship*, 224 (noting that the Constitution's framers "failed to grapple with the relationship of state and national citizenship").

154. *American Insurance Company v. 356 Bales of Cotton*, 26 U.S. 511, 542 (1828).

155. *People v. De La Guerra*, 40 Cal. 311 (1870).

156. Act of Sept. 9, 1850, Ch. 49, 9 U.S. Statutes 446 (1850).

157. Larson, *New Mexico's Quest for Statehood*, 56.

158. As historian Howard Lamar has noted, the congressional act establishing New Mexico as a territory "was an internal colonial system, a device for eventual self-government, a guarantor of property, and a bill of rights rolled into one act." Lamar, *The Far Southwest*, 98.

159. See, generally, Ramirez, "The Hispanic Political Elite."

160. For analyses that adopt a model of annexation rather than colonialism, see Gonzáles, "Inverted Subnationalism"; Montejano, *Anglos and Mexicans*. These models are not mutually exclusive, but rather probably operated together to explain the region's development under American rule.

Notes to Chapter 2

1. According to some sources, Estevan (sometimes spelled Esteban) spoke six indigenous languages. *The First Immigrants, From Slave to Explorer*, permanent exhibition at the Arab American National Museum, Dearborn, Michigan.

2. Accounts written by the Spanish explorers consistently refer to Estevan by first name only, suggesting that his Spanish contemporaries viewed him as racially subordinate. In some accounts, the diminutive of Estevan (Estevanico) was

used, connoting , his low social status. See Gutiérrez, *When Jesus Came*, 39–40; Prince, *A Concise History*, 59–65; Bancroft, *History of the Pacific States*, 27–34.

3. Sando, *Pueblo Nations*, 50.

4. Ibid., 51–53.

5. Gutiérrez, *When Jesus Came*, 39–40. At least one Zuni oral history account is quite similar to the Spanish story of Estevan's death. Ilahiane, "Estevan De Dorantes," 6.

6. Ilahiane, "Estevan De Dorantes," 7.

7. Ibid., 2.

8. Menchaca, *Recovering History*, 70.

9. Ibid., 43, 71–72.

10. *The First Immigrants, From Slave to Explorer*, permanent exhibition at the Arab American National Museum, Dearborn, Michigan.

11. Ibid.

12. Ilahiane, "Estevan De Dorantes," 8.

13. Ibid., 2–3, 9.

14. Ibid., 3.

15. Menchaca, *Recovering History*, 42–43 (noting the difficulty of knowing the precise number of African slaves, since the official census varied according to the age and health of slaves [e.g., healthy children were counted as one-quarter of a person, and so on]).

16. Gutiérrez, *When Jesus Came*, 44.

17. Gutiérrez reports that, in the winter of 1540 (the Spaniards' first in New Mexico), "Coronado's troops extracted blankets and corn from the Tiguex pueblos by force . . . satisfied their lust with Indian women," executed a hundred warriors, and massacred hundreds more. Ibid., 45.

18. Alonso, *Thread of Blood*, 53 (emphasis added).

19. Ibid.

20. Menchaca, *Recovering History*, 61.

21. Knight, "Racism, Revolution, and Indigenismo," 72.

22. Alonso, *Thread of Blood*, 67; Wade, *Blackness and Race Mixture*, 10–11, 297; White, "*It's Your Misfortune*," 14.

23. Alonso, *Thread of Blood*, 65–67; Kraemer, "Dynamic Ethnicity," 96; Menchaca, *Recovering History*, 66.

24. Alonso, *Thread of Blood*, 54.

25. Menchaca, *Recovering History*, 66.

26. Legal scholars Devon Carbado and Mitu Gulati define "identity performance" as "the choices that person makes about how to present her difference" (i.e., racial difference). Carbado and Gulati, "The Fifth Black Woman," 701; see also Carbado and Gulati, "Working Identity." See, generally, Butler, *Bodies That Matter*. The larger point is that racial identity is not (and has not been histori-

cally) merely about a person's membership in a particular, ascribed category, but also about how a person chooses to present his or her racial identity, which can vary in different contexts.

27. Weber, ed., *Foreigners in Their Native Land*, 33–35 ("First Census of Los Angeles, 1781").

28. Gutiérrez, *When Jesus Came*, 103.

29. Bancroft, *History of the Pacific States* 36; Prince, *A Concise History*, 67.

30. Gutiérrez, *When Jesus Came*, 103.

31. Ibid.

32. See ibid., 103 (noting that "nearly 90 percent of the population that was not wholly Indian was native born in New Mexico").

33. Historian José Antonio Esquibel describes the period from 1693 to 1720 as "the formative era of New Mexico's [Spanish] colonial society." Esquibel, "The Formative Era," 64–65.

34. Rodríguez, *The Matachines Dance*, 161 n. 2; see also Gutiérrez, *When Jesus Came*, 130–40. All but one Pueblo community (Isleta) participated in the revolt.

35. Esquibel, "The Formative Era," 65.

36. Ibid., 66–67.

37. Ibid., 68–76.

38. Ibid., 68–69.

39. My analysis draws heavily from Gutiérrez, although he puts *genízaros* at the bottom of the hierarchy. Gutiérrez, *When Jesus Came*, 148–49.

40. Ebright and Hendricks define *genízaros* broadly to include "as the primary markers of Genízaro status the elements of servitude or captivity and Indian blood. Such a definition includes nomadic Indians who lost their tribal identity, spent time as captives and/or servants, and who were living on the margins of Spanish society." Ebright and Hendricks, *Witches of Abiquiu*, 4; see also Gutiérrez, *When Jesus Came*, 149–51, 154.

41. Kraemer, "Dynamic Ethnicity," 96.

42. The same census reported nearly 7,300 Pueblo Indians living in eighteen communities. Ibid., 90.

43. Recent studies of Hispanics in Colorado's San Luis Valley—a region settled by Mexican Americans from northern New Mexico in the mid-1800s and whose current Hispanic residents descend almost exclusively from those early settlers—show conclusively that this population derived historically from mating between indigenous females and European males. One study concluded that, based on DNA variation, "the Hispanic population of the San Luis Valley today more closely resembles an Amerindian population . . . than it does a European population. Over 85 percent of San Luis Valley Hispanics tested possess pure Amerindian/Asian haplotypes." Merriweather et al., "Mitochondrial versus Nuclear Admixture Estimates," 157; see also Bonilla et al., "Admixture in the Hispanics of the San Luis Valley."

44. Ibid.

45. Esquibel, "The Formative Era," 66; see also Kraemer, "Dynamic Ethnicity," 86.

46. Sánchez, *Telling Identities*, 56–58.

47. Menchaca, *Recovering History*, 158.

48. For a summary, see ibid., 158–63.

49. Ortiz, *The Pueblo Indians of North America*, 80; see also Hall and Weber, "Mexican Liberals," 19.

50. Sando, *Pueblo Nations*, 83.

51. Ortiz, *The Pueblo Indians of North America*, 80.

52. See, generally, Weber, ed., *Foreigners in Their Native Land*, 88–90; Zoraida Vázquez, *México al Tiempo de su Guerra con los Estados Unidos*, 29–31.

53. White, *"It's Your Misfortune,"* 65.

54. Historian Deena J. González has done the most comprehensive research to date on the aggregate trends of intermarriage between Mexican females and Euro-American males. She found that no more than 2 percent of Mexican women were married to Euro-American men in Santa Fe in 1850 and 1870. She concludes that historians have tended to exaggerate the extent of such intermarriage. González, *Refusing the Favor*, 72–74, 113–14; see also Deutsch, *No Separate Refuge*.

55. Here I am using "Anglo-American" to refer, not strictly to Americans of British descent, but more generally to the racial legacy of the early British colonists in North America. I also use it to emphasize the nineteenth-century development of Anglo-Saxon race consciousness as the foundation for American white supremacy. See, generally, Horsman, *Race and Manifest Destiny*.

56. On the history of Anglo-American contact with Indians, see, generally, Newton, *Cohen's Handbook*, 6–84; Zinn, *A People's History*; see also Cornell and Hartmann, *Ethnicity and Race*, 110; Fredrickson, *Racism*, 68–69.

57. Perea et al., *Race and Races*, 181.

58. Ibid., 184.

59. Ibid., 176.

60. Zinn, *A People's History*, 23.

61. Fredrickson, *Racism*, 80–81; see also Bell, *Race, Racism and American Law*, 33.

62. Horsman, *Race and Manifest Destiny*, 230.

63. See, for example, Horsman, *Race and Manifest Destiny*, 215.

64. Merk, *Manifest Destiny*, 38–39.

65. Foley, *The White Scourge*, 5 (emphasis added).

66. For analyses of the genre of travel literature as perpetuating stereotypes of Mexicans, see González, *Refusing the Favor*, 44–65; see also, generally, Paredes, "The Mexican Image."

67. See, generally, Streeby, "American Sensations."

68. Davis, *El Gringo*, 17.
69. Ibid., 22, 28, 114–15.
70. Ibid., 157–58.
71. Ibid., 215–16.
72. Ibid., 316, 325.
73. Ibid., 217.
74. Ibid., 221. This and other contemporary accounts by Euro-American men are the source of an enduring stereotype of Latinas as innately oversexed and sexually promiscuous.
75. I do not invoke the word "progressive" to imply that Prince's views were liberal or consensual on their own terms, although they were relative to the dominant racial narrative. Nor is my use of the term in any way connected with the Progressive Era of the early twentieth century.
76. For a general discussion of "dominant" racial theories and how they change, see Omi and Winant, *Racial Formation*, 11.
77. Some analyses place Indians higher than Mexican Americans in New Mexico's post–World War II racial hierarchy. Anthropologist Sylvia Rodríguez describes "'the tri-ethnic trap'—a situation in which Hispanos, unable to advance beyond clear-cut secondary economic status and faced with the steady and irrevocable loss of their traditional land base, must abide by a tourism-engendered Anglo glorification of Indian culture, as well as the federal protection and even restoration of Indian lands, sometimes at the expense of Hispano ownership." Rodriguez, "Land, Water and Ethnic Identity," 321; see also Masco, *Nuclear Borderlands*, 187.
78. In a May 1879 article, all Indians are entirely omitted in the description of New Mexico's population. In a November 1876 article, the *New York Times* described the population in these terms: "They are about seven parts Spanish, more familiarly known as 'greasers' to two parts civilized Indian and one part American."
79. Mexicans in New Mexico were portrayed as lazy, resistant to progress, and generally unwilling to do the work required to fully exploit the region's agricultural, mining, and ranching potential. *New York Times*, November 7, 1876; May 19, 1879.
80. For example, a front-page article in 1876 began with the sentence, "The people of New Mexico do not blend well," and continued by describing the conflict between "greasers" and "Americans." *New York Times*, November 7, 1876.
81. Another *New York Times* editor concluded that "New-Mexico can wait [for admission to the Union]—not merely until [Congress reconvenes], but until it has population enough to constitute a fairly large and intelligent town meeting." *New York Times*, June 29, 1876.
82. "The Mexicans predominating in the population 10 to 1, *the minority, rep-*

resented by the Americans or whites, naturally falls in with the customs of the majority in religious observances." *New York Times,* May 19, 1879 (emphasis added).

83. Ibid.

84. *New York Times,* November 7, 1876.

85. Ibid.

86. For examples, see *New York Times,* January 26 and February 6, 1882; July 8, 1885. American Studies scholar Gabriel Meléndez analyzes an 1899 article in the *Atlantic Monthly* that was titled, simply, "The Greaser," concluding that "the modern American spirit would be likely to predicate the downfall of the Greaser, upon one fact, that he is lacking in 'enterprise.'" Melendez, *So All Is Not Lost,* 43–44. "Greaser" also was used regularly, if less frequently, by the New Mexico press, particularly in the southeastern part of the territory. In 1906, for example, the *Hagerman* (New Mexico) *Messenger* wrote that "the greaser is doomed; he is too lazy to keep up; and smells too badly to be endured." Stratton, *The Territorial Press,* 132.

87. For a description of the law, see Haney López, *White by Law,* 145.

88. *New York Times,* January 26, 1882 (emphasis in original).

89. Ibid.

90. Ibid.

91. *New York Times,* February 28, 1882.

92. See, generally, McWilliams, *North from Mexico;* Montgomery, *The Spanish Redemption.*

93. Prince, *A Concise History,* 20.

94. Prince had previously rejected President Hayes's offer of the governorship of the Idaho Territory. Walter, "Ten Years After," 372.

95. Ibid.

96. Prince reported this tally of cases in his letter of resignation to President Arthur, May 9, 1882.

97. Prince showed his political ambitions early, resigning his judgeship in 1882 to run unsuccessfully for election to be New Mexico's nonvoting delegate to Congress, arguably the most important elected position in the territory.

98. Larson, *New Mexico's Quest for Statehood,* 144.

99. Walter, "Ten Years After," 375.

100. A friend of the Princes for nearly twenty-five years, Paul Walter, would later write that their parties were New Mexico's high society and remark that a wide range of New Mexicans attended these soirees, "including even Indians." Ibid., 374.

101. Gómez, "Race, Colonialism and Criminal Law," 1186.

102. *Territory v. Romine,* 3 NM 114 (1881).

103. *Lyles v. Texas,* 41 Tex. 172 (1874).

104. *Territory v. Romine,* 3 NM 114, 123 (1881).

105. Ibid.

106. New Mexico Territory had to "look" like states in other respects, as well, including having railroads, public buildings, mining, agricultural cultivation, and institutions such as a university, a penitentiary, and an insane asylum—all of which, Prince noted, had been established in the territory by 1890. Prince, "Claims to Statehood," 348, 350.

107. Ibid., 346.

108. Walter, "Ten Years After," 373.

109. Ibid., 374.

110. Prince, *Historical Sketches of New Mexico*, 347.

111. Stephen Elkins, a Euro-American attorney who was then serving as New Mexico's nonvoting delegate to Congress, had made a similar argument in a speech to Congress in May 1874. Summarizing his argument, Robert Larson said, "Elkins made full use of the historical argument that New Mexico was entitled to admission 'by reason of the promises and assurances made by our Government,' previous to the ratification of the Treaty of Guadalupe Hidalgo" (a reference to Kearny's speeches on the eve of the American occupation). Larson, *New Mexico's Quest for Statehood*, 117. In 1889, New Mexico was represented by Antonio Joseph as its delegate, who again made the argument that the history of the war and the Treaty of Guadalupe Hidalgo obligated Congress to advance New Mexico to statehood. Ibid., 154.

112. Prince, *Historical Sketches of New Mexico*, 349.

113. Ibid.

114. Ibid., 351.

115. Ibid.

116. Stratton, *The Territorial Press*, 129; see also ibid., 111.

117. Ibid., 132.

118. Ibid.

119. For discussions of the role of the Santa Fe Ring—which included Prince and Catron as core members—in advocating for statehood, see Durán, "We Come as Friends," 88; Lamar, *The Far Southwest*, 121–46; Larson, *New Mexico's Quest for Statehood*, 142–46.

120. Larson, *New Mexico's Quest for Statehood*, 145 (quoting an 1896 letter written by Catron).

121. Ibid., 143.

122. In addition, during this time several bills were introduced that concerned New Mexico statehood, some of which aroused anti-Mexican sentiment. For example, in 1889, when New Mexico was included in an omnibus statehood bill with Washington, Montana, and South Dakota, several newspapers responded by attacking New Mexico's Mexican population. Ibid., 148. According to the *Chicago Tribune*, New Mexico's people were "not American, but 'Greaser,' persons ignorant of our laws, manners, customs, language, and institutions" who were "grossly illit-

erate and superstitious." Prince responded to press reports such as these, as well as to a congressional report very critical of the New Mexican population. Ibid., 151.

123. See ibid., 117, 332.

124. According to Larson, only the "occasional article" in the national press said something favorable about New Mexico, and then it was "usually brief and unenthusiastic." Ibid., 131.

125. Ibid., 123–24.

126. Ibid., 124 (quoting a March 3, 1875 article). The *Cincinnati Commercial* noted disapprovingly in the same article that court proceedings were conducted in English in only two of fourteen counties. Ibid.

127. Ibid., 125.

128. Ibid., 119.

129. Ibid., 126.

130. Ibid.

131. Ibid., 128, 130.

132. *New York Times,* November 7, 1876.

133. Ibid. (emphasis added).

134. *New York Times,* May 19, 1876.

135. Ibid.

136. For a discussion of Beveridge's role as leader of the opposition to New Mexico statehood, see Larson, *New Mexico's Quest for Statehood,* 207–10; see also Bowers, *Beveridge and the Progressive Era,* 182, 193–97.

137. Weston, *Racism in U.S. Imperialism,* 48 (quoting a 1901 Senate speech by Beveridge). Anthropologist and legal scholar Mark Weiner has drawn similar conclusions about Beveridge in a different context: "American imperialist policy, for Beveridge, thus arose 'not from necessity, but from the irresistible impulse, from instinct, from racial and unwritten laws inherited from our forefathers.'" Weiner, *Americans without Law,* 66 (quoting Beveridge).

138. Weiner, *Americans without Law,* 51 (quoting a 1900 Senate speech by Beveridge).

139. Larson, *New Mexico's Quest for Statehood,* 207.

140. Ibid., 68 (quoting a campaign speech by Beveridge). Bowers's biography celebrates Beveridge as the leading national proponent for imperialism: in Beveridge, he concludes, "Imperialism, defiant, unafraid, had found a voice." Ibid., 70. "He alone, among Republican orators, took imperialism as his theme [and] it was his first speech in the Senate on our Philippine policy that made him a national figure." Ibid., v–vi.

141. Summarizing Beveridge's conclusions about the Phillipines, Bowers reports: "He had convinced himself . . . that the [Filipino] people were unfit for self-government, that their country was enormously rich with resources scarcely touched because of the lack of capital; that commerce would thrive under a stable government; that the climate was fit for American occupation." Ibid., 109.

142. Weston, *Racism in U.S. Imperialism,* 47 (quoting a 1901 article written by Beveridge).

143. Larson also notes Beveridge's close ties to President Roosevelt as a factor in his assumption of the committee chairmanship. Larson, *New Mexico's Quest for Statehood,* 207.

144. The House passed the bill on May 9, 1902.

145. Bowers, *Beveridge and the Progressive Era,* 197.

146. Bowers reports that, prior to undertaking the hearings, Beveridge had tried to line up witnesses calculated to interest Eastern newspaper editors—professors from Columbia, Yale, and Harvard who would testify about New Mexico's poor agricultural potential, and novelists and artists who would interest "the public in the fight." Ibid., 193.

147. Larson, *New Mexico's Quest for Statehood,* 209–13 (describing Beveridge's direct communication with editors of the *Saturday Evening Post, Washington Times, Outlook,* and *Review of Reviews*). Moreover, there is evidence that Beveridge got the idea for the whistle-stop from anti-statehood newspapermen. Ibid., 209.

148. On a fourteen-day tour, the subcommittee held hearings in three Oklahoma cities (over two days), two Arizona cities, and five New Mexico towns (over the course of nine days in the territory).

149. See "New Statehood Bill"; see also Larson, *New Mexico's Quest for Statehood,* 213.

150. In Las Vegas, thirteen of the twenty witnesses had Spanish surnames; in Santa Fe, twelve of eighteen witnesses had Spanish surnames. "New Statehood Bill," 309 (Index of Witnesses).

151. The 225-page report was followed by an additional 100 pages of appendices, including lists of jurors and other documents submitted by district court clerks—documents Beveridge relied on to conclude that Mexican Americans dominated New Mexico's legal system. For example, "Exhibit H" consisted of a series of form documents used in the justice of the peace courts, all written in Spanish. "New Statehood Bill," Exhibit H. The five index topics (listed in order from highest to lowest number of witnesses testifying) were the following: "Census—language and racial division" (twenty-one witnesses); "Population, racial division and language" (sixteen witnesses); "United States courts—language, crimes, and interpreters" (twelve witnesses); "Petty courts (justice of the peace and police)—language used, crimes charged, etc." (twelve witnesses); "Newspapers (Spanish and English)" (nine witnesses). A total of seventy witnesses testified in the hearings, with only thirty-five persons testifying about topics that did not include race or language. These topics were the following: "Schools" (fifteen witnesses); "General statements—occupation, resources, development" (ten witnesses); "County and municipal government offices" (six witnesses); "Irrigation"

(three witnesses); "Banks" (one witness). At least two of these topics—schools and government offices—involved questioning witnesses about racial demographics and language usage, suggesting that these themes were even more pervasive than this analysis suggests. "New Statehood Bill" (Index of Topics).

152. Larson, *New Mexico's Quest*, 211–212, 217.

153. In his history of the statehood fight, Robert Larson calls Quay "a shrewd and unscrupulous politician" and points to earlier charges of abuse of his position to further his financial holdings in sugar stocks. Larson, *New Mexico's Quest for Statehood*, 208.

154. Ibid., 213 (quoting a 1902 letter from Beveridge to a newspaper editor). See also Bowers, *Beveridge and the Progressive Era*, 182, 193.

155. Larson, *New Mexico's Quest for Statehood*, 213.

156. Bowers's celebratory biography clearly takes this view. See, generally, Bowers, *Beveridge and the Progressive Era*. The portrayal of Beveridge as an anti-corruption reformer is prevalent, though less central, in Larson's study. See, generally, Larson, *New Mexico's Quest for Statehood*.

157. Bowers, *Beveridge and the Progressive Era*, 194 (quoting a letter written by Beveridge, November 29, 1902); see also Larson, *New Mexico's Quest for Statehood*, 214–15.

158. See Larson, *New Mexico's Quest for Statehood*, 141–42 (citing Democratic governor Edmund G. Ross's 1885 essay on New Mexico politics).

159. For a general discussion that does not focus on race, see Melzer, "New Mexico in Caricature."

160. See also ibid., 340.

161. Bowers, *Beveridge and the Progressive Era*, 217 (quoting a 1905 Senate speech).

162. Melzer, "New Mexico in Caricature," 345.

163. Larson, *New Mexico's Quest for Statehood*, 267.

164. See ibid., 267–68; see also Melzer, "New Mexico in Caricature," 354.

165. Larson, *New Mexico's Quest for Statehood*, 279.

166. Ibid., 296.

167. For an analysis that links Prince's racial ideology to a concerted effort to draw tourists and immigrants to New Mexico, see Nieto-Phillips, *The Language of Blood*, 163–65.

168. Rodríguez, "Tourism, Whiteness, and the Vanishing Anglo," 196. Whereas Rodríguez traces the tricultural harmony myth to the New Deal period, I have argued here that its origins are in the late nineteenth century.

169. Sylvia Rodríguez has noted the dynamic in contemporary race relations in Taos: "While racism as an issue has surfaced as such during the past two decades, there is nevertheless a strong taboo against discussing it openly in public or ethnically mixed company, although thinly veiled allusions and pointed insin-

uations are often made." Rodriguez, "Land, Water, and Ethnic Identity in Taos," 358.

170. Stratton, *The Territorial Press*, 117.

171. Larson, *New Mexico's Quest for Statehood*, 1.

NOTES TO CHAPTER 3

1. Prince, *A Concise History*, 95.

2. Ortiz, "The Pueblo Revolt," 50.

3. There were significant differences within each strata, of course, but here my focus is race, rather than status, class, or other differences.

4. A contemporary scholar contends, "Because Mexico had recognized Pueblo Indians as citizens, it follows that under the Treaty of Guadalupe Hidalgo, the Pueblo Indians became citizens of the United States." Newton, *Cohen's Handbook*, 322.

5. Merry, *Colonizing Hawaii*, 12.

6. Most scholars trace the gap between Mexican Americans' legal status as white and their social status as non-white to the post–World War II period, but I argue here that it is rooted in the mid-nineteenth-century conquest of Mexico. See Gross, "Texas Mexicans and the Politics of Whiteness"; Haney López, "Retaining Race"; Martínez, "The Legal Construction of Race"; Martínez, "Legal Indeterminacy, Judicial Discretion"; Sheridan, "Another White Race"; Wilson, "Brown over 'Other White.'"

7. Gómez, "Race, Colonialism and Criminal Law," 1143–44.

8. On the history of Mexican Americans in Las Vegas, see generally Arellano, "Through Thick and Thin."

9. As late as 1880, thirty-four years after the American occupation, no county had more than two thousand Euro-American residents, and many had only a few Euro-American residents. Using census data, I have estimated that the proportion of Euro-Americans in New Mexico counties in the late nineteenth-century ranged from a low of 3 percent (in Valencia County) to a high of 57 percent (in Grant County, a mining district). Since the census counted Mexican Americans as "white" at this time, there is no official tally of Euro-Americans and Mexican Americans. I used census data and other data to estimate the figures.

10. For example, in my research on nineteenth-century court proceedings in Doña Ana, San Miguel, and Taos counties from the 1850s to the 1880s, I encountered no more than a handful of Mexican American lawyers who practiced in the territorial courts. In the almost seventy-year period between the end of the war with Mexico and when New Mexico became a state, six hundred lawyers practiced in New Mexico; among these, Euro-American men outnumbered Mexican

American men five to one. Reichard, "Paternalism, Ethnicity, and the Professionalization of the Bar in Territorial New Mexico," 10.

11. Williams, "Dependency Formations," 157–60.

12. Ibid.

13. The first Mexican American generation with a sizable bilingual segment came of age in the 1880s and 1890s—the same generation that gave birth to Mexican American literary and press expression in New Mexico. See Meléndez, *So All Is Not Lost;* Meyer, *Speaking for Themselves.* In addition, several Mexican American witnesses at the 1902 hearings of the Senate Committee on Territories (the so-called Beveridge Committee) were born in the late 1850s and had learned English as young adults (Enrique Armijo, school principal; Enrique H. Salazar, newspaper editor), whereas justice of the peace Jesus María Tafolla, who was born in 1837, spoke no English. "New Statehood Bill." See also Gómez, "Race, Colonialism and Criminal Law," 114 n. 31.

14. On the role of language in anti-Mexican racism, see, generally, Perea, "Demography and Distrust," 269; see also Delgado and Stefancic, eds., *The Latino Condition,* 557–624.

15. In using the phrase "psychological inducement," I am borrowing from sociologist W. E. B. Du Bois's concept of "the psychological wages of whiteness." In his monumental study *Black Reconstruction in America,* Du Bois argued that white workers earned, in effect, "a sort of public and psychological wage" in the form of "public deference and titles of courtesy because they were white," which proved a palatable substitute for wages that had been undercut by the reliance on black labor made cheaper because of racial discrimination. Du Bois, *Black Reconstruction in America,* 701; see also Roediger, *The Wages of Whiteness.*

16. In the 1849 U.S.-led campaign against the Navajos, for instance, six different Pueblos (Cochiti, Jemez, San Felipe, Santa Ana, Santo Domingo, and Zia) contributed between five and fourteen volunteers to the Pueblo Militia. McNitt, ed., *Navaho Expedition,* lxxix.

17. Alfonso Ortiz, "The Pueblo Revolt," 50.

18. I do not intend to overstate the extent to which multiple, diverse Pueblo communities resembled Mexican village society in the region. I agree with Hall and Weber that "the two societies coexisted but were separate in many ways. Since 1598, when Spanish-Mexicans first began to settle among them, the Pueblos had borrowed new kinds of animals, foods, technology, and ideas from their neighbors, but they had borrowed selectively. The essentials of Pueblo culture—language, religion, society—had remained intact." Hall and Weber, "Mexican Liberals," 5. An additional, important point is the extent to which Pueblos resisted hispanicization; these resistance strategies were violent and overt in the Pueblo Revolt of 1680, but they existed in myriad other ways both before and after that time. My objective here is merely to emphasize that the new, American colonizers would have seen significant similarities between the two groups.

19. Prior to the 1870s, most New Mexico counties had little court activity. In San Miguel County, for example, there were few criminal prosecutions prior to 1870; in Taos County, there were even fewer—only a handful between 1855 and 1866. These conclusions are based on my review of docket records. San Miguel County District Court Records and Taos County District Court Records, New Mexico State Records Center and Archives. See also Gómez, "Race, Colonialism and Criminal Law," 1136; Lamar, *The Far Southwest*, 108; see also, generally, Hunt, *Kirby Benedict*.

20. See Gómez, "Race, Colonialism and Criminal Law," 1147.

21. Ibid., 1147–48; Reichard, "Justice Is God's Law," 139 (table 5).

22. These positions tended to be filled by Mexicans. Gómez, "Race, Colonialism and Criminal Law," 1173.

23. Similarly, in his analysis of the Spanish-language press in New Mexico, Gabriel Meléndez has argued that the formation and maintenance of newspapers in Spanish, under the leadership of Mexican editors, played an important role in affirming Mexicans' cultural and political resistance to American domination. Meléndez, *So All Is Not Lost*, 7.

24. In some counties, Euro-American defendants also were overrepresented, compared to Mexican Americans. See Gómez, "Race, Colonialism and Criminal Law," 1158–64.

25. For example, between 1876 and 1883, every sheriff of San Miguel County was Mexican American. Ibid., 1171.

26. Ibid., 1172.

27. Ramirez, "The Hispanic Political Elite," 214.

28. Ibid., 203.

29. My review of records for all ninety-three criminal trials in the county over a seven-year period showed that one-third of defendants were tried by all-Mexican petit juries and another one-third by majority-Mexican petit juries. The records were not sufficient to draw conclusions about the remaining trials, but it is highly likely that they similarly involved all-Mexican or majority-Mexican petit juries. Gómez, "Race, Colonialism and Criminal Law," 1165–66.

30. Ibid., 1168–71.

31. Within this category I include the territorial legislatures (which went into effect in 1851, after Congress established New Mexico as a federal territory), representative constitutional conventions around the statehood issue (three conventions to draft a state constitution for New Mexico were held prior to New Mexico becoming a federal territory [in 1848, 1849, and 1850], and many were held throughout the territorial period), and "unofficial" legislatures that met before Congress formally organized the New Mexico Territory.

32. These estimates are based on my calculations, utilizing primary sources such as the New Mexico Blue Book and a range of secondary sources.

33. Ramirez, "The Hispanic Political Elite," 439. Ramirez's estimate included

perhaps a dozen men who were half Euro-American and half Mexican American, whom he put in the Euro-American or Mexican American category depending on their surname. Ramirez, "The Hispanic Political Elite," 440.

34. Ibid., 373, 401–2.

35. See Perea, "Demography and Distrust," 316–23.

36. For examples of scholarship that tends to treat Mexican American political elites as pawns of Euro-American elites living in New Mexico, see Ganaway, *New Mexico and the Sectional Controversy*; Lamar, *The Far Southwest*; Larson, *New Mexico's Quest for Statehood*; Twitchell, *The Leading Facts of New Mexico History*.

37. See, generally, Ramirez, "The Hispanic Political Elite."

38. Although Congress nullified acts of the New Mexico territorial legislature only a few times, it is very likely that the threat of congressional nullification influenced the majority-Mexican legislatures' actions many times. Ramirez, "The Hispanic Political Elite," 435.

39. Ibid.

40. Holzka, "Taos Honors 'Champion of the Common People'"; Baca, "The Taos Priest."

41. Martínez and other Mexican priests were targeted by Euro-American Archbishop Jean-Baptiste Lamy. When he arrived in New Mexico in 1852, Lamy initiated an overt campaign to replace Mexican priests with priests born in France, Italy, and Spain. Twitchell, *History of the Military Occupation*, 337–39. I rely on Twitchell's account with some hesitation, noting that he had an undisguised anti-Martínez, pro-Lamy bias (he describes Lamy's suspension of Martínez thusly: "No alternative was left to Bishop [*sic*] Lamy, after all sorts of fatherly advice and admonitions had been unheeded, but to suspend Father Martínez from the exercise of every priestly function"; and he describes Martínez as "very crafty" and motivated to oppose the U.S. occupation because it "was a death blow to his power and prestige"). On the roots of anti-Catholic sentiment as it affected the U.S. conquest of New Mexico, see Durán, "We Come As Friends," 30–35.

42. A testament to its lasting popularity, Cather's novel was selected by *Time* magazine as one of the 100 best English-language novels written between 1923 and 2005. www.time.com, last visited January 30, 2007.

43. Rael-Gálvez, "Identifying Captivity," 105–6; Lamar, *The Far Southwest*, 34–36.

44. Rael-Gálvez, "Identifying Captivity,"109; see also Bancroft, *History of the Pacific States*, 311 n.3.

45. Rael-Gálvez, "Identifying Captivity," 109–12 (noting also that Martínez had conflicts with Charles Bent, the American governor assassinated in the 1847 rebellion).

46. Ibid.

47. Twitchell, *History of the Military Occupation*, 337–38 n. 264.

48. Martínez also owned the only printing press in the region during the Mex-

ican period (and through the first few decades of the American period), which he used to publish textbooks for his pupils, a short-lived newspaper, and the many treatises he wrote. Twitchell, *History of the Military Occupation*, 337–38 n. 264.

49. "Indians of the United States," Hearings of the Committee on Indian Affairs, 599–602.

50. For a defense of Martínez, see Martínez, "Betrayal or Benevolence."

51. Weber, *On the Edge of Empire*, 78.

52. For two perspectives on Indian rights in Mexico, compare Hall and Weber, "Mexican Liberals," 8, 19; and Rosen, "Pueblo Indians and Citizenship," 21 n. 1.

53. Article VII, Proposed New Mexico State Constitution of 1850.

54. Ibid.

55. Senate Bill 225, Thirty-first Congress, 1st Session, May 8, 1850 ("A Bill to admit California as a State into the Union; to establish Territorial Governments for Utah and New Mexico, etc.").

56. *United States v. Lucero*, 1 N.M. 422, 456 (1869).

57. Bancroft, *History of the Pacific States*, 650–51. Like Father Martínez, Gallegos was among the fiercely nationalist Mexican priests ousted by Archbishop Lamy.

58. Laguna Pueblo and Taos Pueblo men voted in the election. Bancroft, *History of the Pacific States*, 650 n. 23.

59. Twitchell, *History of the Military Occupation*, 309; Ganaway, *New Mexico and the Sectional Controversy*, 61 (citing the congressional report). Gallegos's election travails were not at an end, however. When he was up for reelection in 1855, he faced Miguel Antonio Otero; rather than support their fellow priest, newly appointed French and Italian priests backed Otero to signal their support for Lamy. Gallegos won the election by 99 votes, but Otero appealed, this time alleging that 1,400 Mexicans who had retained their Mexican citizenship (rather than become U.S. citizens) had voted illegally. Congress sided with Otero and he was seated as delegate. See Bancroft, *History of the Pacific States*, 650–51.

60. 25 U.S.C. § 180 (1983).

61. See *United States v. Lucero*, 1 N.M. 422, 425 (1869) (quoting the full text of the unpublished trial court opinion, United States v. Ortiz [1867]).

62. Three of seven lawyers for the defendants (who sought Indian lands as squatters or purchasers) were former New Mexico Supreme Court justices. Rosen, "Pueblo Indians and Citizenship," 25 n. 31.

63. Lamar, *The Far Southwest*, 131.

64. Gómez, "Race, Colonialism and Criminal Law," 1147 n. 39.

65. Slough's ruling was issued in 1867; by the time Watt's opinion was published in 1869, Slough had been killed and replaced by Watts as Chief Justice. Poldervaart, *Black-Robed Justice*, 72. On the duel with a legislator that resulted in Slough's death, see ibid.

66. *United States v. Lucero*, 1 N.M. 422, 454-457 (1869).

67. See, generally, Rosen, "Pueblo Indians and Citizenship."

68. See, generally, *United States v. Lucero*, 1 N.M. 422 (1869). On December 22, 1858, Congress confirmed the titles of Spanish land grants to seventeen Pueblos in New Mexico. *United States v. Lucero*, 1 N.M. 422, 435 (1869).

69. Ibid., 441.

70. As I have noted, the chief justice quoted the full opinion of the trial judge, Chief Justice Slough, who had died by the time the Lucero opinion was released. As to the other two appellate judges, the chief justice specifically alluded to their familiarity with New Mexico's Pueblo Indians in order to bolster the opinion's authority, stating that, commutatively, the judges had known "the conduct and habits of these Indians for eighteen or twenty years." *United States v. Lucero*, 441.

71. Ibid., 442.

72. Ibid., 425-426

73. Ibid., 427.

74. Ibid., 1 N.M. 422, 427 (1869).

75. Ibid., 427.

76. Ibid.

77. *De La O v. Acoma*, 1 NM 226 (1857).

78. *United States v. Joseph*, 94 U.S. 614 (1877).

79. *United States v. Sandoval*, 231 U.S. 28 (1913).

80. See, e.g., Twitchell, *The Leading Facts of New Mexican History*, 309–10 n. 234.

81. Gutiérrez, *When Jesus Came*, 149. It is more likely that Otero's early-twentieth-century biographers (and possibly himself and his parents) shared the progressive racial view's tendency to designate elite Mexicans as "Spanish."

82. Lamar, *The Far Southwest*, 90.

83. Ibid., 91 (describing Otero's many "Southern connections" in politics).

84. Twitchell, *History of the Military Occupation*, 309–10 n. 234; Rael-Gálvez, "Identifying Captivity," 192. Providing a glimpse into the extent of Euro-American historians' unwillingness to credit even elite Mexicans with agency and self-determination, Loomis Ganaway, writing in 1944, claimed Otero did not have an opinion on slavery until his marriage and attributed his pro-slavery views to his wife's influence. Ganaway, *New Mexico and the Sectional Controversy*, 61, 90. There exists no parallel literature describing the influence of Mexican American women on their Euro-American husbands in the years before and immediately following the American occupation.

85. Lamar, *The Far Southwest*, 90.

86. Ibid., 91.

87. Ganaway, *New Mexico and the Sectional Controversy*, 89. On the other hand, Bancroft refers to contemporary references to an 1861 speech by Otero "which incited the New Mexicans to rebellion," but states that he (Bancroft) had not been able to confirm such reports. Bancroft, *History of the Pacific States*, 684

n. 9. According to Bancroft, the Southern cause was largely rejected in New Mexico, "the masses favoring the Union cause, and furnishing five or six thousand troops, volunteers, and militia, to resist the [Confederate] invasion" and "without avail, most of the wealthy and influential families being pronounced Union men." Bancroft, *History of the Pacific States*, 684.

88. Twitchell, *History of the Military Occupation*, 310 n. 234.

89. Rael-Gálvez, "Identifying Captivity," 197. Brooks speculates that most blacks in New Mexico in 1860 were slaves accompanying their masters, who were army officers. Brooks, *Captives and Cousins*, 309–10.

90. The most complete analysis is provided by Larson. As to why it took almost sixty-four years from the ratification of the Treaty of Guadalupe Hidalgo for New Mexico to become a U.S. state, Larson concludes that New Mexico's distinctive ethnic character and partisan politics were the most critical factors. Larson, *New Mexico's Quest for Statehood*, 303–4.

91. Ganaway, *New Mexico and the Sectional Controversy*, 59.

92. See Lamar, *The Far Southwest*; Larson, *New Mexico's Quest for Statehood*.

93. Rael-Gálvez, "Identifying Captivity," 198. See also Brooks, *Captives and Cousins*, 329 (quoting the same letter).

94. Of thirteen delegates to the convention, ten were Mexican. Ganaway, *New Mexico and the Sectional Controversy*, 40.

95. Congressional Globe, 30th Congress, 2nd Session, Tues., Dec. 19, 1848. See also Ganaway, *New Mexico and the Sectional Controversy*, 40–41.

96. Ibid., 49–52.

97. Ibid., 40–41.

98. Bancroft, *History of the Pacific States*, 684, 686; Durán, "Francisco Chávez," 22–23.

99. An Act Concerning Free Negroes, New Mexico Laws, 1857. The law appears typical of other, contemporaneous so-called "black codes" passed by states that banned slavery. Legislators in such states were motivated by the racist fear that they would be "overrun" by blacks from the South, whether they were illegally fleeing their owners or had been manumitted. For a discussion of these laws, see Berwanger, *The Frontier against Slavery*, 18–32, 118–19.

100. Ibid.

101. Offending black males were to be punished more harshly than offending white (including Mexican) females, with male violators subject to two to three years hard labor and female violators subject to a fine of $100 to $200. Ibid.

102. For historical studies that focus on inter-racial intimacy in New Mexico, see Brooks, *Captives and Cousins*; Gútierrez, *When Jesus Came*. For a legal history of miscegenation laws involving various racial groups, see Moran, *Inter-racial Intimacy*; see also Lubin, *Romance and Rights*.

103. Foley, *The White Scourge*, 208.

104. Chap. XXVI, Laws of New Mexico (1859). New Mexico's slave code never

became law as such because Congress repealed it in May 1860. H.R. Res. 64, 36th Cong. (1st Sess. 1860). Recall that under federal territorial status, the New Mexico legislature's acts were subject to review and approval by Congress.

105. Ibid. See also *People v. Hall*, 4 Cal. 399 (1854).

106. Berwanger, *The Frontier against Slavery*, 30–59. For a different approach to the laws known as the black codes—as laws that arose in the South after emancipation—see Du Bois, *Black Reconstruction*, 166.

107. Berwanger, *The Frontier against Slavery*, 31.

108. Fehrenbacher, *The Dred Scott Case*, 3.

109. Ganaway, *New Mexico and the Sectional Controversy*, 68. Otero's letter became widely available when an anti-slavery organization published it in a pamphlet in English and Spanish that was widely distributed in Washington and New Mexico. Ibid., 68 n. 29. Ganaway notes that "when this letter was made public, Otero did not deny its authenticity, although he had an opportunity of doing so in a number of public letters which he issued early in 1861." Ibid.

110. Ibid., 73–74.

111. See Rael-Gálvez, "Identifying Captivity."

112. Chap. XXVI, §30, Laws of New Mexico (1859).

113. Brooks, *Captives and Cousins*, 346 n. 63 (citing June 9, 1865, proclamation by President Andrew Johnson); see also Rael-Gálvez, "Identifying Captivity," 277, 279.

114. Rael-Gálvez, "Identifying Captivity," 292–93.

115. Ibid., 312–13 n. 597.

116. Ibid., 294–95 (quoting Santistevan's grand jury testimony); see also Brooks, *Captives and Cousins*, 352.

117. For a defense of Indian slavery by a Mexican American contemporary of Santistevan raising similar themes, see Brooks, *Captives and Cousins*, 346–47 (quoting Felipe Delgado, New Mexico Superintendent of Indian Affairs in 1865).

118. The federal grand jury empanelled to hear these charges in 1868 would have been similar in racial composition to grand juries and petit juries at the county-level, territorial district court. In the Taos County District Court in the 1860s and 1870s, the larger group of potential jurors (from which specific grand jurors and petit jurors were selected) had no more than three Euro-Americans and many had none. Taos County District Court Records, New Mexico State Records Center and Archives.

119. During the 1870s, Santistevan was appointed jury commissioner for the April 1871, September 1874, March 1877, and September 1879 terms of court. He served as grand jury interpreter in the April 1873, April 1875, September 1875, March 1876, September 1876, March 1877, and April 1879 terms. Taos County District Court Records, New Mexico State Records Center and Archives.

120. For more detailed descriptions, see, generally, Brooks, *Captives and Cousins*; Gutiérrez, *When Jesus Came*; Rael-Gálvez, "Identifying Captivity."

121. Historian James Brooks argues that a regional exchange in people (especially women and children) of different nomadic Indian tribes predated the Spanish conquest. Brooks, *Captives and Cousins*, 124.

122. Gutiérrez, *When Jesus Came*, 152.

123. Ibid., 153–54.

124. Brooks concludes that Mexican captives "continued to face a range of possible fates from full cultural assimilation through subordinate labor status to resale among the expectant capitalists of American Texas." Brooks, *Captives and Cousins*, 324. He describes the experience of José Andrés Martínez, a mestizo who was taken captive by Mescalero Apaches as a ten-year-old in 1866. After being renamed Andalí, he grew up with the Apaches; as an adult, he returned to his birth family, only to decide to return to live permanently with the Apaches, where he eventually played a role as a translator and spokesman for a Kiowa, Apache, and Comanche delegation to Washington, D.C., in the 1880s. Ibid., 356.

125. Ibid., 327, 331–37.

126. Ibid.

127. Rael-Gálvez, "Identifying Captivity," 249.

128. Brooks, *Captives and Cousins*, 331–32.

129. Rael-Gálvez, "Identifying Captivity," 277, 279.

130. Ibid., 286–87.

131. Ibid., 288.

132. For similar reasons, scholars have gravitated toward the study of American Indians who owned black slaves (common among the Five Civilized Tribes, who formally sided with the Confederacy during the Civil War) and black plantation owners who owned black slaves. See generally, Wickett, *Contested Territory*.

133. Rael-Gálvez, "Identifying Captivity," 301, 306–9.

134. Bancroft, *History of the Pacific States*, 681. Like the majority of Euro-American and Mexican American elites whose history he chronicles, Bancroft conceived of Indian slavery as benign, claiming that "in most instances" it had improved the living conditions of the slaves. Ibid.

135. Rael-Gálvez, "Identifying Captivity," 274.

136. Ibid., 276.

137. Brooks, *Captives and Cousins*, 403 app. C.

138. Ibid., 351–52.

139. Ibid.

140. For example, Rael-Gálvez traces the case of Tomás Heredia's lawsuit against José María García: Heredia fled García's home, arguing that the peonage contract under which he worked was illegal. Multiple justices of the peace in Doña Ana County sided with García and ordered Heredia to return to him. On a habeas corpus petition to the territorial supreme court, the justices reasoned that "peonage must be as illegal as Negro slavery" and ordered Heredia freed.

Rael-Gálvez, "Identifying Captivity," 284–85 (citing records of the New Mexico Supreme Court [no published opinion exists]).

141. The first master-servant law was enacted by the territorial legislature in 1851 and was expanded in a variety of ways in the 1850s and 1860s. Ibid., 188 (citing the various pieces of legislation). The legislature formally abolished peonage in 1867, but the practice apparently continued well into the next decade. Brooks, *Captives and Cousins*, 349 n. 70.

142. Brooks, *Captives and Cousins*, 348.

143. Rael-Gálvez, "Identifying Captivity," 200 (citing legislation enacted in 1859).

144. Gómez, "Race, Colonialism and Criminal Law," 1156 n. 65 (describing probate judges and the probate court).

145. Rael-Gálvez powerfully observes: "While terms such as 'genízaro' and 'criado' were much more common, 'guardianship' may also have begun to be used in similar ways. As is true with all these euphemisms, however, what this reveals is precisely what it attempts to hide: a continually constructed ideology of a legally mandated benevolence, which while read outside of slavery, was in fact constitutive of an uniquely situated colonial paternalism, hierarchy and racism." Ibid., 201.

146. See, e.g., *Jaremillo* [sic] *v. Romero* (1857).

147. Gómez, "Race, Colonialism and Criminal Law," 1158 (noting that the territorial supreme court curtailed the power of justices of the peace in several cases in the 1860s).

148. Rael-Gálvez, "Identifying Captivity," 286–87.

149. One result of the U.S. Army's Indian wars of the 1860s was the largest number of baptisms of nomadic Indians ever recorded in Catholic records. Ibid., 215. As Rael-Gálvez notes, these military campaigns revealed a shift "from the wars against slavery to the wars against Indians." Ibid., 211. Admittedly, Mexicans, as army volunteers and in other support capacities, supported this assault on Navajos and other nomadic tribes. See ibid., 203 n. 387 (citing an 1860 proclamation exhorting Mexican men to "create a force of 1,000 men" to fight the "savage" Navajos).

150. White, *"It's Your Misfortune,"* 100.

151. Rael-Gálvez, "Identifying Captivity," 292. Oddly, Griffin's emancipations apparently occurred at the time he issued arrest warrants for and subpoenas of the alleged slaveholders—before the federal grand jury had an opportunity to consider (and, in these cases, reject) indictments.

152. Ibid., 270.

153. Reliance on 1898 as the beginning of U.S. imperialism cuts across the political spectrum, with even left-leaning scholars evoking that year as the start of "the New American Empire." Smith, *Civic Ideals*, 429; see also Weston, *Racism in*

U.S. Imperialism (arguing that American imperialism began in 1893 with efforts to annex Hawaii). For recent legal scholarship on U.S. imperialism in Puerto Rico, see, e.g., Malavet, *America's Colony*; Román, *The Other American Colonies*.

154. Lipsitz, *The Possessive Investment in Whiteness*, 4–5.

NOTES TO CHAPTER 4

1. For an excellent study of colonialism and the transition in property regimes, see Montoya, *Translating Property*.

2. Legal scholar Emlen Hall argues that, in the case of some community grants, many Mexican Americans later became owners via homesteading and other types of public domain ownership. Hall, "San Miguel del Bado," 413. Yet Hall's analysis does not indicate how prevalent this might have been, either in the case of specific grants or more generally.

3. *United States v. Sandoval*, 167 U.S. 278 (1897).

4. *Scott v. Sandford*, 60 U.S. 393 (1856).

5. *In re Rodriguez*, 81 F. 337 (W.D. Tex. 1897).

6. Transcript of Record, United States v. Julian Sandoval, U.S. Supreme Court (hereafter, Sandoval Transcript), 1.

7. Sandoval Transcript, 50, 56.

8. Ebright, *Land Grants*, 173.

9. La Madrid, *Hermanitos Comanchitos*, 33.

10. Ibid., 27–28. The Comanches not only were the most powerful military force in the region, but also controlled a thriving economy that included a human slave trade. "The Comanches built the most dynamic economy that the southern plains had ever seen. Based on horse raising, buffalo hunting, the preservation of meat, and hide tanning, it was labor-intensive and involved an ever-growing workforce. Trading contacts and ties in New Mexico were pursued aggressively." Ibid., 32.

11. Other types of grants—individual and empresario—were distributed by the Spanish and Mexican authorities in order to achieve other goals. See Montoya, *Translating Property*, 163–65. Community grants included two subtypes: those awarded to mestizo settlers and those awarded to Pueblo Indian communities. The community land grants bear some resemblance to the *ejido* system of land distribution in twentieth-century Mexico.

12. Gómez, "The History and Adjudication of the Common Lands," 1056.

13. Farago, "Mediating Ethnicity and Culture," 24.

14. For the five conditions that accompanied the 1794 grant, see Sandoval Transcript, 2–3.

15. "The principal difference between a community land grant and an individual grant was that the common lands of a community land grant were held in

perpetuity and could not be sold or otherwise alienated, while an individual grant could be transferred." "Treaty of Guadalupe Hidalgo: Findings and Possible Options Regarding Longstanding Community Land Grant Claims in New Mexico," U.S. Government Accountability Office Report to Congress, June 2004 (hereafter GAO Report), 17.

16. Gómez, "The History and Adjudication of the Common Lands," 1043–51, 1058.

17. Ibid., 1053, 1057–58. See also Hall, "San Miguel del Bado," 417.

18. Sandoval Transcript, 1.

19. For a compelling history of Pecos Pueblo, see Hall, *Four Leagues of Pecos.*

20. Ebright, *Land Grants*, 173.

21. Sandoval Transcript, 3.

22. Ebright, *Land Grants*, 171.

23. Gutiérrez, *When Jesus Came*, 149, 154. Gutiérrez traces his family roots to *genízaro* ancestors. Public lecture at University of New Mexico, March 6, 2006.

24. Kraemer, "Dynamic Ethnicity," 96. One result was the strategic manipulation of *genízaro* and mestizo status depending on political and economic utility in particular contexts. Ibid. For a fascinating history of Abiquiu, a *genízaro* community grant established in 1754, that illustrates just such transformations and manipulations, see Ebright and Hendricks, *The Witches of Abiquiu.*

25. GAO Report, 97. This probably is a conservative estimate. Kosek, *Understories*, 9. For a scathing critique of the GAO Report, see Ebright, "The GAO Land Grant Report."

26. GAO Report, 97.

27. *United States v. Sandoval*, 167 U.S. 278 (1897); Hall, "San Miguel del Bado," 415.

28. Westphall, *The Public Domain*, 71.

29. Ibid.

30. I estimated this number based on data compiled by geographers Warren Beck and Ynez Haase. Beck and Haase, *Historical Atlas of New Mexico*, Map 59 (National Forests). Only two national forests in New Mexico were designated outside this time frame (the former Pecos River National Forest, 1892, and the Datil National Forest, 1931).

31. Kosek, *Understories*, 42.

32. For an analysis of the sovereignty/property ownership distinction as it affected Indian lands, see Banner, *How the Indians Lost Their Land*, 6–7.

33. Act of March 3, 1851, 9 U.S. Statutes 631 (1854).

34. "The land unsuccessfully claimed under the act or not presented to the board by 1853 automatically became part of the public domain of the United States." Fritz, *Federal Justice*, 140.

35. Act of July 22, 1854, 10 U.S. Statutes 308 (1854).

36. "For each claim, the act directed the surveyor general for New Mexico to

recommend first to the secretary of the interior and then to Congress whether the new sovereign [the U.S.] should honor the claim, thus segregating the land from the public domain, or reject it, in which case the claimed land would join that to be opened to public settlement or otherwise dealt with under American public land law." Hall, *Four Leagues of Pecos*, 78. See also GAO Report, 41–43; Gómez, "The History and Adjudication of the Common Lands," 1069–70.

37. Gonzáles, "Struggle for Survival," 303.

38. An act to establish a court of private land claims, 26 U.S. Statutes 854 (1891). Despite the act's broad mandate, keep in mind that it was designed to deal only with the non-California portion of the Mexican Cession.

39. See Gómez, "The History and Adjudication of the Common Lands"; Perea et al., *Race and Races*, 284–91. The case remains infamous among today's advocates for land grant rights. At a recent subcommittee hearing of the New Mexico legislature, an heir to a communal land grant that was denied under the holding in *United States v. Sandoval* testified about the lasting impact of the case. Land Grant Committee Hearings, August 23, 2006. For a different perspective see Hall, "San Miguel del Bado," 413.

40. "In the said territories, property of every kind, now belonging to Mexicans now established there, shall be inviolably respected. The present owners, the heirs of these, and all Mexicans who may hereafter acquire said property by contract, shall enjoy with respect to it, guaranties equally ample as if the same belonged to citizens of the United States." Article VIII, Treaty of Guadalupe Hidalgo, 9 U.S. Statutes 922 (1848).

41. A testament to how effective the proposed Article X would have been in keeping land in the ceded territory in the hands of Mexicans is the fact that Polk forwarded the treaty to the Senate with the express recommendation that the article be excised. Ebright, "Land Grant Adjudication," 54. Malcolm Ebright, the widely recognized authority on land grant law, believes that, had the spirit of the proposed article been followed (that is, that Mexican law and practice had been followed by American courts in deciding the validity of claims in the Mexican Cession), the outcomes of land claims would have been dramatically different. Instead, he contends, two kinds of bad law resulted, both of which took the majority of lands in New Mexico out of Mexican American hands: "improperly confirmed grants are now valuable private property" and improperly rejected grants "are now U.S. government land" administered by the U.S. Forest Service and the Bureau of Land Management. Ibid., 54.

42. Griswold del Castillo, *The Treaty of Guadalupe Hidalgo*, 180 (emphasis added).

43. As Mexican historian Josefina Zoraida Vázquez points out, it must be remembered that the Mexicans could not have been in a weaker bargaining position. While the treaty was being negotiated and ratified, Mexico City was occupied by American forces and American military personnel repeatedly threatened

to continue the invasion by moving to capture cities further south. Mexico's acting president had to plead with the Mexican Congress to ratify the treaty in May 1848 by assuring legislators that "the cession of territory was the least that could be agreed upon . . . as large as are the territories of Texas, Upper California, and New Mexico." Zoraida Vázquez, "The Significance in Mexican History of the Treaty of Guadalupe Hidalgo," 82. See also Ebright, "Land Grant Adjudication," 53. On the Mexican perspective of the war, see, generally, Zoraida Vázquez, *México al Tiempo de su Guerre con Los Estados Unidos.*

44. For a scholarly discussion, see Griswold del Castillo, *The Treaty of Guadalupe Hidalgo,* 181, 183. Known as "the Protocol of Querétaro," the clarification was made in writing after negotiations between Mexican and American diplomats on May 26, 1848, a few days before the formal ratification of the treaty on May 30, 1848. See also GAO Report, 31, 178.

45. Stuart Banner makes an analogous point in his analysis of the interaction of conquest and contract law in the ultimate transfer of land from the Indians to Euro-American whites. "In the end, the story of the colonization of the United States is still a story of power, but it was a more subtle and complex kind of power than we conventionally recognize. It was the power to establish the legal institutions and the rules by which land transactions would be enforced. The threat of physical force would always be present, but most of the time it could be kept out of view because it was not needed." Banner, *How the Indians Lost Their Land,* 6.

46. A congressional committee in 1858 expressed frustration with the system: "It is now ten years since the surveyor general of the Territory [of New Mexico] was authorized to examine and report to us the private land claims of its people; and, although protected, as is supposed, by treaty, in the enjoyment of their property, no man in that Territory, without some action of Congress, can say that his title, however acquired, would hold against any claimant who might purchase his lands from the government." "Claims in the Territory of New Mexico," Report to accompany H.R. Bill No. 605, Committee on Private Land Claims, House of Representatives, 35th Congress, 1st Session, Report. No. 457, May 29, 1858, 1.

47. Sandoval Transcript, 4.

48. Ibid., 64–66.

49. Ibid., 65.

50. Hall, "San Miguel del Bado," 417.

51. Schiller, "Adjudicating Empire."

52. Gómez, "The History and Adjudication of the Common Lands" 1071. For a discussion of strikingly similar concerns two decades earlier in California, see Fritz, *Federal Justice,* chap. 5.

53. Gómez, "The History and Adjudication of the Common Lands" 1071.

54. Julian, "Land-Stealing in New Mexico," 18.

55. Ibid. (emphasis added).

56. Sandoval Transcript (Surveyor General Julian's report to Congress, December 6, 1886), 67.

57. For those who answer with a resounding "no," see Gómez, "The History and Adjudication of the Common Lands," 1071–72; Schiller, "Adjudicating Empire."

58. Act of March 3, 1891, 26 U.S. Statutes 854. Congress charged the court with resolving land claims in the federal territories of New Mexico, Arizona, and Utah and the states of Nevada, Colorado, and Wyoming. GAO Report, 77.

59. Gómez, "The History and Adjudication of the Common Lands," 1069–70.

60. For a description of the act, see Fritz, *Federal Justice*, 139–40.

61. Ramirez, "Hispanic Political Elite," 51.

62. See Gómez, "The History and Adjudication of the Common Lands," 1073 n. 261.

63. Ibid. It is not known whether Catron followed through with the recommended amendments.

64. Ibid., 1077 n. 284; see also Hall, "San Miguel del Bado," 417 n. 10.

65. *Biographical Directory*, 1541.

66. Sandoval Transcript, 57.

67. Bradfute, *The Court of Private Land Claims*, 27.

68. Sandoval Transcript, 22–23.

69. Ibid., 54–55. The transcript lists the witness as "Mariano Varos," but his name was very likely "Barros" misspelled as "Varos."

70. Ibid., 17.

71. Ibid.

72. Ibid., 25.

73. Ibid.

74. Ebright, *Land Grants*, 45; see also Fritz, *Federal Justice*, chap. 5.

75. *United States v. Sandoval*, 291, 294. See also GAO Report, 98.

76. Gómez, "The History and Adjudication of the Common Lands," 1042.

77. For recent studies that describe Mexican Americans' transition to a wage-labor economy in northern New Mexico in the broader political economy, see Kosek, *Understories*; Masco, *Nuclear Borderlands*; Montoya, *Translating Property*.

78. Gonzáles, "Hispanic Land Grants," 305.

79. "The problem of territorial government and its relationship to slavery arose in the 1780s, when the first state cessions of western lands made it clear that the central government of the new United States was about to take on certain attributes of empire." Fehrenbacher, *The Dred Scott Case*, 74.

80. Fehrenbacher, *The Dred Scott Case*, 99. Note that when Congress admitted the Orleans Territory as the State of Louisiana in 1812, it changed the name of the Louisiana Territory to the Missouri Territory.

81. Fehrenbacher, *The Era of Expansion*, 125, 128.

82. Ibid., 135.

83. Ibid.; see also Bauer, *The Mexican War*, 78.

84. Bauer, *The Mexican War*, 136.

85. Lamar, *The Far Southwest*, 63.

86. For descriptions of the Compromise of 1850, see Fehrenbacher, *The Dred Scott Case*, 160–63; Larson, *New Mexico's Quest for Statehood*, 55–57; White, *"It's Your Misfortune,"* 159.

87. Congress paid Texas $10 million to relinquish its claims regarding its western border with New Mexico; Texas previously had claimed that its western border extended to include Santa Fe (New Mexico's capital).

88. See Cover, *Justice Accused*, 175 (describing the 1850 Fugitive Slave Act and concluding that it significantly modified the 1793 act); Smith, *Civic Ideals*, 262 (referring to the Fugitive Slave Act as "horrifically Kafkaesque").

89. Fehrenbacher describes nonintervention this way: "Down until 1861, no free state was ever formed out of territory in which nonintervention had been the rule. In practical terms, nonintervention had meant popular sovereignty, and popular sovereignty had always meant slavery." Fehrenbacher, *The Dred Scott Case*, 138. Four years later, with the creation of the Kansas-Nebraska Territory, the question of slavery in the territories again appeared. The region was north of the 36th parallel, so the Missouri Compromise should have governed, yet southerners won out, and the nonintervention provision that had been applied to Utah and New Mexico in 1850 governed. Ibid., 181.

90. Ibid., 185.

91. Scott's federal suit that eventually went to the Supreme Court actually was the second suit he filed to obtain his freedom. The first time, he sued in Missouri state court; he won at trial but then lost in the Missouri Supreme Court.

92. On the requirements for diversity jurisdiction, see Shreve and Raven-Hansen, *Understanding Civil Procedure*, 118–25. The defendant, Sanford, had recently purchased Scott. The Supreme Court misspelled his name and the case went on to be known as *Scott v. Sandford*.

93. For a description of Scott's life and details of his travels in various states and territories, see Fehrenbacher, *The Dred Scott Case*, 240–49.

94. By this time, Scott had lived for more than two years in regions where slavery was prohibited. Under some existing state laws, this made him a free man.

95. Fehrenbacher speculates that the woman's owner either sold or gave her to Scott. The Scotts would go on to have four children: two boys who died in infancy and two daughters who were parties in Scott's history-making suit for freedom. Fehrenbacher, *The Dred Scott Case*, 244.

96. It was common for officers who owned slaves to require them to accompany them to war. General Zachary Taylor (later president) fought in the U.S.–Mexico War with the assistance of his slave "Ben," as noted in Chapter 1. Stephen Kearny, who led the Army of the West, owned two slaves who were with him at Fort Leavenworth, Kansas, when he departed for the invasion of New Mexico.

According to his biographer, Kearny's slaves were a wedding gift from his father-in-law, General William Clark (of Lewis and Clark fame). Although we know few details, Kearny's biographer reports that the Iowa Territory courts considered the legality of Kearny keeping a slave in a region north of the 36th parallel. Clarke, *Stephen Watts Kearny*, 49–51, 69.

97. It is speculative, but one wonders whether Scott was influenced by the fact that many black slaves had escaped slavery by going to Mexico. An estimated 4,000 black slaves escaped to Mexico from Texas between 1835 and 1860. Horne, *Black and Brown*, 16.

98. For example, in slavery cases prior to *Dred Scott*, the Supreme Court had decided questions "on narrow jurisdictional grounds or on points of state law in order to avoid making broad pronouncements on slavery, one way or the other." Gatell, "Roger B. Taney," 666; see also Fehrenbacher, *The Dred Scott Case*, 365 (arguing that Taney "could have and should have remanded the case to the lower court with instructions to dismiss it for want of jurisdiction," after reaching the conclusion that he was not a federal citizen).

99. Justices McLean and Curtis dissented; for a discussion, see Fehrenbacher, *The Dred Scott Case*, 324–34.

100. Because the ruling so radicalized abolitionists, many have said the case made the Civil War inevitable.

101. Fehrenbacher, *The Dred Scott Case*, 366.

102. As Fehrenbacher puts it, Taney's purpose in *Dred Scott* was "to launch a sweeping counterattack on the antislavery movement and to reinforce the bastions of slavery at every rampart and parapet." Ibid., 341.

103. Fehrenbacher, *The Dred Scott Case*, 377; see also 365–88.

104. *Scott v. Sandford*, 60 U.S. 393, 446 (1856).

105. Ibid., 447, 449-50 (1856).

106. Ibid., 451-52 (1856).

107. Act of March 26, 1790, Ch. 3, 1 Stat. 103 (1790). After the Civil War, Congress amended the statute to allow both whites and persons of African descent to naturalize. Act of July 14, 1870, Ch. 255, §7, 16 Stat. 254 (1870).

108. Taney wrote the opinion in *Fremont v. United States*, 58 U.S. 542 (1854), and voted with the majority in *De Arguello v. United States*, 59 U.S. 539 (1855) and *United States v. Ritchie*, 58 U.S. 525 (1854), all three deciding questions about land titles in light of the Treaty of Guadalupe Hidalgo. Taney also took part in *Fleming v. Page*, 50 U.S. 603 (1850), a decision concerning the legality of customs collection during the period between the start of the U.S.–Mexico War and the peace treaty. For a discussion of Taney's role in a case involving the effect of the Treaty of Guadalupe Hidalgo, see Lawson and Seidman, *The Constitution of Empire*, 152–66. For an analysis of Taney's decisions in cases involving Spanish and Mexican land grants, see Luna, "Chicanas/os, 'Liberty' and Roger B. Taney."

109. Taney's failure to acknowledge the collective grant of citizenship to Mexicans was all the more meaningful because he expressly compared African Americans to another racial group: American Indians. Like Mexicans, Indians were ranked by Taney above blacks in the racial hierarchy. As members of sovereign nations, they were outside the polity, but he stated that they could become citizens by renouncing their tribal affiliation.

110. *Scott v. Sandford*, 60 U.S. 393, 450-451 (emphasis added).

111. Román, *The Other American Colonies*, 24.

112. Ibid., 37.

113. One category of white Euro-American settler citizens who had not held state citizenship in the past was those emigrating directly from European countries.

114. Anthropologist and legal scholar Mark Weiner has described citizenship law and race as mutually constitutive: "minority groups were characterized in terms of their relative legal capacity—their ability or inability to uphold legality as a general idea and to follow specific forms of legal behavior—and this characterization served to justify a group's place in the circle of national civil life." Weiner, *Americans without Law*, 2.

115. See Weiner, *Americans without Law*, 6 ("citizenship is not simply a narrow legal matter of rights but also one of identity and cultural acceptance"); see also Brubaker, *Citizenship and Nationhood*, 182; Ngai, *Impossible Subjects*, 6.

116. See, generally, Smith, *Civic Ideals*; Kettner, *The Development of American Citizenship*.

117. Smith, *Civic Ideals*, 323.

118. Act of July 14, 1870, Ch. 255, § 7, 16 Stat. 254 (1870).

119. *Plessy v. Ferguson*, 163 U.S. 537 (1896).

120. See generally, Williams, *The American Indian*.

121. See Newton, *Cohen's Handbook*, 894–98.

122. For example, consider the relative political and cultural assimilation of the Cherokee, Chotaw, Chicasaw, Creek, and Seminole Tribes (the so-called Five Civilized Tribes) living in what became Oklahoma, who supported the Confederacy in the Civil War because of slave owners among their people. For a history of Indian, black, and white relations in Oklahoma, see Wickett, *Contested Territory*.

123. Chinese Exclusion Act, 8 U.S.C. § 261-299 (1882).

124. On racial discrimination against the Chinese, see, generally, Hing, *Making and Remaking Asian America*; McClain, *In Search of Equality*; Takaki, *Strangers from a Different Shore*; Yamamoto et al., eds., *Race, Rights and Reparations*.

125. Haney López, *White by Law*, 42.

126. Ibid., 44.

127. López, "Undocumented Mexican Migration," 143 n. 145.

128. Sánchez, *Becoming Mexican American*, 50.

129. Ibid., 38–62.

130. For a study of appellate cases involving naturalization and claims to white status, see Haney López, *White by Law.*

131. In fact, the 1882 ban triggered the development by the Chinese of routes into the United States via Mexico, since there was relatively little reinforcement of the border. See Sánchez, *Becoming Mexican American,* 50; Lúpez, "Undocumented Mexican Migration," 649–50.

132. In 1907–8, a diplomatic accord between the United States and Japan essentially ended Japanese immigration, which by then had led to 400,000 Japanese workers coming to the United States after the Chinese Exclusion Act. Yamamoto et al., *Race, Rights and Reparation,* 32–35; see also López, "Undocumented Mexican Migration," 655; Ngai, *Impossible Subjects,* 18.

133. Ibid., 19; Lipsitz, *The Possessive Investment in Whiteness,* 2–3; López, "Undocumented Mexican Migration," 649–50.

134. *In re Rodriguez,* 81 F. 337, 348 (W.D. Tex, 1897). The judge took the unusual step of soliciting additional briefing in the case from "several members of the bar"; two of these attorneys filed briefs with the court (along with those submitted by the parties). Ibid.

135. "Handbook of Texas On-line" (joint project of the University of Texas, Austin General Libraries and the Texas State Historical Association), www.tsha. utexas.edu/handbook/online (last accessed August 28, 2006).

136. De León, *"In Re Rodriguez,"* 1.

137. Rodríguez signed his naturalization papers with an X mark. De León, *"In Re Rodriguez,"* 14 n. 3.

138. *In re Rodriguez,* 81 F. 337, 355 (W.D. Tex, 1897).

139. Ibid., 349.

140. Ibid.

141. Haney López, *White by Law,* 61, 243 n. 54; Ngai, *Impossible Subjects,* 54. A local newspaper described Rodríguez as "very dark." De León, *"In Re Rodriguez,"* 3.

142. *In re Rodriguez,* 81 F. 337, 349 (W.D. Tex, 1897).

143. Ibid., 354.

144. Ibid., 353.

145. Ibid., 350.

146. For an analysis of legal indeterminacy in twentieth-century cases involving Mexican Americans, see Martínez, "Legal Indeterminacy."

147. Ibid., 350 (emphasis added).

148. Menchaca, *Recovering History,* 228.

149. See Weber, ed., *Foreigners in Their Native land,* 145–46, 148.

150. Ngai, *Impossible Subjects,* 54.

151. Ibid., 18.

152. Rodríguez, "Unstable Victory of White *Mexicanidad,*" 12.

153. Ibid.

154. What I have termed here the reverse one-drop rule for Mexican Americans may have an analogue for American Indians. Historian Murray Wickett observes: "Because whites were willing to recognize mixed-blood Indians as partially white, there existed the possibility of ultimate assimilation over time—a possibility that was never extended to African Americans. The fact that through intermarriage and miscegenation Native Americans could be absorbed into white society while African Americans could not meant that the government and white settlers themselves adopted very different attitudes and proposed very different answers to race relations in the west in the late nineteenth century." Wickett, *Contested Territory*, 41.

155. A concrete example of how this worked is offered by historian Linda Gordon in her study of a dispute in an Arizona mining community that led Euro-Americans to draw a boundary that included Jews, Irish, French Canadians, and Italians—but not Mexicans—as "white." Gordon, *The Great Arizona Orphan Abduction*, 115–16. For studies describing how Jews, Irish, and Italians became "white," see Brodkin, *How Jews Became White Folks*; Ignatiev, *How the Irish Became White*; Jacobson, *Whiteness of a Different Color*.

156. 163 U.S. 537 (1896).

157. Nash, "The Hidden History of Mestizo America," 20.

158. Rodriguez, *Changing Race*, 91.

159. Ibid.

160. Ibid.; see also Bair, "Remapping the Black/White Body," 415; Sharfstein, "Crossing the Color Line," 654; Telles, *Race in Another America*, 80.

161. Harris, "The Story of *Plessy v. Ferguson*," 203, 204, 211.

162. Harris describes the test case brought by the Citizens Committee to Test the Constitutionality of the Separate Car Law. Ibid., 202–5.

163. Ibid., 210.

164. Ibid.

165. *Plessy v. Ferguson*, 163 U.S. 537, 552 (1896).

166. Senate Debate, January 2, 1902, 568. Unless otherwise indicated, all references to the Senate debate on the omnibus statehood bill are to this page.

167. It was Beveridge who had conducted whistle-stop hearings in 1902 in five New Mexico towns in order to make the point that the Territory's Mexican majority was racially and linguistically "unfit" for statehood.

168. About one-quarter of those on the tribal rolls of the Five Civilized Tribes were full-blooded Indians at the turn of the century. Wickett, *Contested Territory*, 38–39.

169. In fact, Indians opposed Oklahoma statehood for this very reason. Wickett, *Contested Territory*, 169–70.

170. For two important recent studies on race in Latin America that make comparisons to the United States, see Sawyer, *Racial Politics in Post-Revolutionary Cuba*; Telles, *Race in Another America*.

Notes to the Epilogue

1. For studies of how these groups became white, see Brodkin, *How Jews Became White Folks*; Ignatiev, *How the Irish Became White*; Jacobson, *Whiteness of a Different Color*. For studies on poor whites' questionable white status, see Foley, *The White Scourge*; Roediger, *The Wages of Whiteness*.

2. On the distinction between assignment and self-assertion of racial and ethnic identities, see Cornell and Hartmann, *Ethnicity and Race*, 27.

3. I use the terms "Hispanic" and "Latino" interchangeably. Both are pan-ethnic terms that include Mexican Americans, Puerto Ricans, Cuban Americans, and those from other Spanish-speaking countries.

4. Omi and Winant, *Racial Formation*, 3.

5. See Mezey, "Erasure and Recognition"; Rodríguez, *Changing Race*.

6. Skrentney, *The Minority Rights Revolution*, 151–52.

7. As a Texan, Johnson was personally familiar with the difference Mexican Americans could make in an election. The 1975 expansion of the Voting Rights Act to include language minorities also increased interest in Mexican Americans. Fraga et al., "*Su Casa Es Nuestra Casa*," 515.

8. For a description of these events based on interviews with participants on the advisory committee, see Gómez, "The Birth of the 'Hispanic' Generation"; Gómez, "What's in a Name?"

9. Gómez, "The Birth of the 'Hispanic' Generation," 46.

10. "Race and Hispanic Origin," 2.

11. "The Hispanic Population," 2.

12. "Race and Hispanic origin," 4.

13. "The Hispanic Population," 2; Tienda and Mitchell, eds., *Multiple Origins, Uncertain Destinies*, 19.

14. "The Hispanic Population," 2–3.

15. "Race and Hispanic Origin," 7.

16. For a discussion of how the census race categories have changed generally over time, see Rodríguez, *Changing Race*, 65–86.

17. Moore and Pachón, *Hispanics in the United States*, 51.

18. Rodríguez, *Changing Race*, 75.

19. Ibid.

20. See, generally, Carrasco, "Latinos in the U.S."

21. Sánchez, *Becoming Mexican American*, 209–11.

22. Kosek, *Understories*, 116. In the same era Colorado set up a blockade at the New Mexico border to keep out "the Mexicans from New Mexico"—who had since the mid-1800s migrated seasonally to work in Colorado. Ibid.

23. Gómez, "What's in a Name?" 57.

24. Moore, "Foreword," 12.

25. Tienda and Mitchell, *Multiple Origins, Uncertain Destinies*, 39.

26. "Race and Hispanic Origin," 1.

27. For the text of census questions as they pertain to Latino identity, see Tienda and Mitchell, eds., *Multiple Origins, Uncertain Destinies*, 42–43. In 1970, no specific questions about Hispanic ethnicity were included, but in their place were three questions on national origin: (i) "Where was this person born?" (ii) "Is this person's origin or descent . . . " (choose one: Mexican, Puerto Rican, Cuban, Central or South American, Other Spanish, Other); (iii) "What country was his [*sic*] father born in?" Ibid.

28. Ibid.; see also Tafoya, "Shades of Belonging," 4.

29. Tienda and Mitchell, *Multiple Origins, Uncertain Destinies*, 43. The specific instruction for the race question in 2000 was: "What is this person's race? Mark one or more races to indicate what this person considers himself/herself to be." This is the first census in which respondents were invited to check multiple categories.

30. "Race and Hispanic Origin," 1.

31. Tafoya, "Shades of Belonging," 4; see also Bonilla-Silva, *Racism without Racists*, 185–86; Tienda and Mitchell, *Multiple Origins, Uncertain Destinies*, 23, 40–45.

32. Tafoya, "Shades of Belonging," 1.

33. Brubaker, *Citizenship and Nationhood*, 182 (emphasis in original). For a collection of essays exploring similar themes and Latinos, see Flores and Benmayor, *Latino Cultural Citizenship*.

34. Tienda and Mitchell, *Multiple Origins, Uncertain Destinies*, 39–40.

35. Moore and Pachón, *Hispanics in the United States*, 51.

36. Tienda and Mitchell, *Multiple Origins, Uncertain Destinies*, 41.

37. For a study that finds that the order of similar questions outside the census matters, see Bonilla-Silva, *Racism without Racists*, 201 n. 28.

38. Logan, "How Race Counts," 3 (table 3).

39. Sociologist Clara Rodríguez suggests a different set of three explanations in response to the more narrow, though related, question of why substantial numbers of Latinos chose "some other race": (1) Hispanics are indicating their mixed-race heritage; (2) Hispanics misunderstand the race question; (3) Hispanics have a different definition of race. Rodríguez, *Changing Race*, 130–31.

40. Glazer, "Reflections on Race," 319.

41. Rodríguez, *Changing* Race, 130–31; Tienda and Mitchell, *Multiple Origins, Uncertain Destinies*, 41.

42. Sociologist George Yancey makes this claim expressly. Yancey, *Who Is White?* Sociologist David Skrentny makes it implicitly, frequently referencing this data point in his recent book. Skrentny, *The Minority Rights Revolution*. For a similar interpretation of Skrentney, see Johnson, "Review," 316.

43. Sociologist Eduardo Bonilla-Silva makes this argument expressly. Bonilla-Silva, *Racism without Racists*, 187. Sociologists Edward Murguia and Rogelio

Saenz make it implicitly. See Murguia and Saenz, "An Analysis of the Latin Americanization of Race."

44. See Rodríguez, *Changing Race*, 131; Tafoya, "Shades of Belonging," 3, 21; Tienda and Mitchell, *Multiple Origins, Uncertain Destinies*, 41.

45. Tienda and Mitchell, *Multiple Origins, Uncertain Destinies*, 41–44.

46. Moreover, some evidence suggests that these numbers may inflate the proportion of Hispanics who truly identify as white—in other words, Hispanics who check "white" seem to be much more ambivalent than Hispanics who check "some other race." In her study for the Pew Hispanic Center, demographer Sonya Tafoya reported that Hispanics who selected "some other race" were much more likely than Hispanics who identified as white to stick with their census choice when asked their racial identity in a subsequent survey. Tafoya, "Shades of Belonging," 22.

47. Tienda and Mitchell, *Multiple Origins, Uncertain Destinies*, 19.

48. Bonilla-Silva, *Racism without Racists*, 187. These figures are based on the 5 percent questionnaire of the 2000 census. See also Tafoya, "Shades of Belonging."

49. Bonilla-Silva, *Racism without Racists*, 187. The number of Latinos who identify as black may well reflect anti-black racism (and internalized racism) that stems both from the long history of black oppression in the United States and the strong anti-black strand in the Spanish-Mexican racial legacy which I discussed in Chapter 2.

50. The data in this paragraph are drawn from the 5 percent questionnaire for the 2000 census, as reported by Bonilla-Silva, *Racism without Racists*, 187 (table 8.2).

51. This certainly is the case, although Mexican Americans and Puerto Ricans report significantly warmer feelings toward blacks than do Cuban Americans, for example. Ibid., 189. Political scientist Mark Sawyer reports that Cubans are more than twice as likely as Mexican Americans and Puerto Ricans to believe that African Americans face "little or no discrimination." Sawyer, *Racial Politics in Post-Revolutionary Cuba*, 173. For an analysis of the degree to which blacks have internalized anti-black racism, see Bonilla-Silva, *Racism without* Racists, 151–76.

52. Moore, "Foreword," 4.

53. See, generally, García, *Mexican Americans*.

54. See, generally, Haney López, *Racism on Trial*.

55. Sawyer, *Racial Politics in Post-Revolutionary Cuba*, 155–57.

56. Cornell and Hartmann, *Ethnicity and Race*, 157–58; see also Sawyer, *Racial Politics in Post-Revolutionary Cuba*, 156.

57. "Cubans in the United States," 4.

58. Tafoya, "Shades of Belonging," 2.

59. Ibid., 2, 21.

60. Ibid., 12.

61. Ibid.

62. Telles and Ortíz, "Americano Dreams, Mexican American Realities," 10.7.

63. Ibid.

64. Ibid., 8.16.

65. Tienda and Mitchell, *Multiple Origins, Uncertain Destinies*, 4.

66. Ibid., 88–93 (summarizing the data).

67. Telles and Ortiz, "Americano Dreams, Mexican American Realities," 5.1 (citing seven studies).

68. Ibid., 10.4, 5.5.

69. Del Pinal and Ennis, "The Racial and Ethnic Identity of Latin American Immigrants," 3.

70. Tafoya, "Shades of Belonging," 7.

71. Ibid.

72. Lieberman, "51% of Riot Arrests Were Latino," *Los Angeles Times*, June 18, 1992, B3.

73. Tafoya, "Shades of Belonging," 7 (data compiled from table 3).

74. Suro and Escobar, "2006 National Survey of Latinos," 4.

75. Fraga et al., "Su Casa Es Nuestra Casa," 516.

Bibliography

Books, Articles, Dissertations, and Manuscripts

Abramson, Jeffrey. *We, the Jury: The Jury System and the Ideal of Democracy*. New York: Basic Books, 1994.

Acuña, Rodolfo. *Occupied America: A History of Chicanos*. 3d ed. New York: HarperCollins, 1988.

Alemán, Jesse. "Historical Amnesia and the Vanishing Mestiza: The Problem of Race in *The Squatter and the Don* and *Ramona*," *Aztlán* 27 (2002): 59–93.

———. "The Other Country: Mexico, the United States, and the Gothic History of Conquest," *American Literary History* 18 (2006): 406–26.

Allen, Theodore W. *The Invention of the White Race*. New York: Verso, 1994.

Almaguer, Tomás. *Racial Fault Lines: The Historical Origins of White Supremacy in California*. Berkeley: University of California Press, 1994.

Alonso, Ana María. *Thread of Blood: Colonialism, Revolution, and Gender on Mexico's Northern Frontier*. Tucson: University of Arizona Press, 1995.

Alschuler, Albert, and Andrew G. Deiss. "A Brief History of the Criminal Jury in the United States," *Chicago Law Review* 61 (1994): 867–928.

Arellano, Anselmo. "Through Thick and Thin: Evolutionary Transitions of Las Vegas Grandes and Its Pobladores." Ph.D. diss., University of New Mexico, 1990.

Ayres, Edward L. *Vengeance and Justice: Crime and Punishment in the Nineteenth-Century American South*. New York: Oxford University Press, 1984.

Baca, Karla. "The Taos Priest," *Santa Fe New Mexican*, July 17, 2006.

Bair, Barbara. "Remapping the Black/White Body: Sexuality, Nationalism, and Biracial Antimiscegenation Activisim in 1920s Virginia," in *Sex, Love, Race: Crossing Boundaries in North American History*, ed. Martha Hodes. New York: New York University Press, 1999.

Ball, Larry D. *The United States Marshals of New Mexico and Arizona Territories, 1846–1912*. Albuquerque: University of New Mexico Press, 1978.

Bancroft, Hubert Howe. *History of the Pacific States of North America, Arizona and New Mexico, 1530–1888*. San Francisco: A. L. Bancroft, 1969 [1889].

Banner, Stuart. *How the Indians Lost Their Land: Law and Power on the Frontier*. Cambridge: Harvard University Press, 2005.

Bardaglio, Peter W. " 'Shameful Matches': The Regulation of Interracial Sex and

Marriage in the South before 1900," in *Sex, Love, Race: Crossing Boundaries in North American History*, ed. Martha Hodes. New York: New York University Press, 1999.

Barrera, Mario. *Race and Class in the Southwest: A Theory of Racial Inequality.* Notre Dame: University of Notre Dame Press, 1979.

Bauer, K. Jack. *The Mexican War: 1846–1848.* New York: Macmillan, 1974.

Beck, Warren A., and Ynez D. Haase. *Historical Atlas of New Mexico.* Norman: University of Oklahoma Press, 1969.

Bell, Derrick. *Race, Racism, and American Law.* 5th ed. New York: Aspen, 2004.

Benedict, Kirby. *A Journey through New Mexico's First Judicial District in 1864: Letters to the Editor of the Santa Fe Weekly New Mexican.* Los Angeles: Western-lore Press, 1956 [1864].

Berger, Bethany R. " 'Power over This Unfortunate Race': Race, Politics and Indian Law in *United States v. Rogers*," *William and Mary Law Review* 45 (2004): 1957–2052.

Berwanger, Eugene H. *The Frontier against Slavery: Western Anti-Negro Prejudice and the Slavery Extension Controversy.* Urbana: University of Illinois Press, 1967.

Beveridge, Albert J. "Cuba and Congress," *North American Review* 62 (1901): 535–50.

Bieber, Ralph Paul. "The Papers of James J. Webb, Santa Fe Merchant, 1944–61," *Washington University Studies, Humanistic Series* 11 (1924): 255–305.

Blanton, Carlos K. "George I. Sanchez, Ideology, and Whiteness in the Making of the Mexican American Civil Rights Movement, 1930–1960." *Journal of Southern History* 72 (August 2006): 569–604.

Bodine, John J. "A Tri-Ethnic Trap: The Spanish Americans in Taos." Paper presented at the annual meeting of the American Ethnological Society, 1968.

Bonilla, Caroline, et al. "Admixture in the Hispanics of the San Luis Valley, Colorado, and Its Implications for Complex Trait Gene Mapping." *Annals of Human Genetics* 68 (2004): 139–53.

Bonilla-Silva, Eduardo. *Racism without Racists: Color-Blind Racism and the Persistence of Racial Inequality in the United States.* 2d ed. Lanham: Rowman and Littlefield, 2006.

Bonnell, Victoria E. "The Uses of Theory, Concepts and Comparison in Historical Sociology," *Comparative Studies in Society and History* 22 (1980) 156–73.

Bourke, John G. "The American Congo," *Scribner's Magazine* 15, no. 5 (May 1894).

Bowers, Claude G. *Beveridge and the Progressive Era.* New York: Houghton Mifflin, 1932.

Brack, Gene M. *Mexico Views Manifest Destiny, 1821–1846: An Essay on the Origins of the Mexican War.* Albuquerque: University of New Mexico Press, 1975.

Bradfute, Richard Wells. *The Court of Private Land Claims: The Adjudication of Spanish and Mexican Land Grant Titles, 1891–1904.* Albuquerque: University of New Mexico Press, 1975.

Brading, D. A. *The Origins of Mexican Nationalism.* Los Angeles: UCLA Center for Latin American Studies, 1985.

Briggs, Charles L., and John R. Van Ness, eds. *Land, Water and Culture: New Perspectives on Hispanic Land Grants.* Albuquerque: University of New Mexico Press, 1987.

Brodkin, Karen. *How Jews Became White Folks and What That Says about Race in America.* New Brunswick, NJ: Rutgers University Press, 1998.

Brooks, James F. *Captives and Cousins: Slavery, Kinship, and Community in the Southwest Borderlands.* Chapel Hill: University of North Carolina Press, 2002.

Brubaker, Rogers. *Citizenship and Nationhood in France and Germany.* Cambridge: Harvard University Press, 1992.

Bustamante, Adrian. "Los Hispanos: Ethnicity and Social Change in New Mexico." Ph.D. diss., University of New Mexico, 1981.

———. "The Matter Was Never Resolved: The *Casta* System in Colonial New Mexico, 1693–1823," *New Mexico Historical Review* 66 (1991): 143–63.

Butler, Judith. *Bodies That Matter: On the Discursive Limits of "Sex."* New York: Routledge, 1993.

Camarillo, Albert. *Chicanos in a Changing Society: From Mexican Pueblos to American Barrios in Santa Barbara and Southern California, 1848–1930.* Cambridge: Harvard University Press, 1979.

Cameron, Christopher David Ruiz. "One Hundred Fifty Years of Solitude: Reflections on the End of the History Academy's Dominance of Scholarship on the Treaty of Guadalupe Hidalgo," *Southwest Journal of Law and Trade in the Americas* 5 (1998): 83–107.

Carbado, Devon W., and Mitu Gulati. "Working Identity." *Cornell Law Review* 85 (2000): 1259–1308.

———. "The Fifth Black Woman." *Journal of Contemporary Legal Issues* 11 (2001): 701–29.

Carrasco, Gilbert Paul. "Latinos in the U.S.: Invitation and Exile," in *Immigrants Out!*, ed. Juan F. Perea. New York: New York University Press, 1997.

Cartwright, Brad. "Reconsidering Race and Manifest Destiny: John O'Sullivan, Young America and Pan-Ethnic Expansion in the 1840s," *QWERTY* 9 (1999): 291–300.

Chávez, Thomas E. *An Illustrated History of New Mexico.* Albuquerque: University of New Mexico Press, 1992.

Cheetham, Francis. "The First Term of the American Court," *New Mexico Historical Review* 1 (1926): 23–41.

Christensen, Carol, and Thomas Christensen. *The U. S.–Mexican War.* San Francisco: Bay Books, 1998.

Clarke, Dwight L. *Stephen Watts Kearny: Soldier of the West.* Norman: University of Oklahoma Press, 1961.

Clary, David Allen. "The Question of United States Federal Policy toward New Mexico, 1846–1851." Unpublished manuscript, 1968.

Comaroff, Jean, and John Comaroff. *Of Revelation and Revolution.* Chicago: University of Chicago Press, 1997.

Cornell, Stephen, and Douglas Hartmann. *Ethnicity and Race: Making Identities in a Changing World.* Thousand Oaks, CA: Pine Forge Press, 1998.

Courtwright, David T. *Violent Land: Single Men and Social Disorder from the Frontier to the Inner City.* Cambridge: Harvard University Press, 1966.

Cover, Robert. *Justice Accused: Antislavery and the Judicial Process.* New Haven: Yale University Press, 1975.

Crail-Rugotzke, Donna. "A Matter of Guilt: The Treatment of Hispanic Inmates by New Mexico Courts and the New Mexico Territorial Prison, 1890–1912," *New Mexico Historical Review* 74 (1999): 295–314.

Crawford, Stanley. *Mayordomo: Chronicle of an Acequia in Northern New Mexico.* Albuquerque: University of New Mexico Press, 1988.

Crutchfield, Jane A. *Tragedy at Taos: The Revolt of 1847.* Plano: Republic of Texas Press, 1995.

"Cubans in the United States." Washington, DC: Pew Hispanic Center, Aug. 25, 2006.

Cutter, Charles R. *The Legal Culture of Northern New Spain.* Albuquerque: University of New Mexico Press, 1995.

Cutts, James Madison. *The Conquest of California and New Mexico by the Forces of the United States 1846 and 1847.* Albuquerque: Horn and Wallace, 1965 [1847].

Davis, W. W. H. *El Gringo: New Mexico and Her People.* Lincoln: University of Nebraska Press, 1982 [1857].

DeBuys, William. *Enchantment and Exploitation: The Life and Hard Times of a New Mexico Mountain Range.* Albuquerque: University of New Mexico Press, 1985.

De León, Arnoldo. "*In Re Rodriguez*: An Attempt at Chicano Disenfranchisement in San Antonio, 1896–1897." Self-published manuscript, 1979.

Del Pinal, Jorge, and Sharon Ennis. "The Racial and Ethnic Identity of Latin American Immigrants in Census 2000." Paper presented at the annual meeting of the Population of the Association of America. Unpublished manuscript, March 2005.

Delgado, Richard, and Jean Stefancic, eds. *The Latino Condition: A Critical Reader.* New York: New York University Press, 1998.

Deutsch, Sarah. *No Separate Refuge: Culture, Class and Gender on an Anglo-Hispanic Frontier in the American Southwest, 1880–1940.* New York: Oxford University Press, 1987.

Deverell, William. *Whitewashed Adobe: The Rise of Los Angeles and the Remaking of Its Mexican Past*. Berkeley: University of California Press, 2004.

DeVoto, Bernard. *The Year of Decision, 1846*. Boston: Houghton Mifflin, 1942.

Dressler, Joshua. *Understanding Criminal Law*, 3d ed. New York: Lexis Publishing, 2001.

Du Bois, W. E. B. *Black Reconstruction in America, 1860–1880*. New York: Simon and Schuster, 1962.

Durán, Tobias. "Francisco Chavez, Thomas B. Catron, and Organized Political Violence in Santa Fe in the 1890s," *New Mexico Historical Review* 59 (1984): 291–310.

———. "'We Come As Friends:' Violent Social Conflict in New Mexico, 1810–1910." Ph.D. diss., University of New Mexico, 1985.

Durand, John. *The Taos Massacres*. Elkhorn, WI: Puzzlebox Press, 2004.

Dykstra, Robert R. *The Cattle Towns*. New York: Alfred A. Knopf, 1971.

Ebright, Malcolm. *Land Grants and Lawsuits in Northern New Mexico*. Albuquerque: University of New Mexico Press, 1994.

———. "Land Grant Adjudication in New Mexico Under the Treaty of Guadalupe Hidalgo," in *The Treaty of Guadalupe Hidalgo, 1848: Papers of the Sesquicentennial Symposium, 1848–1998*, ed. John Porter Bloom. Las Cruces, NM: Doña Ana County Historical Society, 1999.

———. "The GAO Land Grant Report: A Whitewash and Slap in the Face," *La Jicarita News* (Chamisal, New Mexico) 9 (July 2004), 4.

Ebright, Malcolm, and Rick Hendricks. *The Witches of Abiquiu: The Governor, the Priest, the Genízaro Indians, and the Devil*. Albuquerque: University of New Mexico Press, 2006.

Edwards, Frank S. *A Campaign in New Mexico with Colonel Doniphan*. Albuquerque: University of New Mexico Press, 1996.

Eisenhower, John S. D. *So Far from God*. New York: Random House, 1989.

Ellickson, Robert C. *Order without Law: How Neighbors Settle Disputes*. Cambridge: Harvard University Press, 1991.

Escobar, Edward J. *Race, Police and the Making of a Political Identity: Mexican Americans and the Los Angeles Police Department, 1900–1945*. Berkeley: University of California Press, 1999.

Esquibel, José Antonio. "The Formative Era for New Mexico's Colonial Population, 1693–1700," in *Transforming Images: New Mexican Santos In-Between Worlds* ed. Claire Farago and Donna Pierce. University Park: Pennsylvania State University Press, 2006.

Farago, Claire. "Mediating Ethnicity and Culture: Framing New Mexico as a Case Study," in *Transforming Images: New Mexican Santos In-Between Worlds* ed. Claire Farago and Donna Pierce. University Park: Pennsylvania State University Press, 2006.

Farago, Claire, and Donna Pierce, eds. *Transforming Images: New Mexican Santos In-Between Worlds.* University Park: Pennsylvania State University Press, 2006.

Fehrenbacher, Don E. *A Basic History of California.* Princeton: D. Van Nostrand Company, 1964.

———. *The Era of Expansion: 1800–1848.* New York: John Wiley and Sons, 1969.

———. "The Mexican War and the Conquest of California," in *Essays and Assays: California History Reappraised,* ed. George H. Knoles. San Francisco: California Historical Society, 1973.

———. *The Dred Scott Case: Its Significance in American Law and Politics.* New York: Oxford University Press, 1978.

Fine, Michelle, et al., eds. *Off White: Readings on Power, Privilege and Society.* New York: Routledge, 2004.

Flanigan, Daniel J. *The Criminal Law of Slavery and Freedom, 1800–1868.* New York: Garland, 1987.

Flores, William V., and Rina Benmayor. *Latino Cultural Citizenship: Claiming Identity, Space and Rights.* Boston: Beacon Press, 1997.

Foley, Neil. *The White Scourge: Mexicans, Blacks and Poor Whites in Texas Cotton Culture.* Berkeley: University of California Press, 1997.

Foos, Paul. *A Short, Offhand, Killing Affair: Soldiers and Social Conflict during the Mexican-American War.* Chapel Hill: University of North Carolina Press, 2002.

Fraga, Luis R., et al., "Su Casa Es Nuestra Casa: Latino Politics Research and the Development of American Political Science," *American Political Science Review* 100 (2006): 515–21.

Francaviglia, Richard V. "The Geographic and Cartographic Legacy of the U.S.–Mexican War," in *Dueling Eagles: Reinterpreting the U.S.–Mexican War, 1846–1848,* ed. Richard V. Francaviglia and Douglas W. Richmond. Fort Worth: Texas Christian University Press, 2000.

Francaviglia, Richard V., and Douglas W. Richmond, eds. *Dueling Eagles: Reinterpreting the U.S.–Mexican War, 1846–1848.* Fort Worth: Texas Christian University Press, 2000.

Frankenberg, Ruth. *White Women, Race Matters: The Social Construction of Whiteness.* Minneapolis: University of Minnesota Press, 1993.

Fredrickson, George M. *White Supremacy: A Comparative Study in South African and American History.* New York: Oxford University, 1981.

———. *Racism: A Short History.* Princeton: Princeton University Press, 2002.

Friedman, Lawrence. *Crime and Punishment in American History.* New York: Basic Books, 1993.

Friedman, Lawrence M., and Robert C. Percival. *The Roots of Justice: Crime and Punishment in Alameda County, California, 1870–1910.* Chapel Hill: University of North Carolina Press, 1981.

Fritz, Christian G. *Federal Justice: The California Court of Ogden Hoffman, 1851–1891.* Lincoln: University of Nebraska Press, 1991.

Ganaway, Loomis. *New Mexico and the Sectional Controversy, 1846–1861*. Albuquerque: University of New Mexico Press, 1944.

García, Mario T. *Mexican Americans: Leadership, Ideology, and Identity, 1930–1960*. New Haven: Yale University Press, 1989.

Garrard, Lewis H. *Wah-To-Yah and the Taos Trail*. Palo Alto, CA: American West Publishing Co., 1968 [1848].

Gatell, Frank Otto. "Roger B. Taney," in *The Justices of the United States Supreme Court, 1789–1969: Their Lives and Major Opinions*, ed. Leon Friedman and Fred L. Israel. New York: Chelsea House, 1969.

Gillmer, Jason A. "Poor Whites, Benevolent Masters, and the Ideologies of Slavery." *North Carolina Law Review* 85 (2007): 489–570.

Glazer, Nathan. "Reflections on Race, Hispanicity, and Ancestry in the U.S. Census," in *The New Race Question: How the Census Counts Multiracial Individuals*, ed. Joel Perlmann and Mary C. Waters. New York: Russell Sage Foundation, 2002.

Goldberg, Carole. "Descent into Race," *UCLA Law Review* 49 (2002): 1373.

Gómez, Laura E. "What's in a Name? The Politics of *Hispanic* Identity." A.B. thesis, Harvard College, 1986.

———. "The Birth of the 'Hispanic' Generation: Attitudes of Mexican-American Political Elites toward the Hispanic Label," *Latin American Perspectives* 75 (1992): 45–58.

———. "Race, Colonialism and Criminal Law: Mexicans and the American Criminal Justice System in Territorial New Mexico," *Law and Society Review* 34 (2000): 1129–1201.

———. "Race Mattered: Racial Formation and the Politics of Crime in Territorial New Mexico," *UCLA Law Review* 49 (2002): 1395–1416.

———. "Off-White in an Age of White Supremacy: Mexican Elites and the Rights of Indians and Blacks in Nineteenth-Century New Mexico," *UCLA Chicano-Latino Law Review* 25 (2005): 9–59.

Gómez, Placido. "The History and Adjudication of the Common Lands of Spanish and Mexican Land Grants," *Natural Resources Journal* 25 (1985): 1039–80.

Gómez Quiñones, Juan. *Chicano Politics: Reality and Promise, 1940–1990*. Albuquerque: University of New Mexico Press, 1990.

Gonzáles, Phillip. "The Political Construction of Latino Nomenclatures in Twentieth-Century New Mexico," *Journal of the Southwest* 35 (1993): 158–85.

———. "Inverted Subnationalism: The Ethnopolitics of Hispano Identity, 1850–1935." Unpublished manuscript, 2000.

———. "La Junta de Indignacion: Repertoire of Hispano Collective Protest in New Mexico, 1884–1933," *Western Historical Quarterly* 31 (2000): 161–86.

———. *Forced Sacrifice as Ethnic Protest: The Hispano Cause in New Mexico and the Racial Attitude Confrontation of 1933*. New York: P. Lang, 2001.

———. "Struggle for Survival: The Hispanic Land Grants of New Mexico," *Agricultural History* 77 (2003): 293–324.

Gonzáles, Phillip, and Ann Massmann. "Loyalty Questioned: Nuevomexicanos in the Great War." *Pacific Historical Review* 75 (2006): 629–66.

Gonzáles-Berry, Erlinda, and David R. Maciel, eds. *Contested Homeland: A Chicano History of New Mexico.* Albuquerque: University of New Mexico Press, 2000.

González, Deena J. *Refusing the Favor: The Spanish-Mexican Women of Santa Fe, 1820–1880.* New York: Oxford University Press, 1999.

———. "On the Lives of Women and Children in the Aftermath of the United States–Mexican War," in *The Treaty of Guadalupe Hidalgo, 1848: Papers of the Sesquicentennial Symposium, 1848–1998*, ed. John Porter Bloom. Las Cruces, NM: Doña Ana County Historical Society, 1999.

Gordon, Linda. *The Great Arizona Orphan Abduction.* Cambridge: Harvard University Press, 1999.

Grassham, John William. "Charles H. Beaubien, 1800–1864." M.A. thesis, New Mexico State University, 1983.

Gregg, Josiah. *Commerce of the Prairies: The Journal of a Santa Fe Trader.* Philadelphia: J. B. Lippincott, 1933 [1844].

Gregory, Steven, and Roger Sanjek, eds. *Race.* New Brunswick, NJ: Rutgers University Press, 1994.

Griego, Alfonso. "Good-Bye My Land of Enchantment: A True Story of Some of the First Spanish-Speaking Natives and Early Settlers of San Miguel County, Territory of New Mexico." Self-published manuscript, 1981.

Griswold del Castillo, Richard. *The Treaty of Guadalupe Hidalgo: A Legacy of Conflict.* Norman: University of Oklahoma Press, 1990.

———. "The Treaty of Guadalupe Hidalgo and New Mexico: Borders, Boundaries and Limits," in *The Treaty of Guadalupe Hidalgo, 1848: Papers of the Sesquicentennial Symposium, 1848–1998*, ed. John Porter Bloom. Doña Ana County Historical Society, 1999.

Gross, Ariela. "Litigating Whiteness: Trials of Racial Determination in the Nineteenth-Century South," *Yale Law Journal* 108 (1998): 109–188.

———. "Texas Mexicans and the Politics of Whiteness," *Law and History Review* 21 (2003): 195.

Gutiérrez, David. "Significant to Whom?" *Western Historical Quarterly* 24 (1993): 519–39.

———. *Walls and Mirrors: Mexican Americans, Mexican Immigrants, and the Politics of Ethnicity.* Berkeley: University of California Press, 1995.

Gutiérrez, Ramon A. *When Jesus Came, the Corn Mothers Went Away: Marriage, Sexuality, and Power in New Mexico, 1500–1846.* Stanford: Stanford University Press, 1991.

Hall, G. Emlen. *Four Leagues of Pecos: A Legal History of the Pecos Grant, 1800–1933.* Albuquerque: University of New Mexico Press, 1984.

———. "San Miguel del Bado and the Loss of the Common Lands of New Mexico Community Land Grants," *New Mexico Historical Review* 66 (1991): 413–32.

Hall, G. Emlen, and David J. Weber. "Mexican Liberals and the Pueblo Indians, 1821–1829," *New Mexico Historical Review* 59 (1984): 19.

Haney López, Ian. *White by Law: The Legal Construction of Race.* New York: University Press, 1996.

———. "Retaining Race: LatCrit Theory and Mexican American Identity," *Harvard Latino Law Review* 1 (1997): 297.

———. *Racism on Trial: The Chicano Fight for Justice.* Cambridge: Harvard University Press, 2003.

———. "Race and Colorblindness after *Hernandez* and *Brown*," in *"Colored Men" and "Hombres Aquí": Hernandez v. Texas and the Emergence of Mexican-American Lawyering,* ed. Michael A. Olivas. Houston: Arte Público Press, 2006.

Harris, Cheryl I. "The Story of *Plessy v. Ferguson:* The Death and Resurrection of Legal Formalism," in *Constitutional Law Stories,* ed. Michael C. Dorf. New York: Foundation Press, 2004.

Hay, Douglas. "Crime and Justice in Eighteenth- and Nineteenth-Century England," in *Crime and Justice: An Annual Review of Research,* ed. Norval Morris and Michael Tonry. Chicago: University of Chicago Press, 1980.

Hay, Douglas, et al. *Albion's Fatal Tree: Crime and Society in Eighteenth-Century England.* New York: Pantheon, 1975.

Hersch, Joni. "Skin Color and Wages among New U.S. Immigrants." Unpublished manuscript, April 2006.

Hietala, Thomas R. *Manifest Design: Anxious Aggrandizement in Late Jacksonian America.* Ithaca, NY: Cornell University Press, 1985.

Hindus, Michael. *Prison and Plantation: Crime, Justice, and Authority in Massachusetts and South Carolina, 1767–1878.* Chapel Hill: University of North Carolina Press, 1980.

Hing, Bill Ong. *Making and Remaking Asian America through Immigration Policy, 1850–1990.* Palo Alto: Stanford University Press, 1994.

Hobsbawm, Eric. *Bandits.* New York: Delacorte Press, 1969.

Hochschild, Jennifer L. "Multiple Racial Identifiers in the 2000 Census, and Then What?" in *The New Race Question: How the Census Counts Multiracial Individuals,* ed. Joel Perlmann and Mary C. Waters. New York: Russell Sage Foundation, 2002.

Holzka, Kathryn. "Taos Honors 'Champion of Common People,'" *Albuquerque Journal,* July 15, 2006.

Horne, Gerald. *Black and Brown: African Americans and the Mexican Revolution, 1910–1920.* New York: New York University Press, 2005.

Horsman, Reginald. *Race and Manifest Destiny: The Origins of American Racial Anglo-Saxonism.* Cambridge: Harvard University Press, 1981.

Hunt, Aurora. *Kirby Benedict: Frontier Federal Judge*. Glendale: A. H. Clark, 1961.

Huntington, Samuel P. *Who Are We? The Challenges to America's National Identity*. New York: Simon and Schuster, 2004.

Ignatiev, Noel. *How the Irish Became White*. New York: Routledge, 1995.

Ilahiane, Hsain. "Estevan De Dorantes, the Moor or the Slave?" *Journal of North African Studies* 5 (2000): 1–14.

Inciardi, James A. "Outlaws, Bandits and the Lore of the American Wild West," in James A. Inciardi, Alan A. Block, and Lyle A. Hallowell, *Historical Approaches to Crime: Research Strategies and Issues*. Beverly Hills, CA: Sage Publications, 1977.

Ireland, Robert M. "The Nineteenth-Century Criminal Jury: Kentucky in the Context of the American Experience," *Kentucky Review* 4 (1983): 52–70.

Jacobson, Matthew F. *Whiteness of a Different Color: European Immigrants and the Alchemy of Race*. Cambridge: Harvard University Press, 1998.

Jenkins, Myra Ellen. "Rebellion against America: The Occupation of New Mexico, 1846–1847." Unpublished manuscript, 1949.

Jenkins, Myra Ellen, and Albert H. Schroeder. *A Brief History of New Mexico*. Albuquerque: University of New Mexico Press, 1974.

Johannsen, Robert W. *To the Halls of the Montezumas: The Mexican War in the American Imagination*. New York: Oxford University Press, 1985.

Johnson, Kevin R. "Review of *The Minority Rights Revolution* by John D. Skrentny," *American Journal of Legal History* 47 (2006): 315–17.

Johnson, Kevin R., and Bill Ong Hing. Book review. "Huntington: *Who Are We? The Challenges to America's National Identity*." *Michigan Law Review* 103 (2005): 1347–90.

Jones, Sondra. *The Trial of Don Pedro Leon Lujan: The Attack against Indian Slavery and Mexican Traders in Utah*. Salt Lake City: University of Utah Press, 2000.

Juárez, José Roberto, Jr. "The American Tradition of Language Rights: The Forgotten Right to Government in a 'Known Tongue.'" *Law and Inequality: A Journal of Theory and Practice* 13 (1995): 443–642.

Julian, George. "Land-Stealing in New Mexico." *North American Review* 145 (1887): 17–31.

Kadish, S. J. ed., *Encyclopedia of Crime and Justice*, vol. 3. New York: Free Press, 1983.

Kawashima, Yasuhide. *Puritan Justice and the Indian*. Middletown, CT: Wesleyan University Press, 1986.

Keleher, William A. *Turmoil in New Mexico, 1846–1868*. Albuquerque: University of New Mexico Press, 1982 [1951].

Kerson, Paul E. "The American Testament: How and Why Governor L. Bradford Prince Rebuilt Flushing, New York, in Santa Fe, New Mexico." Unpublished manuscript, 1997.

Kettner, James H. *The Development of American Citizenship, 1608–1870*. Chapel Hill: University of North Carolina Press, 1978.

Knight, Alan. "Racism, Revolution, and Indigenismo: Mexico, 1900–1940," in *The Idea of Race in Latin America*, ed. Richard Graham. Austin: University of Texas Press, 1990.

Koch, Lena Clara. "Federal Indian Policy in Texas, 1845–1860." M.A. thesis, University of Texas, 1922.

Kochlar, Rakesh. "The Wealth of Hispanic Households: 1996 to 2002." Washington, DC: Pew Hispanic Center, Oct. 18, 2004.

Kosek, Jake. *Understories: The Political Life of Forests in Northern New Mexico*. Durham, NC: Duke University Press, 2006.

Kraemer, Paul. "The Dynamic Ethnicity of the People of Spanish Colonial New Mexico in the Eighteenth Century," in *Transforming Images: New Mexican Santos In-Between Worlds*, ed. Claire Farago and Donna Pierce. University Park: Pennsylvania State University Press, 2006.

La Madrid, Enrique R. *Hermanitos Comanchitos: Indo-Hispano Rituals of Captivity and Redemption*. Albuquerque: University of New Mexico Press, 2003.

Lamar, Howard. *The Far Southwest, 1846–1912: A Territorial History*. New Haven: Yale University Press, 1966.

Langum, David J. "California Women and the Image of Virtue," *Southern California Quarterly* 59 (1977): 245–50.

———. *Law and Community on the Mexican California Frontier: Anglo-American Expatriates and the Clash of Legal Traditions, 1821–1846*. Norman: University of Oklahoma Press, 1987.

Larson, Robert W. *New Mexico's Quest for Statehood, 1846–1912*. Albuquerque: University of New Mexico Press, 1968.

———. *New Mexico Populism: A Study of Radical Protest in a Western Territory*. Boulder: Colorado Associated University Press, 1974.

Lavender, David. *Bent's Fort*. Garden City, NY: Doubleday, 1954.

Lawson, Gary, and Guy Seidman. *The Constitution of Empire: Territorial Expansion and American Legal History*. New Haven: Yale University Press, 2004.

Lazarus-Black, Mindie. *Legitimate Acts and Illegal Encounters: Law and Society in Antigua and Barbuda*. Washington, DC: Smithsonian Institution Press, 1994.

Lazarus-Black, Mindie, and Susan F. Hirsch, eds. *Contested States: Law, Hegemony, and Resistance*. New York: Routledge, 1994.

Lehmann, Terry. "Contrast and Conflict in the Development of Two Southwestern Towns." Ph.D. diss., Indiana University, 1974.

Levinson, Irving W. "Wars within Wars: Mexican Guerillas, Domestic Elites, and the United States of America, 1846–1848." Self-published manuscript, 2005.

Lieberman, Paul. "51% of Riot Arrests Were Latino," *Los Angeles Times*, June 18, 1992, B3.

Limerick, Patricia Nelson. *The Legacy of Conquest*. New York: Norton, 1987.

Limón, José E. *American Encounters: Greater Mexico, the United States, and the Erotics of Culture.* Boston: Beacon Press, 1998.

Lipsitz, George. *The Possessive Investment in Whiteness: How White People Profit from Identity Politics.* Philadelphia: Temple University Press, 1998.

Logan, John R. "How Race Counts for Hispanic Americans." Lewis Mumford Center for Comparative Urban and Regional Research, State University of New York, Albany, July 14, 2003.

López, Gerald P. "Undocumented Mexican Migration: In Search of a Just Immigration Law and Policy." *UCLA Law Review* 28 (1980–81): 615–714.

Loyola, Sister Mary. "The American Occupation of New Mexico, 1821–1852, Chaps. 1–2," *New Mexico Historical Review* 14 (1939): 34–75.

———. "The American Occupation of New Mexico, 1821–1852, Chaps. 3–5," *New Mexico Historical Review* 14 (1939): 142–286.

Lubin, Alex. *Romance and Rights: The Politics of Inter-racial Intimacy.* Jackson: University Press of Mississippi, 2005.

Luna, Guadalupe T. "On the Complexities of Race: The Treaty of Guadalupe Hidalgo and *Dred Scott v. Sandford*," *University of Miami Law Review* 53 (1999): 691–716.

———. "Chicanas/os, 'Liberty' and Roger B. Taney," *University of Florida Journal of Law and Public Policy* 12 (2000): 33–55.

Malavet, Pedro. *America's Colony: The Political and Cultural Conflict between the United States and Puerto Rico.* New York: New York University Press, 2004.

Martínez, George. "Legal Indeterminacy, Judicial Discretion and the Mexican-American Litigation Experience: 1930–1980," *U.C. Davis Law Review* 27 (1994): 555.

———. "The Legal Construction of Race: Mexican-Americans and Whiteness," *Harvard Latino Law Review* 2 (1997): 321.

Martínez, Oscar J. "On the Size of the Chicano Population: New Estimates, 1850–1870," *Aztlán* 6 (1975): 43–65.

Martínez, Ramiro, Jr. "Coming to America: The Impact of the New Immigration on Crime," in *Immigration and Crime: Race, Ethnicity and Violence*, ed. Ramiro Martínez, Jr., and Abel Valenzuela. New York: New York University Press, 2006.

Martínez, Stephen C. "Civic Ideals in New Mexico: The Sacred Quest for Citizenship, 1848–1922." Ph.D. diss., University of New Mexico, 2006.

Martínez, Vicente M. "Betrayal or Benevolence: The Role of Padre Martínez and the 1846 Treason Trials and Executions." Unpublished manuscript, August 2006.

Masco, Joseph. *The Nuclear Borderlands: The Manhattan Project in Post–Cold War New Mexico.* Princeton: Princeton University Press, 2006.

McClain, Charles J. *In Search of Equality: The Chinese Struggle against Discrimination in Nineteenth-Century America.* Berkeley: University of California Press, 1994.

McGrath, Roger. *Gunfighters, Highwaymen, and Vigilantes: Violence on the Frontier*. Berkeley: University of California Press, 1984.

McKanna, Clare V., Jr. *Homicide, Race, and Justice in the American West, 1880–1920*. Tucson: University of Arizona Press, 1997.

McNitt, Frank, ed. *Navaho Expedition: Journal of a Military Reconnaissance from Santa Fe, New Mexico to the Navaho Country Made in 1949*. Norman: University of Oklahoma Press, 1964 [1850].

McWilliams, Carey. *North from Mexico: The Spanish-Speaking People of the United States*. Philadelphia: J. B. Lippincott, 1949.

Mead, Robert A. "Statehood for a Conquered Land," in *Prestatehood Legal Materials: A Fifty-State Research Guide*, ed. Michael Chiorazzi and Marguerite Most. New York: Haworth Information Press, 2005.

Meinig, Donald William. "The Shaping of America: A Geographical Perspective on 500 Years of History," *Transcontinental America* 3 (1998): 1850–1915.

Meléndez, A. Gabriel. *So All Is Not Lost: The Poetics of Print in Nuevomexicano Communities, 1834–1958*. Albuquerque: University of New Mexico Press, 1997.

———, ed. *The Biography of Casimiro Barela*. Albuquerque: University of New Mexico Press, 2003.

Melzer, Richard. "New Mexico in Caricature: Images of the Territory on the Eve of Statehood," *New Mexico Historical Review* 62 (1987): 335–60.

Menchaca, Martha. "Chicano Indianism: A Historical Account of Racial Repression in the United States," *American Ethnologist* 20 (1993): 583–603.

———. *Recovering History, Constructing Race: The Indian, Black, and White Roots of Mexican Americans*. Austin: University of Texas Press, 2001.

Merk, Frederick. *Manifest Destiny and Mission in American History: A Reinterpretation*. New York: Alfred A. Knopf, 1963.

Merriweather, D. Andrew, et al. "Mitochondrial versus Nuclear Admixture Estimates Demonstrate a Past History of Directional Mating." *American Journal of Physical Anthropology* 102 (1997): 153–59.

Merry, Sally Engle. "Law and Colonialism," *Law and Society Review* 25 (1991): 889–922.

———. *Colonizing Hawaii: The Cultural Power of Law*. Princeton: Princeton University Press, 2000.

Meyer, Doris. *Speaking for Themselves: Neomexicano Cultural Identity and the Spanish-Language Press, 1880–1920*. Albuquerque: University of New Mexico Press, 1996.

Mezey, Naomi. "Erasure and Recognition: the Census, Race and the National Imagination," *Northwestern University Law Review* 98 (2003): 1701–68.

Miller, Darlis A. *The California Column in New Mexico*. Albuquerque: University of New Mexico Press, 1982.

Mirandé, Alfredo. *Gringo Justice*. Notre Dame: University of Notre Dame Press, 1987.

Mitchell, Pablo. "Accomplished Ladies and Coyotes: Marriage, Power, and Straying from the Flock in Territorial New Mexico, 1880–1920," in *Sex, Love, Race: Crossing Boundaries in North American History*, ed. Martha Hodes. New York: New York University Press, 1999.

———. *Coyote Nation: Sexuality, Race, and Conquest in Modernizing New Mexico, 1880–1920*. Chicago: University of Chicago Press, 2005.

Mitchell, Timothy. *Colonising Egypt*. Berkeley: University of California Press, 1988.

Mocho, Jill. *Murder and Justice in Frontier New Mexico, 1821–46*. Albuquerque: University of New Mexico Press, 1997.

Monkkonen, Eric H. *The Dangerous Class: Crime and Poverty in Columbus, Ohio, 1860–1885*. Cambridge: Harvard University Press, 1975.

———. *The Frontier*. Westport, CT: Meckler, 1991.

———. "Racial Factors in New York City Homicides, 1800–1874," in *Ethnicity, Race, and Crime: Perspectives Across Time and Place*, ed. D. F. Hawkins. Albany: State University of New York Press, 1995.

Montejano, David. *Anglos and Mexicans in the Making of Texas, 1836–1986*. Austin: University of Texas Press, 1987.

———. "On the Question of Inclusion," in *Chicano Politics and Society in the Late Twentieth Century*, ed. David Montejano. Austin: University of Texas Press, 1999.

———. "Who Is Samuel P. Huntington? Patriotic Reading for Anglo Protestants Who Live in Fear of Reconquista," *Texas Observer* 96 (2004): 12.

Montgomery, Charles H. *The Spanish Redemption: Heritage, Power, and Loss on New Mexico's Upper Rio Grande*. Berkeley: University of California Press, 2002.

Montoya, María E. "L. Bradford Prince: The Education of a Gilded Age Politician," *New Mexico Historical Review* 66 (1991): 179–201

———. "The Dual World of Governor Miguel A. Otero: Myth and Reality in Turn-of-the-Century New Mexico," *New Mexico Historical Review* 67 (1992): 13–31.

———. *Translating Property: The Maxwell Land Grant and the Conflict over Land in the American West, 1840–1900*. Berkeley: University of California Press, 2002.

Moore, Joan W. "Foreword," in Edward E. Telles and Vilma Ortiz, "Americano Dreams, Mexican American Realities." Unpublished manuscript, April 2006.

Moore, Joan W., and Harry Pachón. *Hispanics in the United States*. Englewood Cliffs, NJ: Prentice-Hall, 1985.

Moran, Rachel. *Inter-racial Intimacy: The Regulation of Race and Romance*. Chicago: University of Chicago Press, 2001.

Morrison, Michael A. *Slavery and the American West: The Eclipse of Manifest Destiny and the Coming of the Civil War*. Chapel Hill: University of North Carolina Press, 1997.

Murguia, Edward, and Rogelio Saenz. "An Analysis of the Latin Americanization of Race in the United States," *Race and Society* 5 (2002): 87–103.

Nader, Laura, and Harry F. Todd, eds. *The Disputing Process: Law in Ten Societies.* New York: Columbia University Press, 1978.

Nash, Gary B. "The Hidden History of Mestizo America," in *Sex, Love, Race: Crossing Boundaries in North American History*, ed. Martha Hodes. New York: New York University Press, 1999.

Nash, Gerald D. "New Mexico in the Otero Era: Some Historical Perspectives," *New Mexico Historical Review* 67 (1992): 1–12.

Nevins, Allan. *Frémont: Pathmaker of the West.* New York: D. Appleton-Century, 1939.

Newton, Nell Jessup, et al., eds. *Cohen's Handbook of Federal Indian Law.* Newark, NJ: LexisNexis, 2005.

Ngai, Mae M. *Impossible Subjects: Illegal Aliens and the Making of Modern America.* Princeton: Princeton University Press, 2004.

Nieto-Phillips, John. *The Language of Blood: The Making of Spanish American Identity in New Mexico: 1880s–1930s.* Albuquerque: University of New Mexico Press, 2004.

Nostrand, Richard L. "Mexican Americans circa 1850," *Annals of the Association of American Geographers* 65 (1975): 378–90.

———. *The Hispano Homeland.* Norman: University of Oklahoma Press, 1992.

Oboler, Suzanne. *Ethnic Labels, Latino Lives: Identity and the Politics of (Re)Presentation in the United States.* Minneapolis: University of Minnesota Press, 1995.

Olivas, Michael A., ed. *"Colored Men" and "Hombres Aquí": Hernandez v. Texas and the Emergence of Mexican-American Lawyering.* Houston: Arte Público Press, 2006.

———. "Introduction: Commemorating the 50th Anniversary of *Hernandez v. Texas*," in *"Colored Men" and "Hombres Aquí": Hernandez v. Texas and the Emergence of Mexican-American Lawyering*, ed. Michael A. Olivas. Houston: Arte Público Press, 2006.

Omi, Michael, and Howard Winant. *Racial Formation in the United States from the 1960s to the 1990s.* New York: Routledge and Kegan Paul, 1994.

Ortiz, Alfonso, ed. *Handbook of North American Indians.* Washington, DC: Smithsonian Institution, 1979.

———. *The Pueblo Indians of North America.* New York: Chelsea House, 1994.

———. "The Pueblo Revolt," in *Po'pay: Leader of the First American Revolution*, ed. Joe S. Sando and Herman Agoyo. Santa Fe, NM: Clear Light Publishing, 2005.

Ortiz, Roxanne Dunbar. *Roots of Resistance: Land Tenure in New Mexico, 1680–1980.* Los Angeles: UCLA Chicano Studies Research Center Publications, 1980.

Padilla, Felix M. *Latino Ethnic Consciousness: The Case of Mexican Americans and Puerto Ricans in Chicago*. Notre Dame: University of Notre Dame Press, 1985.

Paredes, Americo. *"With His Pistol in His Hand": A Border Ballad and Its Hero*. Austin: University of Texas Press, 1958.

Paredes, Patricia P. "Latinos and the Census: Responding to the Race Question," *George Washington Law Review* 74 (2005): 146–63.

Paredes, Raymund A. "The Mexican Image in American Travel Literature," *New Mexico Historical Review* 52 (1977): 5–29.

Perea, Juan. "Demography and Distrust: An Essay on American Languages, Cultural Pluralism and Official English," *Minnesota Law Review* 72 (1992): 269.

———. "A Brief History of Race and the U.S.–Mexican Border: Tracing the Trajectories of Conquest," *UCLA Law Review* 50 (2003): 283–312.

Perea, Juan, et al., eds. *Race and Races: Cases and Materials for a Diverse America*. St. Paul, MN: West Group, 2000.

Pierce, Donna, and Cordelia Thomas Snow. "Hybrid Households: A Cross Section of New Mexican Material Culture," in *Transforming Images: New Mexican Santos In-Between Worlds*, ed. Claire Farago and Donna Pierce. University Park: Pennsylvania State University Press, 2006.

Poldervaart, Arie. *Black-Robed Justice: A History of the Administration of Justice in New Mexico from the American Occupation in 1846 until Statehood in 1912*. Santa Fe: Historical Society of New Mexico, 1999 [1948].

Pomeroy, Earl. "California's Legacies from the Pioneers," in *Essays and Assays: California History Reappraised*, ed. George H. Knoles. San Francisco: California Historical Society, 1973.

Prince, L. Bradford. *Historical Sketches of New Mexico*. New York: Leggat Bros., 1883.

———. "Claims to Statehood," *North American Review* 156 (1893): 346–54.

———. *A Concise History of New Mexico*. Cedar Rapids, IA: Torch Press, 1912.

Rael-Gálvez, Estévan. "Identifying Captivity and Capturing Identity: Narratives of American Indian Slavery, Colorado and New Mexico, 1776–1934." Ph.D diss., University of Michigan, 2002.

Ramirez, Carlos Brazil. "The Hispanic Political Elite in Territorial New Mexico: A Study of Classical Colonialism." Ph.D. diss., University of California, Santa Barbara, 1979.

Read, Benjamin M. *Illustrated History of New Mexico*. New York: Arno Press, 1976 [1912].

Reeve, Frank D. "The Federal Indian Policy in New Mexico, 1858–1880, II," *New Mexico Historical Review* 13 (1938): 14.

Reichard, David A. "'Justice Is God's Law': The Struggle to Control Social Conflict and the United States Colonization of New Mexico, 1846–1912." Ph.D. diss., Temple University, 1996.

————. "The Politics of Village Water Disputes in Northern New Mexico, 1882–1905," *Western Legal History* 9 (1996): 9, 33.

————. "Paternalism, Ethnicity, and the Professionalization of the Bar in Territorial New Mexico." Unpublished manuscript, 1998.

————. "Whitening the Bar: Professionalization, Ethnicity, and Power in New Mexico's Justice of the Peace Courts, 1882–1886." Unpublished manuscript, 1996.

Reid, John Phillip. *Law for the Elephant: Property and Social Behavior on the Overland Trail.* San Marino, CA: Huntington Library, 1980.

————. *Controlling the Law: Legal Politics in Early National New Hampshire.* Dekalb: Northern Illinois University Press, 2004.

Reséndez, Andrés. *Changing National Identities at the Frontier: Texas and New Mexico, 1800–1850.* Cambridge: Cambridge University Press, 2004.

Rivera, John-Michael. *The Emergence of Mexican America: Recovering Stories of Mexican Peoplehood in U.S. Culture.* New York: New York University Press, 2006.

Rivera, José A. *Acequia Culture: Water, Land and Community in the Southwest.* Albuquerque: University of New Mexico Press, 1998.

Roberts, Susan A. "A Political History of the New Mexico Supreme Court, 1912–1972," *New Mexico Law Review* 6 (1975): 1–83.

Rodríguez, Annette M. "Unstable Victory of White *Mexicanidad:* Considerations of *In Re Rodriguez* and the 1917 Immigration Act." Unpublished manuscript, December 2006.

Rodríguez , Clara E. *Changing Race: Latinos, the Census, and the History of Ethnicity in the United States.* New York: New York University Press, 2000.

Rodríguez, Sylvia. "Land, Water and Ethnic Identity in Taos," in *Land, Water and Culture: New Perspectives on Hispanic Land Grants,* ed. Charles L. Briggs and John R. Van Ness. Albuquerque: University of New Mexico Press, 1987.

————. "Ethnic Reconstruction in Contemporary Taos," *Journal of the Southwest* 32 (1990): 541–55.

————. *The Matachines Dance: Ritual Symbolism and Interethnic Relations in the Upper Rio Grande Valley.* Albuquerque: University of New Mexico Press, 1996.

————. "Tourism, Whiteness, and the Vanishing Anglo," in *Seeing and Being Seen: Tourism in the American West,* ed. David M. Wrobel and Patrick T. Long. Lawrence: University Press of Kansas, 2001.

Roediger, David R. *The Wages of Whiteness: Race and the Making of the American Working Class.* New York: Verso, 1999.

————. *Colored White: Transcending the Racial Past.* Berkeley: University of California Press, 2002.

Román, Ediberto. *The Other American Colonies: An International and Constitutional Law Examination of the United States' Nineteenth and Twentieth Century Island Conquests.* Durham, NC: Carolina Academic Press, 2006.

Romano, Octavio Ignacio. "The Anthropology and Sociology of the Mexican-Americans: The Distortion of Mexican-American History," *El Grito* 2 (1968): 13–26.

Rosen, Deborah A. "Pueblo Indians and Citizenship in Territorial New Mexico," *New Mexico Historical Review* 78 (2003): 21.

Rosenbaum, Robert J. *Mexicano Resistance in the Southwest: The Sacred Right of Self-Preservation.* Austin: University of Texas Press, 1981.

Said, Edward W. "Foreword," in *Selected Subaltern Studies*, ed. Ranajit Guha and Gayatri Chakravorty Spivak. New York: Oxford University Press, 1988.

Samora, Julian, Joe Bernal, and Albert Pena. *Gunpowder Justice: A Reassessment of the Texas Rangers.* Notre Dame: University of Notre Dame Press, 1979.

Sánchez, George J. *Becoming Mexican American: Ethnicity, Culture, and Identity in Chicano Los Angeles, 1900–1945.* New York: Oxford University Press, 1993.

Sánchez, Rosaura. *Telling Identities: The Californio Testimonios.* Minneapolis: University of Minnesota Press, 1995.

Sando, Joe S. *Pueblo Nations: Eight Centuries of Pueblo Indian History.* Santa Fe, NM: Clear Light Publishers, 1992.

Sando, Joe S., and Herman Agoyo, eds. *Po'pay: Leader of the First American Revolution.* Santa Fe, NM: Clear Light Publishers, 2005.

Saunders, Myra K. "California Legal History: A Review of Spanish and Mexican Legal Institutions," *Law Library Journal* 87 (1985): 487–514.

Sawyer, Mark Q. *Racial Politics in Post-Revolutionary Cuba.* Cambridge: Cambridge University Press, 2006.

Schiller, Mark. "Adjudicating Empire: Mathew G. Reynolds and the Misappropriation of Spanish and Mexican Land Grants." Unpublished manuscript, August 2006.

Schwarz, Philip J. *Twice Condemned: Slaves and the Criminal Laws of Virginia, 1705–1865.* Baton Rouge: Louisiana State University Press, 1988.

Sharfstein, Daniel J. "Crossing the Color Line: Racial Migration and the One-Drop Rule, 1600–1860," *Minnesota Law Review* 91 (2007): 592–656.

Sheridan, Claire. " 'Another White Race': Mexican Americans and the Paradox of Whiteness in Jury Selection," *Law and Historical Review* 21 (2003): 109.

Shirley, Glenn. *Law West of Fort Smith: A History of Frontier Justice in the Indian Territory, 1834–1896.* New York: Henry Holt, 1957.

Shreve, Gene R., and Peter Raven-Hansen. *Understanding Civil Procedure.* 3d ed. New York: Lexis Publishing, 2002.

Simmons, Marc. "History of the Pueblos Since 1821," in *Handbook of North American Indians: Southwest*, ed. Alfonso Ortiz. Washington, DC: Smithsonian Institution, 1979.

Sisneros, Samuel E. "Los Emigrantes Nuevomexicanos: The 1849 Repatriation to Guadalupe and San Ignacio, Chihuahua, Mexico." M.A. thesis, University of Texas, El Paso, 2001.

Skerry, Peter. *Mexican Americans: The Ambivalent Minority.* New York: Free Press, 1993.

Skop, Emily, Brian Gratton, and Myron P. Guttman. "La Frontera and Beyond: Geography and Demography in Mexican American History," *Professional Geographer* 58 (2006): 78–98.

Skrentny, John D. *The Minority Rights Revolution.* Cambridge: Harvard University Press, 2002.

Slifer, D., and J. Duffield. *Kokopelli: Flute Player Images in Rock Art.* Santa Fe, NM: Ancient City Press, 1994.

Smith, Justin H. *The War with Mexico.* New York: Macmillan, 1919.

Smith, Rogers M. *Civic Ideals: Conflicting Citizenship in U.S. History.* New Haven: Yale University Press, 1997.

Soltero, Carlos R. *Latinos and American Law: Landmark Supreme Court Cases.* Austin: University of Texas Press, 2006.

Spicer, Edward H. *Cycles of Conquest: The Impact of Spain, Mexico and the United States on the Indians of the Southwest, 1533–1960.* Tucson: University of Arizona Press, 1962.

Spruhan, Paul. "A Legal History of Blood Quantum in Federal Indian Law to 1935," *South Dakota Law Review* 51 (2006): 1–50.

Starr, June, and Jane F. Collier, eds. *History and Power in the Study of Law: New Directions in Legal Anthropology.* Ithaca, NY: Cornell University Press, 1989.

Steele, Thomas J., Paul Chetts, and Barbe Awalt, eds. *Seeds of Struggle/Harvest of Faith: The Papers of the Archdiocese of Santa Fe Catholic Cuatro Centennial Conference—The History of the Catholic Church in New Mexico.* Albuquerque, NM: LPD Press, 1998.

Stegmaier, Mark J. "The Guadalupe Hidalgo Treaty as a Factor in the New Mexico–Texas Boundary Dispute," in *The Treaty of Guadalupe Hidalgo, 1848: Papers of the Sesquicentennial Symposium, 1848–1998,* ed. John Porter Bloom. Las Cruces, NM: Doña Ana County Historical Society, 1999.

Steinberg, Allen. *The Transformation of Criminal Justice: Philadelphia, 1800–1880.* Chapel Hill: University of North Carolina Press, 1989.

Stephanson, Anders. *Manifest Destiny: American Expansion and the Empire of Right.* New York: Hill and Wang, 1995.

Stevens, T. Rorie. *The Death of a Governor: The Massacre of Charles Bent, First American Civil Governor of the Territory of New Mexico.* Jacksonville, TX: Jayroe Graphic Arts, 1971.

Stoler, Ann Laura. *Race and the Education of Desire: Foucault's History of Sexuality and the Colonial Order of Things.* Durham, NC: Duke University Press, 1995.

Stratton, Porter A. *The Territorial Press of New Mexico, 1834–1912.* Albuquerque: University of New Mexico Press, 1969.

Streeby, Shelley. "American Sensations: Empire, Amnesia, and the U.S.–Mexican War," *American Literary History* (2001): 1–4.

————. *American Sensations: Empire, Amnesia, and the Production of Popular Culture*. Berkeley: University of California Press, 2002.

Sunseri, Alvin R. *Seeds of Discord: New Mexico in the Aftermath of the American Conquest, 1846–1861*. Chicago: Nelson Hall, 1979.

Suro, Robert, and Gabriel Escobar. "2006 National Survey of Latinos: The Immigration Debate." Washington, DC: Pew Hispanic Center, July 13, 2006.

Tafoya, Sonya. "Shades of Belonging." Washington, DC: Pew Hispanic Center, December 6, 2004.

Takaki, Ronald T. *Iron Cages: Race and Culture in Nineteenth-Century America*. New York: Alfred A. Knopf, 1979.

————. *Strangers from a Different Shore: A History of Asian Americans*. New York: Back Bay Books, 1989.

————. *A Different Mirror: A History of Multicultural America*. New York: Back Bay Books, 1993.

Telles, Edward E. *Race in Another America: The Significance of Skin Color in Brazil*. Princeton: Princeton University Press, 2004.

Telles, Edward E., and Vilma Ortiz. "Americano Dreams, Mexican American Realities." Unpublished manuscript, April 2006.

Thomas, David Yancey. "A History of Military Government in Newly Acquired Territory of the United States." Ph.D diss., Columbia University, 1904.

Thompson, Albert W. "Insurrection at Taos," *New Mexico Magazine* 20 (1941): 18.

Thompson, E. P. *Whigs and Hunters: The Origins of the Black Act*. New York: Pantheon, 1975.

Tienda, Marta, and Faith Mitchell, eds. *Multiple Origins, Uncertain Destinies: Hispanics and the American Future*. Washington, DC: National Academies Press, 2006.

Tjarks, Alicia. "Demographic, Ethnic and Occupational Structure of New Mexico, 1790," *The Americas* 35 (1978): 45–88.

Tórrez, Robert J. "The San Juan Gold Rush of 1860 and Its Effect on the Development of Northern New Mexico," *New Mexico Historical Review* 63 (1988): 257.

————. "Crime and Punishment in Spanish Colonial New Mexico," Research Paper no. 34. Albuquerque: University of New Mexico Center for Land Grant Studies, 1990.

————. "The New Mexican 'Revolt' and Treason Trials of 1847." Unpublished manuscript, 1998.

Torruella, Juan R. "Review of *America's Colony*," *Journal of Legal Education* 55 (2005): 432–45.

Twitchell, Ralph Emerson. *History of the Military Occupation of the Territory of New Mexico from 1846–1851 by the Government of the United States*. Chicago: Rio Grande Press, 1909.

————. *The Leading Facts of New Mexican History*. Cedar Rapids, IA: Torch Press, 1911.

Utley, Robert M. *High Noon in Lincoln: Violence on the Western Frontier.* Albuquerque: University of New Mexico Press, 1987.

———. *Billy the Kid: A Short and Violent Life.* Lincoln: University of Nebraska Press, 1989.

———. *Lone Star Justice: The First Century of the Texas Rangers.* New York: Berkley, 2003.

Valencia, Reynaldo Anaya, Sonia R. García, Henry Flores, and José Roberto Juárez, Jr. *Mexican Americans and the Law.* Tucson: University of Arizona Press, 2004.

Valencia-Weber, Gloria. "Racial Equality: Old and New Strains and American Indians," *Notre Dame Law Review* 80 (2004): 333–75.

Volpp, Leti. "The Citizen and the Terrorist," *UCLA Law Review* 49 (2001): 1575.

———. " 'Obnoxious to Their Very Nature': Asian Americans and Constitutional Citizenship," *Citizenship Studies* 5 (2001): 57.

Wade, Peter. *Blackness and Race Mixture: The Dynamics of Racial Identity in Columbia.* Baltimore: Johns Hopkins University Press, 1993.

Waghelstein, John D. "The Mexican War and the American Civil War: The American Army's Experience in Irregular Warfare as a Sub-Set of a Major Conventional Conflict," *Small Wars and Insurgencies* 7 (1996): 139–64.

Waldrep, Christopher. *Roots of Disorder: Race and Criminal Justice in the American South, 1817–1880.* Urbana: University of Illinois Press, 1998.

Walter, Paul A. "Ten Years After," *New Mexico Historical Review* 7 (1932): 371–76.

Weber, David. *The Mexican Frontier: The American Southwest under Mexico.* Albuquerque: University of New Mexico Press, 1982.

———. *On the Edge of Empire: The Taos Hacienda of Los Martínez.* Santa Fe: Museum of New Mexico Press, 1996.

Weber, David, ed. *Foreigners in Their Native Land: Historical Roots of the Mexican Americans.* Albuquerque: University of New Mexico Press, 2003 [1973].

Webster's New Geographical Dictionary. Springfield, MA: G. and C. Merriam, 1980.

Weigle, Marta. *Brothers of Light, Brothers of Blood: The Penitentes of the Southwest.* Albuquerque: University of New Mexico Press, 1976.

Weiner, Mark S. *Americans without Law: The Racial Boundaries of Citizenship.* New York: New York University Press, 2006.

Weston, Rubin Francis. *Racism in U.S. Imperialism: The Influence of Racial Assumptions on American Foreign Policy, 1893–1946.* Columbia: University of South Carolina Press, 1972.

Westphall, Victor. *The Public Domain in New Mexico, 1854–1891.* Albuquerque: University of New Mexico Press, 1965.

———. *Thomas Benton Catron and His Era.* Tucson: University of Arizona Press, 1973.

White, Richard. "Outlaw Gangs of the Middle Border: American Social Bandits," *Western Historical Quarterly* 12 (1981) 387–408.

———. *"It's Your Misfortune and None of My Own": A New History of the American West.* Norman: University of Oklahoma Press, 1991.

Wickett, Murray R. *Contested Territory: Whites, Native Americans and African Americans in Oklahoma, 1865–1907.* Baton Rouge: Louisiana State University Press, 2000.

Williams, Gerry C. "Dependency Formations and the Spanish-American Community: An Interpretative and Theoretical Study of Modernization in New Mexico." Ph.D diss., University of Oklahoma, 1985.

Williams, Robert A., Jr. *The American Indian in Western Legal Thought: The Discourses of Conquest.* New York: Oxford University Press, 1990.

———. "Columbus's Legacy: Law as an Instrument of Racial Discrimination against Indigenous People's Rights of Self-Determination," *Arizona Journal of International and Comparative Law* 8 (1991): 51.

———. "Documents of Barbarism: The Contemporary Legacy of European Racism and Colonialism in the Narrative Traditions of Federal Indian Law," *Arizona Law Review* 31 (1992): 237.

Wilson, Steven H. "Brown over 'Other White': Mexican Americans' Legal Arguments and Litigation Strategy in School Desegregation," *Law and History Review* 21 (2003): 145.

———. "Some Are Born White, Some Achieve Whiteness, and Some Have Whiteness Thrust Upon Them: Mexican Americans and the Politics of Racial Classification in the Federal Judicial Bureaucracy, Twenty-five Years after *Hernandez v. Texas*," in *"Colored Men" and "Hombres Aquí":" Hernandez v. Texas and the Emergence of Mexican-American Lawyering*, ed. Michael A. Olivas. Houston: Arte Público Press, 2006.

Wright, Robert E. "How Many Are a 'Few'? Catholic Clergy in Central and Northern New Mexico, 1780–1851," in *Seeds of Struggle/Harvest of Faith: The Papers of the Archdiocese of Santa Fe Catholic Cuatro Centennial Conference—The History of the Catholic Church in New Mexico*, ed. T. J. Steele, P. Chetts, and B. Awalt. Albuquerque: LPD Press, 1998.

Wunder, John. *Inferior Courts, Superior Justice: A History of the Justices of the Peace of the Northwest Frontier, 1853–1889.* Westport, CT: Greenwood Press, 1979.

Yamamoto, Eric, et al., eds. *Race, Rights and Reparations: Law and the Japanese American Internment.* New York: Aspen Publishers, 2001.

Yancey, George A. *Who Is White? Latinos, Asians, and the New Black/Nonblack Divide.* Boulder, CO: Lynne Rienner, 2003.

Zinn, Howard. *A People's History of the United States: 1492–Present.* New York: Harper Perennial, 1995.

Zoraida Vázquez, Josefina. *México al Tiempo de su Guerra con Estados Unidos.* Mexico City: Fondo de Cultura Economica, 1997.

———. "The Significance in Mexican History of the Treaty of Guadalupe Hidalgo," in *The Treaty of Guadalupe Hidalgo, 1848: Papers of the Sesquicentennial*

Symposium, 1848–1998, ed. John Porter Bloom. Las Cruces, NM: Doña Ana County Historical Society, 1999.

————. "Causes of the War with the United States," in *Dueling Eagles: Reinterpreting the U.S.–Mexican War, 1846–1848*, ed. Richard V. Francaviglia and Douglas W. Richmond. Fort Worth: Texas Christian University Press, 2000.

CASES, STATUTES, AND GOVERNMENT DOCUMENTS

Act of March 26, 1790, 1 Stat. 103. (1790).

Act of September 9, 1850 (Establishing territorial government of New Mexico), Ch. 49, 9 U.S. Statutes 446 (1850).

Act of March 3, 1851, 9 U.S. Statutes 631 (1851).

Act of July 22, 1854, 10 U.S. Statutes 308 (1854).

Act of July 14, 1870, Ch. 255, 16 U.S. Statutes 254 §7 (1870).

American Insurance Co. v. 356 Bales of Cotton, 26 U.S. 511 (1828).

An Act to Provide for the Protection of Property in Slaves in the Territory. Ch. XXVI. Revised Statutes and Laws of the Territory of New Mexico (1859). Repealed by H.R. Res. 64, 36th Cong., 1st Sess., 1860.

An Act Concerning Free Negroes. Art. XXVI, Ch. LXIV. Revised Statutes and Laws of the Territory of New Mexico (1857). Repealed 1865.

Bibliographical Directory of the United States Congress, 1774–1989. Washington, DC: U.S. Government Printing Office, 1989.

Carter v. Territory, 1 N.M. 317 (1859).

Chinese Exclusion Act, 8 U.S.C. § 261-299 (1882).

De Arguello v. United States, 59 U.S. 539 (1855).

De La O v. Acoma, 1 N.M. 226 (1857).

Fleming v. Page, 50 U.S. 603 (1850).

Fremont v. United States, 58 U.S. 542 (1854).

Government Accountability Office Report. "Treaty of Guadalupe Hidalgo: Findings and Possible Options Regarding Longstanding Community Land Grant Claims in New Mexico." Washington, DC: Government Accountability Office, 2004.

Gadsden Purchase Treaty, 10 Stat. 1031 (1853).

Hale v. Kentucky, 303 U.S. 613 (1938).

"The Hispanic Population." Census 2000 Brief, May 2001. U.S. Census Bureau.

Historical Abstracts of the United States Colonial Times to 1970. Part I. Washington, DC: U.S. Department of Commerce, 1975.

In re Rodriguez, 81 F. 337, W.D. Tex., (1897).

"Indians of the United States: Investigation of the Field Service." Hearings before the House Committee on Indian Affairs. House of Representatives, 66th Cong., 2d Sess., 1920.

Jaremillo v. Romero, 1 N.M. 190 (1857).

Lyles v. Texas, 41 Tex. 172 (1874).

New Mexico State Department of Tourism, Official 2004 Brochure.

"New Statehood Bill." (The Beveridge Report) Hearings before the Subcommittee of the Committee on the Territories. House Bill 12543. 57th Cong., 2d Sess., December 10, 1902.

Norris v. Alabama, 294 U.S. 587 (1935).

People v. De La Guerra, 40 Cal. 311 (1870).

People v. Hall, 4 Cal. 399 (1854).

Plessy v. Ferguson, 163 U.S. 537 (1896).

President's Message Regarding Occupation of Mexican Territory, Doc. No. 19. House of Representatives, 29th Cong., 2nd Sess., December 22, 1846 (In answer to a resolution of the House of Representatives of December 15, 1846).

President's Message Regarding New Mexico and California, Ex. Doc. No. 70. House of Representatives, 30th Cong., 1st Sess., July 24, 1848 (In answer to a resolution of the House of Representatives of July 10, 1848).

Proposed New Mexico State Constitution of 1850.

"Race and Hispanic Origin in 2004," in *Population Profile of the United States.* U.S. Census Bureau.

Report to accompany House of Representatives Bill No. 605. Document No. 457, Committee on Private Land Claims, U.S. Congress, House of Representatives, 35th Cong., 1st Sess., May 29, 1858.

Report on Discovery of Conspiracy by Governor Bent. Doc. No. 442, U.S. Congress, Senate, 56th Cong., 1st Sess., 1900.

Revised New Mexico Statutes 126 (The Kearny Code), Chap. XXI §14 (1864 [Sept. 22, 1846]).

Revised New Mexico Statutes, Chap. LVII, § 18-19 (1865).

Scott v. Sandford, 60 U.S. 393 (1856).

Senate Debate on Omnibus Statehood Bill, Congressional Record (Senate), 57th Cong., 2d Sess., Jan. 7, 1902.

Strauder v. West Virginia, 100 U.S. 303 (1880).

Territory v. Romine, 2 N.M. 114 (1881).

Transcript of Record. United States v. Julian Sandoval, Appeal from the Court of Private Land Claims. United States Supreme Court, October Term 1896.

Treaty of Guadalupe Hidalgo, 9 U.S. Statutes 922 (1848).

United States v. Joseph, 94 U.S. 614 (1877).

United States v. Lucero, 1 N.M. 422 (1869).

United States v. Ritchie, 58 U.S. 525 (1854).

United States v. Sandoval, 167 U.S. 278 (1897).

United States v. Sandoval, 231 U.S. 28 (1913).

Virginia v. Rives, 100 U.S. 313 (1880).

Index

235

About the Author

Laura E. Gómez is Professor of Law and American Studies at the University of New Mexico. She is the author of *Misconceiving Mothers: Legislators, Prosecutors, and the Politics of Prenatal Drug Exposure.*

CPSIA information can be obtained
at www.ICGtesting.com
Printed in the USA
LVHW081515291118
598420LV00039B/1521/P